Hands Reaching out of Darkness

REAL ACCOUNTS IN CHRISTIAN MISSIONS

Carlos and Myrtice Owens

ISBN 978-0-7414-3077-9

All Scripture quotations in this book are from the HOLY
BIBLE, NEW INTERNATIONAL VERSION COPYRIGHT
1973, 1978, 1984, International Bible Society. Used by
permission of Zondervan Bible Publishers.
Front page artwork by Jan Owens Phillips;
Pictures inside by Carlos and Myrtice Owens;
Picture on back cover by HPM, Financial Service, Inc.

Published by:

INFINITY
PUBLISHING.COM

Info@buybooksontheweb.com
www.buybooksontheweb.com
Toll-free (877) BUY BOOK
Local Phone (610) 941-9999
Fax (610) 941-9959

Printed in the United States of America

Published August 2015

Contents

Dedication

We dedicate this work to the Glory of God
And
To our daughters, Janice, Ruth, and Debra, who grew up
with us in Africa, and who continued being an integral part
of our lives, even when far away from us.

Acknowledgments

We acknowledge and extend appreciation to the many people who have contributed to this book:

- Our children who shared in our work and added tremendous joy to our lives;

- Our family that held us up in prayer and love;

- Our fellow missionaries, who worked alongside us with their encouragement and influence;

- The International Mission Board who led in planning our work and providing financial support and guidance;

- Pastors and church members who remembered us with their love, support and prayers;

- Our African brothers and sisters who made our stories possible by working alongside us, following our leadership and remaining faithful to the Lord;

- Our dear friends, Evelyn Foote, who critiqued our writing and Connie Davis Bushey who assisted with our pictures;

- Woman's Missionary Union whose influence, encouragement and promotion of missions, especially with the Lottie Moon Christmas Mission Offering, undergirded everything we did;

- Most of all, our Heavenly Father who called us, inspired us, protected us, directed our activities and blessed us with many souls for his Kingdom.

Introduction

Living in Africa for thirty six years afforded us many wonderful experiences and unique encounters with the African people. Our call and subsequent service in the Christian ministry were unquestionably from the Lord and for His glory. From our first days in Africa, we recorded and have recounted what were to us amazing and interesting events from the culture and response of the people. The Lord used many of the incidents written in this book to open doors for witnessing and sharing the love of Christ. It was clear to us that God's hand was on our involvement with the people with whom we lived and worked. Our stories reveal how God brought about remarkable changes in the lives of people.

We have attempted to record these narratives in a style for easy reading and usable as illustrations by church and mission leaders. Each of us has written about incidents from our own separate ministries. Some are written from our teamwork and its consequences. A few stories are included to help the reader catch a glimpse of our family life and of the many changes that came about.

Chapters are written with relation to the places we lived and worked. Because of our moving into areas for pioneering new work, we likely experienced more amusing and unusual incidents than some other missionaries. A historical and geographical note at the beginning of each chapter helps to orient the reader.

We pray that this book will inspire, encourage and influence many in the work and understanding of missions. To see God's power demonstrated in some of the most primitive conditions, we hope to impact the lives of those who read these pages.

Chapter One

Rattling Windows / Open Doors

South West Africa was a German Colony before WW I. After the war, it became a Trust Territory of the League of Nations under South African control. The United Nations declared the territory independent in 1968 as Namibia (Nah-MEE-bee-ah) but South Africa refused to give up her rule and continued using the name, South West Africa. When we transferred from East Africa in 1982, freedom fighters were using terrorist tactics to gain independence.

Myrtice: Bombs and Machine Guns

"Kaboom! Kaboom!" sounded loudly, nearly shaking us out of bed. Bombs were blasting somewhere near by. Shortly, "rat-a-tat-tat" sounds of machine gun fire added to the tension. Surely it was only a few houses away. The terrorists, fighting for freedom of their country, and the South African army were in a close encounter. Our first night in Tsumeb (SUE-meb) in northern Namibia gave us an unraveling feeling; that we might be in serious danger. The shaking knocked pictures askew on the walls and turned over items on tables. All we knew to do was to lie quietly, thinking about the complications of trying to establish a ministry in a war-torn country. After nearly two hours, the gunfire ceased. We were grateful that our children were grown and away from home. We had not realized that we would be right in the midst of the war but had that inner assurance that God wanted us here, after twenty-five years in East Africa.

The next day we learned that opposing forces had met in Nomtsoub (NOME-soob), just down from our street. Some were killed and much damage was done. Very few details of the conflict filtered out into the community. In fact, all war activities were kept hushed and not allowed in the news media.

Bombs exploding in the night brought fear and panic to our neighbors. Terrorists shot and killed one of them late one afternoon as he returned home from work in his pickup truck. He came under machine gun fire while passing along the main road.

The freedom fighters used every available means; land mines, bombs, attacks on vital services and sabotage, to bring chaos in the country, believing that they could incite enough fear to force the South Africans to leave the area. They wanted to rule their own country.

We were unhappy about a war that was killing so many people, but we also felt very sympathetic with the freedom fighters' cause. South Africa was taking advantage of resources for their own country.

Discrimination and apartheid were apparent wherever you went. Many public areas, such as toilet facilities and eating-places, were off limits to non-whites. This made for considerable difficulties for blacks especially when traveling and for us later as we traveled with them for meetings and conferences.

Assuredly from the first day in the country we had felt a firm confirmation that God had sent us to this land to minister to the tribal people. We had full confidence in the Lord's will for us to be here even with all the fighting and felt protected with His Spirit.

One day before the noon hour I was rushing to complete letters that needed to be sent out on the train that goes out three times a week. There was no airmail service, so, to hasten important letters on their way we had to get them in the post office before noon so they would go out on the afternoon train. Gathering all my letters, I bundled them up and climbed into our mission-provided pickup truck and hurried to town. On the way I felt strongly that I needed to go by the little church building where we had recently begun one of our town churches. Therefore, I veered from my regular route to go by the church where we had stored Bible teaching materials. I pulled up outside the church and sat for two or three minutes to decide on the materials I really needed. For some reason, I could not remember exactly what I needed. I didn't want to spend too much time hunting through all the materials, so I sat just a short time trying to remember. Finally, as time was pressing, I decided to go ahead and pick up what I needed on the way back.

Pulling up to the curb in front of the Post Office, I quickly got out. All of a sudden, after I had moved only a step, a terrific 'kaboom' sounded, nearly knocking me over. A huge blast from planted explosives detonating nearly destroyed the postal facilities. Dust and pieces of building blew all around me with the pickup truck protecting me. I stood there absolutely stunned.

Then there was a moment of dead silence before police and army arrived with fire trucks, ambulances and sirens blasting.

Then it hit me. I realized that if I hadn't paused those few minutes at the church, I would have been inside the Post Office getting my mail out of our box.

Tears came to my eyes as I realized how the Lord had been with me, giving me His protection. All I could do was quietly praise the Lord for His intervention in delaying me. No wonder I could not remember what I needed in the church! Immediately I went home to share what had happened with Carlos.

Anxiously he met me at the door. **"I heard a terrible blast in town. What happened?"** he questioned.

I quickly explained the whole situation and how the Lord had cared for me. We hugged and said a prayer of thanksgiving. Also we knew many people were praying for us that day as well as every day. The prayers of the righteous are truly effective!

He has delivered us from such a deadly peril, and he will deliver us. On him we have set our hope that he will continue to deliver us, as you help us by your prayers. Then many will give thanks on our behalf for the gracious favor granted us in answer to the prayers of many." 2Co 1:10-11

Carlos: Under Trees

We had preached under trees at Okomboni (Oh-ko-mm-BOW-nee) on the edge of Tsumeb town for several weeks and had many converts. Okomboni, meaning quarters or location, housed more than two thousand mineworkers. We were persistent in teaching the new converts and had plans to baptize them and organize a church.

One Sunday morning following the service, I was standing aside from the crowd talking with those who had come forward during the service. A stranger, a tall, resolute and very pleasant man, approached and introduced himself as Jesaja (Yea-SA-ya) Shavingi (Shah-VEEN-gee).

He said, "I was walking by and heard your singing. It is the best singing I believe I have ever heard. Where did you get these songs? I have not heard these songs before."

I explained that these were songs our people in America sing in church; Amazing Grace, What a Friend We Have in Jesus, Blessed Assurance and more. We were translating them and teaching them to the people.

Jesaja asked, "Could I attend your services and learn these songs?"

"We would be pleased if you were to do that."

"I am a member of another church. I would not want to join your church. Could I come just to learn the songs?"

"That would be fine. We would be happy to have you."

Each time we were at Okomboni after that day, Jesaja was there learning our songs. He was always very pleasant, happy and seemed to have much joy in whatever he did. We learned that he had come from his village in the north to work in the mine. He would work for two or three months and return to his village for some days, taking back to his family goods he could buy from having worked in the mine. He appeared to be happy as a part of our group and to be able to learn our songs.

One Tuesday morning, when I was at home doing some office work, I looked out the window and saw Jesaja coming down the sidewalk. I went outside, greeted him and invited him in. He appeared to be somewhat distressed. I asked if he had some problem.

He said, "Do you recall the first day we met at Okomboni?"

"Yes, I well remember."

"Do you remember that I told you that I would not join your church?"

"Yes, I remember, and I told you that it would be fine for you to come just to learn our songs."

After some moments of hesitation he said, "I think that I am about to change my mind. You have been preaching about being born again. I want to be born again. Can I be born again like you preach at Okomboni?"

I assured him that he could. We spent quite a long time looking at Bible verses which gave him assurance that he could be born again.

He again said, "I want to be born again."

We prayed with his repeating phrases after me. He confessed Christ as his personal Savior and left our house a very happy man with his new experience and his new birth.

Some time later I baptized those who had accepted Jesus as Savior with plans to organize the church at Okomboni. I told them that, as we had many places to go, we would be back after three weeks and asked them to be thinking of who they would want to be their church leaders. I explained that since we would not be able to be with them every Sunday, they would need to choose their leaders, including their pastor, from among their congregation.

Two days later as I was in town, I came upon one of the men from the church. We greeted and spoke of our joy over the new church at Okomboni. Then he told me something, which startled me. He said that Jesaja had two wives. The news dumbfounded me, as Jesaja had told us that he was a member of another church. As I had already baptized him, we wondered how we could deal with this delicate dilemma. Myrtice and I talked and prayed about it and decided that we would carry on and ask for the Lord's leadership in dealing with the situation as it became necessary.

After the three weeks we returned to Okomboni. I preached and we led the excited and happy people in choosing leaders for their church. They chose all the other leaders, leaving the pastor to the end.

I asked, "Who do you want for your pastor?"

In one accord they all said, "Jesaja. He is our best leader."

Silently I was thinking, "Please, Lord, please help me."

Prayerfully I told them that they could not have Jesaja and showed them in the Bible where it says that the pastor must be the husband of one wife. They accepted my council and chose Kumalu (Koo-MA-lou) who was also a very good leader. He led the church well.

Some weeks passed and Kumalu showed up at our house late one afternoon. He was apparently extremely happy. I asked him why he was so happy.

"We have good news. A man came yesterday and told us that Jesaja's two wives were in the field hoeing. There came a thunder storm and the lightening struck and killed one of them." Then quickly he continued, "Isn't that good news? Now Jesaja has only one wife. He can be a preacher, can't he?"

A bit taken back I was slow in responding. I admit that I had problems with Kumalu's theology.

We grieved with Jesaja in the loss of one of his wives. He went home to bury her and returned to his work in the mine, remaining faithful in the church. All the while he became more involved with his spiritual journey with special interest in learning and using our songs. He studied his Bible, especially the parts which speak of being saved or being born again.

After some months Jesaja gave up his work at the mine and returned to live with his family in Owamboland (Oh-VHAM-bow-land) in the north. He had only been there a few weeks when he wrote requesting that we come. He said that he had been calling the villagers together each afternoon under a large tree. He had been teaching them our songs and, from the Scriptures, how to be born again. He wanted us to assist him in getting a church going in his village. As soon as we could arrange it we went to Omatando (O-ma-TAHN-doe) to visit Jesaja. Knowing that we were coming, he had called the villagers together. We sang and then Jesaja called those who had accepted Jesus to stand with him at the front. More than two dozen, both men and women, joined him. Jesaja shared with us that the headman, who was also present, had given permission to have their meetings under the tree and had promised the church land nearby for a building when they would be able to have one. We rejoiced with more singing and I preached. As we sang again several more joined us at the front.

Jesaja led the Omatando church from its beginning. The church continued to grow and, with our help, built a very nice building accommodating about 200 people. Prior to our coming back to the US, Simeon, the headman accepted Jesus. Jesaja baptized him and he became an active member. Yes, God had a purpose in Jesaja's life and made it possible to use him for His glory.

"All of these must be done for the strengthening of the church." 1Co 14:26b

M: Sudden Shutdown

We were anxious to spread our witness outside of the town and into Owamboland where the greater population lived. The war continued to spread through other areas. We knew that the South African Army checked major roads regularly for land mines before allowing vehicles to pass. The army drove large anti-mine vehicles, looking like huge crickets, for protection since so many land mines were used. Many of the mines were accidentally set off by children. Numerous lives were lost or maimed. We knew any work would take a lot of care and praying.

When we heard that the roads to this area were cleared we were anxious to see the commander of the SA army for permission to work in the area since everything was under his command. We were interested in an area half way to Oshakati, the major town in the north, in a place called Omutsegonime (Omm-Say-go-NEE-may), meaning Lion's Head, where the family of one of the new Christians who worked in the mine lived. He had begged us to go to his village.

On the main army base we endured the passing of command to be finally allowed to see the commander of the large army base in a formal meeting. He agreed that at the present he would grant us permission to work but it could be rescinded anytime fighting broke out. We were so pleased that we could really have a witness there. We had prayed about it and felt this was the place to which God was leading us.

Stopping at one of the shops lined up on the roadside in Omutsegonime, we asked where we could find the headman's house. An older man directed us to the buildings in the highest area. We asked about the dangers but all he would do was shrug his shoulders.

Driving through the deep sand we found the headman's house on the top of a nearby hill. After telling him of our intentions of beginning a church and helping the people with clinics he responded cordially.

"You'll be very welcome here to help us," he said. "Our people have no churches, no medical help and we are just very poor." The headman was a very sharp, intelligent and clean looking man. "I'll be happy to set up a meeting next week. We can hear you and would be thankful for any medical help you can give. We are a long way from medical facilities."

On the day of our return many had gathered around in front of the shop where we had first inquired. The area was bone dry, dust blowing strongly through the air and felt like a hot air blower in our faces. Neither the dust nor the wind seemed to bother them. Many people were standing in front of the shop in a small, open building with a tin roof and no sides. Carlos spoke to the group, explaining who we were and what our intentions were. All seemed very interested and listened well. We shared our purpose of beginning a church and my having primary care clinics for those in need. They all agreed and seemed so pleased that we had come. We were so excited that we were really getting something started in this desolate area. After a short message we sat up tables, unloaded boxes of medicine and I began to see those in need while Carlos visited with others.

Suddenly, six huge army trucks and anti-land mine vehicles pulled up right beside us. Quickly, over twenty men jumped out of the trucks, each with a gun. We were utterly startled. The clinic had only begun for half hour with my seeing barely ten patients; mostly children with terrible eye infections and some with dysentery. I was wearing my white lab coat with South African nursing pins and had medical supplies on a nearby table.

The commander looked straight at me and said, "You must leave now. This is a very dangerous area. Terrorists are nearby and they have been kidnapping medical personnel to treat the wounded. Please leave immediately! You will not be permitted in this area for a long time."

Without question we apologized to the people, had a brief prayer and closed up our work and left in a state of shock, wondering what would be the future here. We had felt so assured that this was the place God was leading us.

Consequently we were not permitted to do any work there for over two years. God had opened the door but the devil had quickly closed this one. We felt a real peace that God was still in control and sometime a witness in Omutsegonime would come. Later we will tell how God did overcome in this village resulting in a strong church and faithful following.

"I have told you these things, so that in me you may have peace. In this world you will have trouble. But take heart! I have overcome the world." Jn 16:33

C: Funeral

It was common for bombs to explode in public places. Two American diplomats died in Oshakati when a bomb exploded next to the gas pump where they were filling their car. Our local bank and Post Office had been damaged. Land mines exploded on major roads and there was the occasional shoot out in a market place or in living quarters. Sometimes we had strict curfews. Other times we were as cautious as we could be, not going out in the late afternoon or evening as terrorists were known to attack late in the evening, usually at sundown, in order to have the night to get away on foot. The South African Army had conscripted the agile and small in stature Bushmen as trackers. They had keen senses of hearing and sight but could only track when there was daylight.

Earlier on, we only traveled outside of Tsumeb in caravans escorted by heavily armed South African soldiers. When the Army felt that an area was clear of terrorists they would allow us to travel without the escort.

We took extreme caution when going into places where terrorists were active. We did venture out with caution into some areas knowing that our safety could be in jeopardy.

We drove one day to the Kavango Region to spy out the area in search for possible places to begin establishing churches. That day we met Moses Tololi (Toe-LOW-lee).

Moses, having been born in Angola, had spent time in Russia training to become a terrorist. He initially returned to northern Namibia to assist in the terrorist activities related to his homeland, Angola, which was just across the Great Kavango River. On returning to Namibia however he was converted and, though still interested in freedom for his people in Angola, his focus changed leaving all interests in terrorism. He married and began his family. We met him there at a funeral.

On this very hot and windy day we were driving along the dusty, dirt road in Kaisosi (Kah-ee-SO-see), a very large African location a few miles outside Rundu town, the

Administrative Headquarters of the Kavango Region when we came upon a very large gathering. We stopped to make inquiry and found that they were mourning the death of the woman who had died in Angola.

This woman had crossed the River to visit her family. While there she became ill and died. Because of the intensity of the civil war in the area they were not able to bring her body back across the river. Neither her husband nor her children were able to attend the burial. Relatives in Angola buried her. Back in Namibia family and friends gathered to mourn the woman's passing. There were several hundred people standing around, sitting on makeshift benches and chairs and some sitting on mats on the ground. They told us about what had happened.

We were paying our respects to the family of the deceased woman when a man approached and asked if I were a preacher. He said that some of those present were Christians but they had no preacher.

When I confirmed that I was a preacher, he asked. "Could you preach for us?"

Not having been in the area very long I felt that I could not preach in the local language having no time for preparation. I asked if there were anyone there who spoke Swahili. I really cannot explain why I asked as Swahili was the language of Eastern Africa where we had served for 25 years -- all the way across the continent.

The answer was "Yes, there is a man here who used to live where they speak Swahili."

The man went into the crowd and soon returned with Moses. How grateful I felt that this unusual opportunity opened to comfort the bereaved family and to share the Gospel. I preached in Swahili and Moses interpreted into the local Luchazi language. The entire crowd listened with eagerness and many expressed appreciation.

Afterwards Moses asked, "Do you plan to have a church in our village?" He said that if we were to have a church there, he wanted to be a part of it. He explained that when he was a child in Angola he attended a mission Sunday school and, since growing up and coming to Namibia, had wondered if he would ever again be able to attend a Sunday school.

Two weeks passed and we returned to Kaisosi where we met with Moses and a number of others who wanted to have a church there. Thankfully some of them had been members and leaders in churches in Angola. We worshipped with them and laid secure plans for a church in Kaisosi. In a matter of five years this church became our largest in the area and had more than 800 baptized members. Moses, demonstrating exceptional leadership, became the Kaisosi pastor and led the church to have an outreach program assisting other villages to have churches. They became involved and assisted in the beginning of 18 more churches. Every three or four months many of the churches would come together at Kaisosi for fellowship. Usually there would be a baptismal service. Their enthusiasm and joy in worship was absolutely exciting to witness.

We stand in awe and amazement at how God used that funeral to open the door of opportunity for the Kaisosi people and the surrounding villages.

And pray for us, too, that God may open a door
for our message. . ." Col 4:3a

Chapter Two

Where and How It Began

The authors, having come from different states and backgrounds, share their lives being brought together to serve the Lord through missions in Africa.

Carlos's Story:

I sat on the back bench with four of my friends next to an open window. We had agreed, "If she heads our way, we will go out the window."

The preaching was finished and the singing of the invitation hymn had begun. As we suspected, she, standing at her normal place at the front of the church and on the left side, looked around and directly at us. She left her place and headed in our direction.

"Here she comes." I thought. I nudged the fellow next to me and we quickly climbed out the open window. The other three followed.

The next night we had the same plan but things went different. Four boys went out the window while I went down the aisle, meeting her about half way. God's Spirit had tugged at my heart. The Lord pulled hard on me and there was no climbing out the window. I hurried on to the front, took the preacher by the hand and made my profession of faith. I publicly accepted Jesus as my Savior that night. I was twelve years old.

Three weeks later I was baptized, along with two women, in the Tennessee River beneath the Scott Fitzhugh Bridge. From that time I was eager to live for Jesus and took every opportunity which came my way to serve Him.

I became a member of the Point Pleasant Baptist Church which had been known as the Baptist Church of Christ at Point Pleasant in the early 1800s. In the mid 1940's when I was saved it was still very much a country church. Many attended by buggy or wagons pulled by mules. I recall that during one revival meeting, mules became tangled in their chains causing quite a commotion. The preacher paused, told the men to go and take care of the mules and continued with his sermon.

My mother told me that before I was born, during revivals, women were accustomed to leaving their babies asleep in their wagons or buggies. From time to time one or two women would go and check on them. On one particular night a group of boys waited until these women had checked on the babies and had gone back into the church. They then switched babies among the wagons. My mother said that you could hear wagons until daybreak the next morning as parents went in search for their babies.

My parents were Raymond and Della Nora Rice Owens. I was the eighth and last of six boys. I had four sisters. I, along with all my siblings except my oldest brother, was born in a three-room log house near Eagle Creek in Henry Co., in west Tennessee.

Dad, during that time was a farmer, blacksmith and railroad worker. About 1936 he built an eight room, two story concrete block house for us on the main highway about a mile away and became a building contractor in 1941. He later, along with his construction work, moved houses and pumped sand from a dredge ditch near where he and my mother lived after the children had left home.

My first schooling was at Point Pleasant School, next to the Point Pleasant Baptist Church. Frank Pflueger's father, John Christian Pflueger and his wife, Eliza, my great grandmother's sister had given land for the church, cemetery and school in 1854. The school was one room with one teacher and eight grades.

I graduated from High School in Paris, the county seat, in the spring of 1948, surrendered to preach while working in Detroit that summer and entered Union University, Jackson, TN that fall.

In late summer of 1949 when I was nineteen, both the Morning Shade and Birds' Creek churches in Henry County called me as pastor; half time at each place. Early the following year Friendship church, also in Henry County, called me to preach for them two Sunday afternoons a month. In September of 1950 Bird's Creek went full time so I resigned Morning Shade but continued preaching for Friendship for another year. I continued at Birds' Creek to February, 1955—my last year at the seminary.

I earned a BA in English from Union University, Jackson, TN. While there during my second year I had my first encounter with foreign missions when missionaries came during a week of mission emphasis. After several personal conferences with them I felt that I wanted to be a foreign missionary. I began praying that God would call me.

At Southern Baptist Seminary, Louisville, KY, I continued praying that God would call me. I met Myrtice there. God had already called her. We began dating.

During a chapel program on missionary day I felt the call and surrendered to serve full time as a foreign missionary.

Myrtice's Story:

The night was so dark! The road went right through the orange groves on my side of town. "I must peddle as fast as I can," I thought to myself as I dreaded the dark road ahead. It really was a scary place as there were no lights at all in this area though I was sixteen years old.

As I stood up from the seat of my bicycle I just couldn't put any pressure on the pedals. A great heaviness came over me and I just had to stop.

"Myrtice, I want you to serve me" came a voice, not audible but as clear as anything to my heart. Overcome with the holiness of the moment, I kneeled there in the road by my bicycle.

I had just heard the first missionary I had ever met in our small First Baptist Church in Dunedin, Florida. I had been deeply impressed with her enthusiasm as she shared the many wonderful things that God had done through her in China. Her presentation of the desperate needs of the people touched a tender spot in my heart. She was tall, thin, wearing a black dress with a Chinese type collar, and her hair pulled sternly back to form a ball on her head. She had never married but had given her life to serve the Lord in China.

"Lord, I love you, but I want to be normal," thinking of her old maid status. I thought all missionary women had to be single to serve. I had dreamed of a having a husband and family. Quickly I felt ashamed I could consider this excuse. "Lord, forgive my selfishness."

"Myrtice, I want you to serve as a nurse, a missionary nurse to help others to know me and my love for them," the Spirit spoke to my heart again.

I was overcome in that moment. I knew I had nothing. I was from a poor family and schooling would be necessary, but without funds how would I prepare myself? Instantly I felt God touching me in a firm but gentle manner.

"Give your life to me for I want you to serve me. I will be with you."

Without hesitation I realized serving God was far more important than any of my desires. I replied to this call of God, "Lord, I don't know how this is possible but I want to serve you with all my heart and to give you my very best. You have given me such joy and life. I want to do what you want me to do." From that moment my commitment was strong and God was with me every step of the way.

Growing up in Florida on the western Gulf coast in a small town called Dunedin, gave me a completely different background from Carlos. Our home was surrounded on three sides with orange groves. Even going to town, we passed through the large areas of the fruit trees. The smell of orange blossoms or the sight of sweet yellow ripe fruit was commonplace for me. So for God to deal with me in an orange grove with the heavily perfumed air of orange blossoms was only a natural way of signifying the sweet aroma of God's call.

In my family of four children, two boys and two girls, I was the youngest. The family rarely thought of church or attended even though our parents claimed Christianity. Father, Leonard, worked as a mechanic in a repair shop of work vehicles of one of the largest citrus groves. Since he had a bad habit of drinking away his pay check every weekend, Mother worked in the fruit business too, packing fruit for shipment. Of course this situation brought much unhappiness as we struggled to have the basics of life.

My older sister married very young and my brothers enlisted extra early in the Navy during WWII, misrepresenting their ages. It was my job to prepare the evening meal before my parents came home. Saturday meant I had to clean the house thoroughly. I also earned extra money baby sitting, working after school in the soda fountain of a drug store and later in Penney's department store in the next town of Clearwater. These responsibilities developed a great sense of independence and reliability. Transportation for me was my old faithful bicycle or local buses.

The summer was the times of the greatest joy to me. We lived right near the Gulf Coast so bicycling to Clearwater Beach or rowing in the Dunedin Bay with a dear friend, looking for scallops or swimming, was so enjoyable. We would often plan together to spend a few days on Paradise Island, rowing over and living in a very crude fisherman's cabin which belonged to her family. Truly it was paradise to me, a place of peace, beauty, fun, and being close to nature.

My first encounter with feeling about God was when I was only four or five years old. Whenever I even heard the name God or Jesus huge tears would come to my eyes. This happened many times but I really did not know why. I had not been around church to even know what this was all about, but this was a very vivid memory to me.

My conversion was really brought about by several circumstances. While I was sitting in a hot car outside a saloon on a very hot Sunday while my parents were inside, I began to realize that this wasn't the direction I wanted my life to go. During that long wait people came out staggering, falling, vomiting, quarreling and fighting. I was repulsed.

I was a fourteen years old now. When I started thinking about this situation there was one thing very clear. I wanted a happier and more satisfying life than my parents had.

When I thought of those who impressed me, my favorite school teacher came to mind. She motivated me to do my best in everything. She was a Christian and let it be known, even in the classroom. I began to realize that going to church must make a difference. She was a faithful Methodist and shared openly about her faith. I decided to visit her church and see if it would make a difference in my life. That visit just wasn't successful. I felt like such a stranger in this place.

After school I often worked at the town's drugstore that had a soda fountain. The manager was so kind and helpful to me. He attended the Presbyterian Church so I decided to go there to find a better direction. Again, I felt so out of place, strange and unaccepted.

"Well, maybe I will try one of the other churches in town, the Baptist," I thought after the last incident.

After parking my bicycle by the side of the church I stood in front under the tree near the entrance to be sure if I really wanted to go in.

Fortunately, a smiling lady came up to me to welcome me, "It's so nice that you have come to join us today. I think I have seen you in town." Evidently she could see my shyness and awkwardness. "Would you sit with me?"

After that warm welcome and someone to feel comfortable with I experienced a life changing situation in the service that day. The worship and the preaching opened my heart to the One that I needed in my life. That very day I wanted Christ in my heart. That hand of this lady reaching out to me made all the difference in the world.

"Where are your parents?" asked the pastor as he was getting ready to baptize me three weeks later.

"They didn't want to come tonight" is all I could say.

In a short time so much had happened to me. I just felt like a new person but my parents were too busy in their concerns to be very involved with me. From that time on I became a part of everything the church had to offer. I had found a loving family fellowship. Fortunately they had mission organizations. So in the next two years I learned the magnificence of the world of missions. I must confess that I often went because I didn't want to miss the delicious cookies that our dear Miss Mary baked for us. Many times I would be the only girl present, but Miss Mary would have the full lesson and let me write a letter to a missionary for whom we had prayed.

When God called me at sixteen in that orange grove, my church teachings had prepared me. My intellect, my heart and my understanding of missions were ripe and ready to answer the Master's call. My favorite verse that spurred me on and kept me focused on God's call was in Romans 12:1-2, "Offer your bodies as living sacrifices, holy and pleasing to God".

After completing Clearwater High School among the top six scholars, I immediately entered Mather School of Nursing in New Orleans, an intriguing city. The studies included classes at Tulane University which excited me to no end.

Life opened possibilities for service through the Baptist Student Union, an organization of college students. Upon seeing the slum area right behind our dorm, I started a 'Saturday Sunday school'. The black children loved the songs, flannel graph stories of the Bible and the fun games. My mission work was beginning!

Every part of nursing was a joy to me. The Lord gave me a deep voice which was soothing to the patients. I tried to learn all I could in and out of school. One of the doctors, knowing my interest in missions, took me to the Leprosarium in southern Louisiana, where he did facial surgery. I observed the patients and learned much about the disease from the staff.

After completing nurses training and state board examinations, I became a registered nurse. I worked for a year between New Orleans and Clearwater, Florida to earn money to enter Florida State University in Tallahassee. Since I had extra credits from Tulane, I earned my Bachelor of Science in Nursing Education and did practice teaching at FSU. I was invited to teach nursing but the call to continue my education at the seminary prevailed after teaching one term.

During college and graduate school, I served as campus nurse, working full time in the infirmary to pay my tuition. Since the doctors didn't like to come out during the night, they provided standing orders to follow until they came the next morning. This gave valuable experience for diagnosing and treating primary care problems.

Summers were enriching by serving in Florida as nurse in our denomination's state youth camps. One summer the camp staff worked with the Seminole Indians, enlightening my interest in primitive lifestyles.

From college I entered Women's Missionary Union Training School in Louisville, Kentucky for graduate studies. The next year it became the Carver School of Missions and Social Work. It was located next to the Southern Seminary where we took over half our classes. This gave opportunity to meet men training for the ministry. After two years I earned a Master's Degree in Religious Education and felt ready to enter foreign missions.

"Here am I, Send me!" Isa 6:8b

C: Joining Forces

Bill said, "Carlos, I want you to meet Myrtice Taylor, Polly's friend. We want the two of you to join us for the early morning Thanksgiving service."

Bill and Polly had been dating for some time. Myrtice and Polly worked together as nurses in the school infirmary. The school was just across the way on the next hill with a small valley connecting them. Most called it "the valley of decision" since many students met life partners there.

"Will you go with us to Crescent Hill Church?"

"OK. Sounds good to me."

We enjoyed the service and afterwards drove around for a time. I liked Myrtice and enjoyed very much being with her. I was impressed with her looks, dedication and her interest in missions. She was from Florida and a mission volunteer. I wanted to be a missionary too so she and I started dating.

While in the seminary, I was also pastor in West Tennessee commuting 250 miles each way on weekends, leaving school at noon on Friday and getting back late on Monday or early Tuesday morning if having come by train.. Myrtice was full time nurse and full time student. We had little time together except in the library in the evenings.

I was moving a bit slow for Myrtice. She, not being sure of my intentions, proceeded with her application for foreign missionary service. One evening in the library she slipped a letter from the Foreign Mission Board over to me. I saw quickly that it was a letter of her acceptance to serve as a nurse in Southern Rhodesia (now Zimbabwe). That was enough for me. Within a few days I asked for permission to visit her and her family in Florida over the Christmas holidays. She said that she would be pleased.

While there I proposed and asked her father for her hand in marriage. Just after midnight on January 1, 1955 as we walked on the Clearwater Beach, she accepted my proposal.

*"For this reason a man will leave his father
and his mother and be united to his wife and
they will become one flesh" Ge 2:24*

M: Interlude

First Baptist, Dover, TN, called Carlos in February 1955. We both received our graduate degrees from the seminary in May and married on June 17 at my home church, First Baptist in Dunedin, Florida. My whole church assisted in helping us have a beautiful wedding from decorating to providing the reception afterwards. They had been so faithful in encouraging my mission call and now participating in helping us as a couple to join forces to go to Africa. Even our wedding included our commitment to the call of God to serve in Africa. Following our honeymoon in Sarasota, Florida we moved into the small parsonage in Dover. Though we hardly had the basics in our house we were so very happy in all we had. It would be a great time of preparing ourselves in this interim for later. Before accepting the church Carlos had informed them of our plans for appointment and going to Africa in mid 1957.

Those two years in Dover were invaluable to our establishing our marriage and working enough to buy the necessities for home furnishings. Carlos developed a good ministry in the church which was evidenced by the numerical growth and activities. He found many challenges in reaching out to the rural community where moonshine was illegally made in many of the hills and hollers. In spite of some encounters with rough ungodly men, he reached many for salvation and baptism into the church. The loving fellowship of the church and its own mission interests strengthened our goals and experience. We particularly loved our special times with the youth group with regular Sunday night fun and food at our house.

Driving over very extremely winding roads to the nearest hospital in Paris, TN became my daily trek to go to my nursing job. Nursing in delivery room, surgical unit, to medical-surgical floors gave me varied experiences and contacts. After becoming highly pregnant with our first daughter, I was asked to teach nursing to one of the new practical nurses classes which I enjoyed immensely.

The night Janice was born Carlos was away for a revival in a church out in the county. I had gone into labor after he had left in early afternoon. I was waiting for his return home to take me to the hospital. To give him a signal I had placed my small packed bag on the porch with the porch light burning. Being a nurse I felt like I had plenty of time but when he returned late, I was in full heavy labor. It excited him so much that he took off with me in the backseat of the car in only a couple of minutes. The winding roads kept him from going very fast heightening his concern that he may not get to the hospital in time having to go twenty-five miles. Soon as the road straightened he began to really hit the accelerator. Nearing midnight in the sleepy town with no cars around, he ran a red light being afraid that he might not get there in time since my groaning had really become so frequent. The blue lights of a police car stopped him giving him more frustration. But the policeman saw the dilemma and quickly escorted us into the hospital emergency area. It wasn't long before he was a proud father holding his beautiful little daughter with a full head of hair to which someone had attached a pink bow.

After our daughter Janice was born, our plans for the foreign field became the center of our focus - preparing for appointment and the time of departure. Our appointment to Tanganyika, East Africa in mid-March 1957, in Richmond, Virginia, was an experience that fulfilled our dreams and call.

Men in the church helped us to crate our goods. Big farewells were given with the church, our home churches and our families. We had a big send off from the church in Dover. They surprised us with a new car to use on the mission field. They had traded ours in without our knowing it. We sailed in June of 1957 from New York on the Queen Mary with little Janice being ten months old. We had a tremendous joy and an eagerness to follow our calling to the other side of the world.

Chapter Three

Dar es Salaam

Dar es Salaam, Arabic for harbor of safety or peace, was a sprawling tropical city of 120,000 people when we arrived in 1957. We were impressed with massive groves of coconut palms, mango, avocado, banana, guava, papaya, and cashew trees most of which had been imported by early settlers. Tropical flowering trees and vines as well as ferns and flowers of many species were in most gardens and along streets.

Fish venders passed daily through most neighborhoods with their blue and red fish and the occasional shark. Others came with chickens.

Breezes blew from the Indian Ocean most of the time and though sometimes uncomfortably hot helped in making for very delightful surroundings.

Tanganyika was a German Colony prior to World War I and became a Trust Territory under Great Britain following that war. The British were there in an administrative capacity when we arrived. Arabs had been in Tanganyika for decades. Their influence was apparent on every hand. Asian Indians came early to assist in the laying of the railroads and were owners of many of the shops and other businesses as well as sisal and kapok plantations in the surrounding area.

M: At Sea

Our big moment had come! Our hearts seemed to bounce with joy and our bodies wanted to jump up and down as little children in excitement for this tremendous moment. It was the most ecstatic feeling we had ever had and hardly believable that a near lifetime of preparation for a work in Africa was being fulfilled. Our emotions had built up to this special time of arrival. Having keenly felt the anticipation of God's calling for many years, this answered our dreams and heart calling. Beautiful Africa!

Our ship was now moving into the peaceful harbor of Dar es Salaam which was surrounded by graceful coconut palms swaying in the light breezes. The water was smooth and glass-like as a tugboat brought our ship into the inner harbor. As we neared the docks the crowd of passengers had the same excitement of arriving at their destination. We all leaned over the railings, straining to see the dock side. Suddenly we could see hundreds of hands waving vigorously—welcoming all aboard. The excitement below paralleled that above on ship. Most of the passengers were returning to their homes and loved ones who were living and working here.

"Welcome to Tanganyika!" shouted the crowd with vigorous hand waves. Our hearts welled up with emotion. Tears filled our eyes when we recognized fellow missionary families who were there to receive us, holding up a big sign of welcome. They were just as excited to receive another couple to add to the brand new mission that was just starting out in East Africa.

Our hearts had been wrenched in saying goodbyes to our loved ones in America, but replaced with the joy of the reality of actually arriving in this beautiful land. We had been on board a ship, with our small daughter, for five and half weeks since leaving New York. Our thoughts whirled with the newness, unimaginable sights, the smells and heat. From leaving all with which we were familiar, we felt the challenge of replacing it with this new and strange world. Our imaginations were overwhelmed with the possibilities of actually putting feet on our dreams and calling.

Coming ashore, we descended the gangplank to this challenging land. After going through customs we met and hugged our dear mission families, all strangers to us but more as family. Seven families had arrived only a few months before to establish new work in East Africa, i.e. Tanganyika, Kenya and Uganda, among millions of people. Three had come from Nigeria and the Foreign Mission Board had appointed and assigned four more families to the area. Three of the seven couples were to establish themselves in

Kenya. The rest were presently beginning work in Tanganyika. Later work would be established in Uganda. These had just completed six months of studying the national language of Swahili. Our mission was to establish a strong witness in this vast and heavily populated region on the eastern side of Africa. We were the eighth couple added to this force to do pioneer missions of evangelism and church planting.

The trip alone was the best orientation to our future country. We sailed on the Queen Mary across the Atlantic to England to board another ship, the Warwick Castle, which would go through the Mediterranean Sea by way of the Red Sea to the eastern side of Africa. The cities at ports of call were like living a story book of adventures in the Port of Gibraltar; Marseilles, France; Genoa, Italy; Port Saidi, Egypt; Aden; Mombasa, Kenya and Zanzibar. Merchants came alongside the ship to sell their wares. At some places we could take day trips out to explore these ancient cities. A sand storm across the Sahara Desert hit our ship while we were passing through the Red Sea, tossing us with the strong winds filled with dust seemingly for days.

Our point of call in Mombasa, Kenya, was special, since one couple of our mission had just settled there. They helped to give us a good orientation of the area and African life.

Sharing the voyage with mainly British expatriates, we received an education in itself of British formalism, etiquette, manners and traditions. This was an unexpected plus since we would be working closely with them in the government and communities. Their traditions and language were absolutely strange to us. Scones were biscuits. Biscuits were cookies. Pudding was dessert. 'Bubbles and squeak' for breakfast was fried leftover potatoes and cabbage! Cars have windscreens for windshields, bonnets for hoods, and boots for trunks and petrol for gasoline. We even had a new English language to learn. Their etiquette and protocol were extremely formal for us easy-going southerners.

The city had streets filled with people walking or riding bicycles, as well as many animals. We were nearly overcome with the heavy heat and humidity. The pot-holed roads added extra bounce to the rough ride while we were driven to our abode. A small flat (apartment) awaited us until further housing was ready right across the road from an African village. All windows were wide open to catch the slightest breezes. The beds were covered with mosquito nets. It was a sweet sleep that night as we tucked in our mosquito nets, listened to the rhythmic beat of the drums and dreamed of the future for which God had prepared us.

C: Studying Swahili

We knew before we arrived, that we would study Swahili in Dar for nine months. Since there was not yet an established language school, we sought the help of Sister Veronica, a University Missions to Central Africa (UMCA) Anglican missionary, who knew Swahili well. We hired her to assist us two afternoons a week. The rest of the time we studied on our own or with the help of conversants, nationals who spoke excellent Swahili, with whom we could practice conversing in the language. We spent as much time as possible with Africans in the market place, in the shops and along the way.

Sister Veronica wore a gray garment similar to a Catholic nun's garb. The white band under her chin was tight and she could hardly open her mouth so did not speak clearly. Being solidly motivated to learn, we threw all our energies into learning the language well. It would be the major means of communicating the Gospel. All went well though, as we both passed the Government Swahili exam subsequent to our leaving language study. We would continue our study and practice of Swahili the rest of our career in East Africa in order to better comprehend and more thoroughly understand the language and more proficiently minister to the people.

While in Dar, a missionary from another country who had been in Tanganyika for more than twenty-five years remarked, "You will never sound like an African. You will always keep your American way of saying things."

His statement became a challenge to us. We worked hard at not only learning the meaning of the language but also the way to pronounce words and phrases and how to use them. Years of being closely related to the Africans and using their language continually in conversation, preaching, and teaching made a difference in this process.

After some years and working daily with the Africans, we began hearing them say that we sounded like them. One day we were carrying on a conversation in Swahili at a petrol (gas) station.

An African standing near by but not seeing us turned around quickly and commented, "Where did you learn Swahili? Were you born here? You speak as we do. On hearing you I thought that you would be black."

How pleased we were to receive such a compliment.

"I have become all things to all men that by all possible means I might save some." ICo. 9:22b

M: Lepers and Oranges

Fascinating to the eye, sometimes repulsive to the nose, the local open market was one of the very first places to visit for food supplies. Piles of beautiful oranges, fresh coconuts, freshly cut ripe banana stocks, tomatoes, fresh greens, dried beans and onions were all measured out in little piles ready for sale.

Soon the nose took over, however, when we passed the tables with sun dried fish. The horrible sickening smell was nearly unbearable. We were also taken back when passing the meat area, seeing carcasses of freshly slaughtered animals hanging in the heat and covered with flies. Was this place to be our main source of food? No American products were available although there were many strange and different imported foods in the market place and in the Asian shops run by the Indians, the main tradesmen in Tanganyika. Hence all meals would be cooked from scratch from here on.

Throughout the market were Arab vendors selling ginger tea and strong coffee poured from brass cone-shaped pots kept warm with small charcoal burners. The small cups were rinsed out in not too clean water between customers. Though we were tempted to experience this interesting custom, our common sense helped us refrain for health's sake.

After passing the piles of beautiful oranges we observed three beggars seated on the ground in a semicircle extending their deformed hands to us begging for money. Having been in the Leprosarium in Louisiana years before, I was shocked to see similar cases. Their flattened noses, deformed ears, nubs of fingers and toes, were all symptoms of leprosy, sitting right here in the food market, next to the oranges. The disease ate away the cartilage of their bodies. Some leprosy, also called Hanson's disease, was found throughout the country. Though leprosy is not supposed to be very communicable, it did bring concern especially in the place where food is sold.

From now on all food would have to be washed or peeled or soaked in antiseptic solution so we could care for our own health. Just ordinary living would take far more care and work than we had ever imagined. We wanted to care for our bodies in order to fulfill the calling of serving God and to honor him.

"Do you not know that your body is a temple of the Holy Spirit, Therefore honor God with your body." ICo. 6:19a, 20

C: Gods May be Asleep

Having seen the Hindu temple, we decided to visit there one day. We stood for a while outside observing the ornate architecture of the building. The priest standing at the top of the long flight of steps leading into the temple came down and greeted us. We told him that we would be pleased if he were to allow us to visit his temple. He smiled with delight and told us to wait.

He turned and ran to the top of the steps where a little bell hangs on a small chain. He took the bell and shook it vigorously. Coming back down to us he motioned with his hands and said that we could come into the temple. He explained that the gods might be asleep and that he must awake them by ringing the bell before allowing visitors to enter the temple.

Climbing the steps with the priest, we found the temple area filled with many ornately carved and molded idols. A woman was standing and praying before a small table in front of one of the idols. As she prayed, she moved rice around with her fingers making designs on the table.

The priest explained that the gods in his temple were just a few of hundreds of gods. As he led us around, he explained how some of them had come to be gods. Pointing to the monkey god he explained, "Many years ago the wife of a king was kidnapped. The king of the monkeys called all the monkeys together and assisted in the rescue of the king's wife. Because of this good deed the king of the monkeys became a god."

Next to the monkey god were that king, his wife and his son, all being gods.

The elephant god was a man's body with an elephant head. Pointing to it the priest said, "A prince was beheaded. Immediately they cut off the head of an elephant and placed it on the prince's shoulders. The prince lived for many years with the elephant's head and became the elephant god, so says the Hindu scriptures."

The priest accompanied us as we descended the long flight of steps. Near the foot of the steps was a "sacred tree" covered with tiny lights which, he said, never were allowed to go out. Nearby was a large pan containing a fire, which, he said was also never allowed to go out. Around the fire were bits of food and money—offerings to the gods of fire and lights.

We were pleased to share with the Hindu priest that the God we worship is a living God, a Spirit who neither slumbers nor sleeps—no bell needed to wake Him up.

"They called on the name of Baal from morning till noon. . But there was no response. . Maybe he is sleeping and must be awakened. . ." IKg 18:25-29

M: Chocolate Pie

During our language study we invited one of our conversants and his wife for supper. Both were secondary school teachers and, according to local standards, were well educated. They appeared to have enjoyed the meal of chicken and rice with vegetables until we came to the dessert. I had cooked a beautiful chocolate meringue pie, one of our favorite desserts. As soon as the wife put the first bite into her mouth she uttered loudly "Aggggghh!" while spitting the pie into her hand. "That's the worst tasting food I have ever eaten," complained the wife. She had never eaten chocolate before, which we naively did not know. Even though she was a school teacher, she had never experienced chocolate.

We learned a terrific lesson that evening concerning the African culture. They don't mind telling you when they don't like something. Later we learned that you can refuse a food gracefully by saying that you do not like it. However you can never say you are not hungry. That is something they have never experienced. We had a very friendly relationship with this couple, but I just did not ever serve anything that had chocolate in it to nationals again!

In like manner we found several foods offensive to them since they were never in their diet. Peanut butter, cheese and, of course, ice cubes were strange and disliked by all we knew. Later while traveling with our pastors and leaders for conferences or ministry, we soon found out that we must carefully choose what filling we put in sandwiches. Since we didn't have lunch meats or cheese in the market, we had to cook something in the kitchen that would be good on sandwiches. Market bread was unwrapped and exposed to all the hands that wanted to check its freshness. Consequently we made our bread in our kitchen. Even making a simple sandwich was a production!

"Show proper respect to everyone" IPe 2:17a

C: Along the Coast

Near the beach and along the coast just outside of the city and in the direction of Bagamoyo (Bah-go-MOW-yoe) there were many very tall coconut palms. Beneath them was, what appeared to be, a very old cemetery. What we saw however, late one afternoon convinced us that the cemetery was very much active. There were some new graves but interestingly on many of the older graves were bits of food.

Upon inquiry, we learned that many believed that the spirits of their ancestors returned at night and must have food. If there were not food for them, the spirits would become angry and harm would come to their family. In the morning, the food was always gone. We found that dogs and other animals roamed the cemetery and ate the food during the night so there was nothing left on the graves in the morning. This led the people to believe that the spirits had come and had eaten. No one dared to go out after dark for fear of wrath from the spirits. Some considered this offering an act of ancestral worship. It appeared to us that the practice was more like witchcraft and served to instill dread and fear in the people.

Taking a break from language study one Saturday morning we visited Bagamoyo, the quaint Arab town on the Indian Ocean coast 45 miles north of the capitol city. This was the port of entry for newspaperman Henry Stanley who came to Africa looking for Dr. David Livingstone. We found little activity in the town on the day we were there. Arabs owned and ran the shops as well as owning the large expanse of coconut groves which extended as far as the eye could see. Young African boys were climbing the palms and throwing down coconuts. There were large mounds of dried, broken coconut pieces still in their shells. Other boys were working diligently to remove the coconut from the shells. The dried pieces, copra, would be shipped in bulk to Europe and made into desiccated coconut for sale for human consumption.

During the early 1800's Bagamoyo was a bustling town, the center of slave and ivory trade. Arab slave and ivory traders brought their commodities to the coastal town where the auctioneers sold them to the highest bidders. Some of the auction stalls or pits remained when we were there—reminders of the cruel handling of humankind. Africans who converted to Islam and assisted the Arabs in the capture and transport of their fellow Africans for sale into slavery never became slaves. They and their descendants made for a firm establishment of the Islam faith among the Africans.

Bagamoyo was the early capital of Tanganyika under Colonial German rule. The Germans shifted the Capital to Dar es Salaam in 1892. A conference of world proportions was held in the town in September, 2002, as an effort to have the town declared a UNESCO World Heritage Site. This unpretentious yet interesting town remains solidly Muslim to this day.

"I will turn the darkness into light." Isa 42:16c

M: Chicken Business

We boiled and filtered the water we consumed and slept under mosquito nets until Carlos could install screens on the doors and windows. Obtaining enough and the right kind of food was a challenge.

Vendors brought all sorts of things to the door but most of our food came from the local market. One day in the market we bought a live chicken. To ensure that it was not sick we kept it in a small pen for three days. Then one day when we were taking the chicken out to prepare it, the yard helper appeared and offered to do it for us. We thanked him, gave the chicken to him and left him to his work. A little later we found the chicken dressed, and lying in the kitchen sink. Stripped of feathers, the carcass was black and blue and its head was still attached as well as the feet. Upon inquiry we found that he had received instructions from a former employer to strangle a chicken and not cut off its head or feet. They wanted to retain the blood. It didn't take long to teach him the proper way to chop or wring off a chicken's head and dress it properly. Having a good country born husband really helped out!

On the next Sunday following church we stopped by a local hotel to have lunch. On going from our car to the restaurant we noticed about a dozen chickens, dressed in the same way as our helper had dressed ours, hanging on a line outside the kitchen door. After lunch we made inquiry about them to the owners of the restaurant.

Confidently they told us that they hang chickens out like this for a few days to 'ripen' them. "Otherwise," he said, "they will be tough. Sometimes we even give them a tablespoon full of brandy before we kill them to make the meat tender."

Then we realized that the chicken we had just eaten was not "tender" but just 'soft'. Without doubt we avoided eating chicken there again. This is one custom that we chose not to adopt.

"As one who is in the Lord Jesus, I am fully convinced that no food is unclean in itself. But if anyone regards something as unclean, then for him it is unclean." Ro 14:14

M: Strange Living

Housing was of every kind and construction in this capital city. There were mud huts with grass or coconut palm frond roofs. Most were without windows for many believed that the spirits of the dead came through the windows at night. Basically they had hard packed dirt floors. Only the wealthier could afford cement flooring. Some had metal roofs and/or siding which made them like ovens in the tropical heat. Some houses were made of cement or mud bricks. Most expatriates had beautiful stucco houses with red tile roofs built by the Germans or British. Many Africans stayed outside the houses most of the time due to the very intense, tropical heat but slept inside at night. Most of their chores were performed outside as pounding the grain for food, cooking and eating. Water was available in taps located through the settlements but only the wealthy had water inside. Many of the ladies and children were seen caring large water pots on their heads.

The city was heavily populated. Everywhere we went we seemed to find masses of people. The Muslims stood out with their white turbans and long white gowns which the men wore. The Muslim women wore the black 'buibui', meaning spider, which covered them from head to foot. They were not permitted to show their faces, only the eyes. The other tribal women wore very colorful khangas which were wraparound cloths bought by the pairs in order to have two pieces for their dress. These cloths had many uses for the ladies. After one was used as a covering on the body, the other may be used to carry her baby on the back, or to cover her head, or wrap up goods to carry them on her head. Many of these cloths were made in Dutch colonies with beautiful designs and texture of cotton. At that time only a small portion of the population wore 'European' type clothing.

Most streets and roads downtown or in the suburbs were always swarming with people, dogs, goats and bicyclists. While driving through the streets we had to keep on the horn and brakes to keep from hitting those on the road. Since very few nationals owned cars most went everywhere on foot.

We often observed many people coming from the same houses. They came from smaller villages in the countryside to find work in the city. Being penniless they found friends or family with whom they could stay. We found out later from a local survey, that some of the rented rooms housed up to 38 in one room! They actually took shifts in sleeping. There was no lack of possibilities to find groups with which to share the Gospel.

> *"When He saw the crowds, He had compassion*
> *on them, because they were harassed and helpless,*
> *Like sheep without a shepherd." Mt 9:36*

C: Soccer Ball

When we arrived there was an estimated 120,000 people living in Dar es Salaam with various African quarters in the city, and Magomeni (Mah-go-MAY-nee) being the largest. One afternoon while we were driving about in Magomeni we noticed about a dozen boys playing soccer in a sandy field under large mango trees. We stopped to watch them and observed that they were playing with a ball about the size of a soft ball made from strips of old cloth rolled loosely into a ball. When they saw us they stopped their game and came over to us.

We asked, "Would you like to have a real soccer ball?"

All together they screamed in Swahili, "Yeah! That would be great, but balls cost money and we don't have any money."

We told them that we would see what we could do and asked them to meet us the next day at about the same time.

The next morning we went into the city and purchased a soccer ball from a local shop. We went back to the ball field that afternoon but found no boys. We stood around a few minutes and two boys meandered over to where we stood. When we showed them the ball they took off in a scurry with shouts of joy.

Within a few minutes there were 30 - 40 boys playing soccer under those mango trees, for the first time with a real soccer ball. Our hearts thrilled at their clamor and shouts of happiness.

After a while, they gathered with us under one of those great mango trees where we taught them choruses, told them of Jesus and that we would return on Sunday when we would again teach them. They agreed to be there.

By Sunday, most of the Muslims in Magomeni had heard of our being there. They did not want their boys involved with Christians. Only a few boys came. We sang choruses with them and told them more stories about Jesus.

We were there again for soccer on Tuesday afternoon and back the next Sunday. The number grew and quite a few adults attended. In the beginning, fellow missionary, Web, and I took turns preaching on alternate Sundays, as neither of us knew much Swahili by then. Myrtice played the portable organ.

God used that soccer ball and our being there to open the way for a significant work in that section of Dar es Salaam. We were pleased to be on the same spot a few months later and to see our Janice, then less than two years old, push the first spade into the sand breaking ground for a church and community center.

"Whoever welcomes one of these little children in my name welcomes me." Mk 9:37a

M: Sewing Seeds

Some men and many children came to the first worship services that we had under the Mango trees. I enjoyed playing our small pump organ to attract passersby to the service as well as accompany the new songs and choruses we were teaching them. Our little daughter, Janice, then only fifteen months old, loved sitting right in the middle of the children. They loved to touch her skin and her pretty blonde pony tail. She was delighted with the attention. It was so dusty and dirty with their sitting in the sand under the trees that it didn't take long for her to be nearly as dark as they were.

The absence of women was a tremendous concern to fellow missionary Betty and me. Something needed to be done to change this situation. Most of the women were of the Muslim faith in this area but we wanted to find a way to reach them. One day while the men were with the boys playing soccer we asked a few ladies passing by what they would like to learn to do. All of these ladies unanimously agreed that they wanted to learn to sew for their children and themselves. We quickly made our plans to design a child's dress and a lady's skirt, make patterns, purchase materials and find a place to meet. Fortunately we were given permission for a room in a nearby school where we could meet after school hours. Advertisements on handmade folders were passed out in the surrounding area to homes and to those attending the worship services.

Being fearful that none would come, we prayed hard for a good turnout. On the date of the first meeting we were absolutely overwhelmed with the large crowd of Muslim women who showed up to sew. We were challenged beyond our abilities, but God worked His wonders by opening an avenue to teach these women to sew and learn stories from the Word of God. Our limited Swahili did not bring too much problem since much is done by demonstration. Copying their own patterns out of newspaper was quite easy, but cutting the paper and cloth with scissors was the hardest task most of them had ever attempted. Holding a pair of scissors properly to cut is a complicated job to anyone who has never done it before. We were able to obtain a few hand-turn sewing machines to enable their learning skills along with simple hand sewing. With much patience and many tries these women were able to proceed with their cutting and sewing diligently.

We kept the main emphasis on building relationships and sharing the love of Christ. I began using my flannelgraph Bible stories at each class which intrigued many of the ladies as well as helped increase my speaking in Swahili. Betty shared from her heart to the concerns of the ladies. After several weeks, we felt God had given a break through when around fifty women graduated in our class with each having made beautiful children's garments by hand. We had a 'tea party' and invited the public to the graduation so they could show their accomplishments. Our greatest pleasure came when some of these same women began to attend our worship services and later some were saved. For the others we know they were touched by the seeds of the Gospel planted in their hearts. We called it 'sewing the seeds' for Christ.

> *"How blessed you will be, sowing your seed by every stream," Isa 32:20a*

C: Different Kind of Closet

We enjoyed meeting and having fellowship with expatriates from around the world, especially since most of them spoke English. Most were British government servants. There were the Indians and Arabs owning many of the shops where we bought groceries, with tantalizing smells from their spicy, aromatic food coming through the open doors to rooms behind the shops.

We soon found friends from among most of these groups. The idols in some of the shops along with incense burners disturbed us, knowing that they worshipped empty and foreign gods. We received invitations into their homes and quickly learned to appreciate their delicious foods. We invited them into to our home for American food and on each occasion, we would have the blessing before the meal, not knowing how they would react to it. The next day after one of these meals the wife of the Indian family called to ask for a copy of the prayer. She wanted her children to learn and say it before their meals. Every opportunity opens doors for sharing God's love.

During language study, before we had begun Swahili services, we attended the Lutheran church on Sunday evenings; the only English service in town. On one occasion the minister was to be away and asked that I preach. In my sermon, I used Fibber Magee's closet to illustrate how clutter often invades our lives. I explained that this came from a radio show where, sometime in each program someone opened the door to Fibber's closet and everything came tumbling out. There were strange looks on the faces of the people but I did not know why until after the service.

On the way out of the church, a British friend said to me, "Carlos, we do not know what you mean by Magee's closet. His closet must be something different from what we know to be a closet." Then he explained that to the British a closet is a "water closet," a small room with a commode. Oops, we had not learned enough of the British terminology!

"We heard a language we did not understand." Ps 82:35c

M: Satisfying Craving

Fellow missionaries, Web and Betty, lived next door. They had finished their language study and were assisting us in ours as well as beginning local work. They had been married twelve years and had no children. They dearly wanted some. Betty loved playing with our Janice and fixing her hair. Her yearning for a child was seen all over her face and gestures. One day Betty announced with a great deal of excitement that she was expecting a child. As it usually goes, she developed a severe craving. Hers was for hot dogs but none were ever available in this country. It became an obsession to her and she spoke of her craving every time we were together. There just were not any hot dogs available in Africa, or as we thought.

One day we noticed in the paper that there was an American ship in port. Carlos got an inspiration. If there were Americans on the ship, surely there must be hot dogs aboard. Being new in the country, however, he knew little about port protocol. Without hesitation he drove into the port area, parked his car and walked through the unattended gate and towards the gangplank of the ship. At the gangplank there was a guard who asked why he was there. He told him of his mission, whereupon the guard laughed and motioned him onto the ship.

"Go and see if you can get some of your American hot dogs," he said.

On board the ship, Carlos made his way to the captain's cabin where the guard told him that one does not just come to the captain like that. You must first have permission.

Carlos explained his mission.

The guard took him to the captain who in turn called for the third mate and said to him, "Give this man some hot dogs and we'll see if he can get off the ship with them."

With a ten pound package of hot dogs in hand, Carlos descended the gangplank to find the same guard who sent him on his way with a big smile and a wave. Later we realized how this must have been an absolute miracle passing into and out of what was supposed to have been a tightly guarded port area, to enter a ship and return with a package of hot dogs.

At home we made our plans for the special hot dog presentation a few days later when other missionaries would be visiting from upcountry. On the day of the special luncheon the hot dogs were prepared in many ways; just plain, with cheese, with chili, wrapped in bacon etc. Special hot dog buns were homemade. When all the guests had arrived and were standing in the living room, Carlos brought out a large platter with all the prepared hot dogs. With a loud scream of excitement Betty then began crying and laughing all at the same time. "Where did you get these hot dogs? I know I could eat them all!"

For a time we feared that the shock might bring on an early labor, but all went well. We will long remember the fun and enjoyment of this special event. Needless to say this was the last time we all had hot dogs in Tanganyika. We really goofed when we failed to count how many hot dogs Betty ate, but it was an unbelievable number. What man won't do to pacify the craving of a pregnant woman, even in Africa!

'He satisfies the thirsty and fills the hungry with good things.
Ps 107:9

C: Four Generations

We met Lewis Pinto, a fourteen-year-old Asian boy, in one of our services. He had taken a keen interest in our work and wanted to accompany us whenever he could.

One afternoon I invited Lewis to join me in going to a village for a service. As we rode along in the Land Rover I asked him, "How long have you been a Christian?"

After some hesitation he said, 'Four generations.'

"What do you mean?"

'Well, my great grandfather was a Christian and my grandfather was also a Christian. My father is a Christian and I am a Christian. I guess that means that I have been a Christian for four generations."

Somewhat taken back with his statement I pulled to the roadside, stopped the Land Rover and took the New Testament from my shirt pocket. I slowly read from the third chapter of the Gospel of John. When I got to verse 16 he stopped me and asked if I would read the verse again.

When I had read the verse the second time, he took the New Testament in his hand and read the verse himself. When he finished he said, "If that were true I am not a Christian now. I have never believed in Jesus for everlasting life."

We talked, read more scripture, answered Lewis' questions and prayed. As we prayed, Lewis confessed his sins and accepted Jesus as his personnel Savior. The weeks and months that followed saw a great change in Lewis. He was happier and had a much more sincere interest in everything he and we did. He grew in his Christian walk, learned more and became a part of sharing Christ with others.

> *". . .and teaching them to obey everything I have commanded you." Mt 28:20a*

M: Transition

This special time in Dar es Salaam and having a part in establishing new work gave us greater anticipation and fuel for our spirits for what was ahead. We finished our language study and packed up our household belongings to move to Mbeya for our first assignment to work in the Mbeya and Tukuyu regions. We were to move into the house of the doctor who had come to build the hospital. They were still there waiting for their new house, under construction next to the hospital, to be finished. They were gracious to invite us to stay with them for a couple of weeks until their house was completed.

I was heavily pregnant with Ruth and soon to deliver, so I flew with Janice to Mbeya in a small propeller plane. Carlos drove our packed car for twelve hours over six hundred miles of rough gravel road. Along the way he observed many villages, great fields of kapok trees, tremendous baobab trees, which appeared to be upside down, sisal and sugar plantations, and game reservations. He was fascinated. Carlos, needing breaks anyway, stopped several times to observe the animals alongside the road and in the fields. He was intrigued by huge herds of elephants, zebra, wildebeests, giraffe, and all kinds of antelope as well as the lions and leopard on the landscape.

We were in Mbeya only about two weeks when we got a call that Wimpy Harper had drowned. He and his family had come from Nigeria to assist in the beginning of our work in East Africa. They had been on furlough and had just returned. Also two new missionary families had just come to the field. A welcome party for fellowship was planned for all the missionaries in Dar es Salaam. Being on the coast of the Indian Ocean they went to the beach for an ice cream party to welcome the Harpers and the two other families. The beautiful blue ocean was enticing to all who enjoyed swimming. Several were in the water when the tide suddenly changed. Immediately a tremendous undertow took most of those who were in the water away from the shore. Several were pulled under the water. Panic set in for all of them.

A missionary doctor who was an exceptionally good swimmer was able to bring almost everyone to shore. Wimpy disappeared under the water quickly. Two of the other men went to help. After searching a long time they found his limp body. They pulled him to shore and began resuscitation. Our doctor did all he could. Before other help arrived it was evident that Wimpy was already gone. According to the custom of the land, they had to bury him the next day in Dar es Salaam because there is no embalming. Our missionaries were devastated with this loss. He left a lovely wife and three children.

Through this painful experience we learned that missionaries also suffer loss. In times like these we too have to depend fully on God's love, grace and strength. His comfort gave us peace and challenged us all to continue to carry the message to the lost as Wimpy would have wanted us to do. We do not understand this tragedy but we all grew in faith and trust to put our burdens in His hands.

Just about everything we saw and heard in Dar es Salaam while in language study was as strange to us as was the vibrations of those drums which we heard every night through our open windows. We began to be engrossed in the rhythm and ways of the African life.

"I press on toward the goal to win the prize for which
God has called me heavenward in Christ Jesus."
Php 3:14

Chapter Four

The Southern Highlands

Mbeya (Mm-BAY-ya) town nestled in the foothills of the Mbeya Mountains was primitive in many ways but impressive. We welcomed the pleasant landscape with much greenery, beautiful flowers, magnificent mountains, rolling hills and valleys. A tall hedge of red poinsettias lined the property beside the road of our house.

The area had many varieties of bananas as well as coffee and tea plantations. The cool air at the one-mile high altitude was exhilarating. This was a welcome change from the miserably hot, sticky weather in Dar es Salaam. Mbeya was the Regional Headquarters of the Southern Highland Province

In Mbeya and in neighboring Rungwe (ROON-gway) District, home of the proud Nyakusya people, we encountered witchcraft, paganism, polygamy, and ancestor worship.

Customs were strange to us. Among other things, we learned that having multiple wives was common. When we heard that a paramount chief had died, our mouths dropped open when learning that he left over 200 wives. His eldest, living brother had inherited his property, including his wives. Our plans and thoughts were racing ahead in search of how to reach these people for Christ.

We were delighted to find that the people in both the Mbeya and Rungwe Districts would be very receptive to the gospel. In the two years and three months we were in the area we saw four churches begun in the Mbeya District and five in Rungwe. Many churches and many outstanding leaders would come out of these two districts in the months and years to follow.

C: Anosisye's Dream

We had just arrived in Mbeya and were settling in when one morning, while having breakfast; we heard a knock at the door. It was Sam, a fellow missionary, who had only recently begun his work in Mbeya town. Joining us for a cup of coffee he shared that a man was at his house asking us to come to his village.

"This is his third time to come. Can we go and talk with him?"

We finished breakfast and went with Sam to his house where I met Anosisye (Ah-no-SEE-shay) Nikubuka (Nee-koo-BOO-kah). He was a very intense, rather tall, middle age man. We listened to his story.

"One night I had a dream. In the dream a man in a white robe told me to go to Mbeya where I would find missionaries who will come to our village. He said that the missionaries would show how we would experience change for the good of our people. I believe that you are the missionaries of whom this one spoke. Please come to our village."

We were stunned and amazed. Even though we had been in Mbeya for a very short time, God seemed already to be at work. We prayed with Anosisye and promised him that we would come to his village. Together we made plans to go on the following Tuesday.

Early Tuesday morning, we set out in our Land Rover. We drove into the Poroto (Po-ROE-toe) Mountains and along the plateau towards Tukuyu (Too-KOO-you) in the Rungwe District.

Along the way we saw large fields of green peas, Irish potatoes and pyrethrum on the hillsides. The tiny white flowers from the pyrethrum plant provide an ingredient for a very fine insecticide.

The dirt road was winding and rough, causing us to bounce erratically from our seats. The roads were dry and very dusty. Then it began raining and we slowly made our way along the muddy tract. It seemed such a long distance and we questioned whether we had understood Anosisye's instructions.

Finally, along the side of the road, we saw Anosisye and several men with him. They warmly welcomed us by their greetings and vigorous hand shakes. The paramount chief and six of his headmen were with Anosisye.

We soon realized that we were in the company of men who strongly influenced the lives of many people in the area. We had a long and profitable visit. Then we planned our next visit for the following Sunday when we would meet with the village leaders and all the people.

On our way home, checking the speedometer, we reflected on how Anosisye had walked 37 miles to Mbeya and back two times, getting no help. Only on his third trip had we agreed to come. On those three trips Anosisye, tugged on by his dream, had walked 222 miles to get help for his people.

A much larger crowd was on the road to meet us when we returned on Sunday. After fond greetings we opened the back of the Land Rover and asked the men if they would assist us by carrying the portable, pump organ into his village. Three men reached in, took the organ and gently placed it on a young woman's head. Off we went. We went along a path to a steep incline and down the path to a small flowing stream. Anosisye explained that the men of the village, with their hoes, had scraped the path clean in order to make our descent easier.

Crossing over the stream on a foot log we passed round, mud huts with grass roofs and through groves of banana trees, some laden with stalks of fruit. We noticed patches of coffee trees with beautiful white blossoms along the way.

After walking quite a long way we arrived at the Paramount Chief's compound. He had prepared a place for us in the midst of his compound, and people had already gathered; some standing and some sitting on the ground.

Again, there were fond greetings in Swahili and Nyakusya, after which Anosisye called the crowd to order. Without delay we began by sharing with them about our mission and our work.

Myrtice played the organ. We taught them a hymn and preached. When we sang again, 17 men stepped forward to tell us that, if we were to have a church in their village, they wanted to be a part of it. Their hearts were ripe unto harvest.

By a dream, God had led this sensitive but persistent man, in search for a better way for his people.

"An angel of the Lord appeared in a dream." Mt 2:19b

M: Unexpected Situations

In beginning the work at our assigned post, we had no idea that the Lord was already at work preparing the way for a tremendous open door to the Mbeya and Rungwe districts. As an evangelist, Carlos was assigned to establish work outside the Mbeya town, and I, personally, was to serve as the Matron, (Director of Nursing) of the new, mission hospital. The settling and adjusting time would take some few weeks, since housing was still not available for us.

It was such a relief to leave the oppressive heat to the cool, clear air of Mbeya. From our house, in every direction, we could see the beautiful green, covered mountains and valleys. Just breathing in the air invigorated us.

When Janice and I arrived, by a small plane, in Mbeya, "Aunt Sally" and "Uncle Jack" welcomed us royally. Sally prepared for us a most refreshing cup of hot tea and cookies on our first afternoon. Tea had never tasted better. We had all adopted the afternoon tea habit from our British neighbors. Right at four o'clock each afternoon, every one paused with that cup of hot tea, served with some type of 'savory' such as a small cucumber sandwich and a sweet, as cake or a biscuit which we called a cookie.

We found that so many of our British friends loved to drop in at that time and truly expected that proverbial tea time. It proved to be the refreshment of choice even to us Americans, who found that it added energy for the rest of the day's work.

The hospital was still under construction and missionary housing for the doctors, at the hospital site, was also not completed. Graciously received by Dr. Jack and Sally, until their house at the hospital was ready, we moved in temporarily with them. We were to reside in their house after they moved into the new housing. Construction was behind schedule, so we expected two or three weeks of living together. Since I was near time for delivery of my expected baby, Sally was very attentive and took care of the basic functions in the house.

Only after a week there, I heard loud scream coming from the kitchen. As I ran in to see what was happening, little Janice ran out. Poor Sally! She could hardly stand. She was rubbing the back of her thigh.

"She bit my leg!" She cried out with a shocked tone. "I didn't even see her and then I felt this piercing bite on my thigh."

"Why did she do it? I was just washing these vegetables. I was absolutely surprised."

I was so embarrassed that our quiet, little daughter would do such a thing. "I am so sorry! I can't imagine why she would bite you. She has never bitten before."

After consoling and helping Sally, we discussed why this twenty-two month old child would bite her.

Only then did we realize that Janice really resented that someone else was taking her mommy's place in the kitchen and she just wasn't happy about it.

Calling Janice, I picked her up, giving her an extra hug. "Aunt Sally is our family. She is helping us. Don't you want to tell her you are sorry?"

Little Janice shyly said, "Sorry, Auntie."

Sally reached over and hugged her. Janice returned a quick little kiss on her cheek. We didn't have any more incidents after that. Janice became very loving and responsive to Sally. All our missionaries were called Aunt and Uncle by our mission children. Our relationship to our fellow missionaries was like one big family.

Within a few days, our beautiful, little daughter, Ruth Ellen, was delivered in the local hospital by a British woman doctor. Her husband was the Regional Judge, since England was still in full control of this trust territory.

I found quickly that the birth procedures were far different from anything I had experienced or had cared for as a delivery room nurse. Most of the birth process was on my own. We did appreciate the government clinic and its services to expatriates. We had many things yet to be learned in this new world.

My doctor kept me occupied with her story about her newly purchased VW Bug that had been ordered from Germany for her. She had sent one of her workers, by bus, to the capitol city, Dar es Salaam, to pick it up and drive it back.

He had never seen the huge elephants that strayed into his path. He had always lived up country where there were no elephants. Fascinated, he just sat there, in the car, in the middle of the road, observing these huge creatures.

After about fifteen minutes they became very hostile, flapped their ears, trumpeted and started charging the small car. Sensing he was in danger, he quickly got out, climbed a nearby tree and watched the elephants charge the car.

With the fierceness of real anger, dozens of them stumped on the vehicle with their large feet until the VW was a flat piece of metal, unrecognizable as a car! Then they passed on their way assured they had gotten rid of that nuisance.

Luckily they didn't bother him, but the car was totally a write-off. He didn't want to see an elephant again! Later, he caught a ride on a lorry (large truck) back to Mbeya, humiliated.

Two weeks later, after Jack and Sally had moved to their new house, I suddenly realized that Janice was not playing in the house. After calling for her several times and getting no answer, I frantically searched inside and out. She was nowhere to be found.

My helper, who was busy with laundry duties, joined me in searching the house and all around the yard. We could not find her. Calling loudly, we still had no response. All we could think of was that she might have wandered off. We went to our Greek neighbor whose teenaged daughters often played with her. They had not seen her but joined us in our search. We continued with our desperate calls. Only being twenty-two months old, with a long blonde ponytail, I knew she could not go too far without being seen. Carlos was away and we had no vehicle to go looking for her.

We all began to go down the gravel roads in different directions. Tears flowed from my eyes. What could happen to such a little girl? I couldn't imagine anyone kidnapping her. We had not seen any hostility or criminal acts since being in the country.

I walked down the gravel road, calling and frantically searching for over an hour. Then, at another intersection, I began going in another direction toward the town. After walking for over a mile from our house, an African man came out of the small hotel at the end of the road about a half block ahead of me.

He called out, "Have you lost a little girl?"

My heart skipped a beat and I burst into a run to the hotel. There she was, sitting on a big chair and enjoying a glass of milk and a biscuit (cookie). Several African workers at the hotel were happily entertaining her.

Profusely thanking the people at the hotel, I quickly picked her up with an extra big hug as my tears were flowing. She looked at me as if nothing had happened, nor had any realization of what she had done. She did not fear the Africans and loved being with them.

All of a sudden it dawned on me. Only then did I realize why this had happened. Every afternoon, I had been taking her for a long walk down one of these roads while I was pregnant. Now the new baby had stopped her daily walk so she just tried it on her own. Oh, the trials of motherhood!

"Train up a child in the way he should go" Pr 22:6

C: Mwakalosi's Wedding

We had been in Mbeya for only a few weeks when someone told us that Mwakalosi (Mwa-kah-LOW-see) would be married at Sinsitila (Seen-see-TEA-la) on Sunday. We looked forward to the occasion, as we had not witnessed an African wedding. We waited for the day with considerable anticipation and expectation. We were in for some surprises.

On this special day we arrived well ahead of 1:00 o'clock, the announced time for the wedding. Already, there was a great crowd gathered which we estimated to exceed 200. They were Mwakalosi's family and friends; chanting and dancing to the beat of many drums. The drummers, dressed scantily, beat their drums with much enthusiasm. We were told that the bride's family and those from her village would arrive with her at the time the service was to begin. We waited in amazement with all the excitement.

Mwakalosi, the son of the second of his father's four wives, had been a Christian for only a short time and wanted a Christian wedding. He wanted the missionary to perform the wedding but he also wanted the tribal activities.

We were gathered in a large, open courtyard with several houses on the circumference; a house for each wife and her children. A rather large, open, covered space was used for different kinds of meetings. Another similar area was for cooking and lesser buildings for storing various types of food. Strips of bark held standing poles together on one side of the opening with lesser poles across the top holding up banana leaves for shade. Underneath were a small table and chairs for us and our local fellow missionaries.

The dry season had begun over a month before and would last for the next five months. The earth was already very dry and dust filled the air from the jumping and running by the dancers.

Beneath the cooking shed, we noticed large pots with fires under them and a sort of a grill with fire under it on which were portions of a cow and two goats. Smoke filled the air. We sat under the makeshift, shed covered with large banana leaves to protect us from the sun; prepared especially for us. Myrtice held Ruth, wrapped in a blanket, while Janice stood near by, watching intensely all the activities.

We asked several times when the ceremony would begin. No one seemed to know when the bride would arrive, as her village was several miles away. She and those from her village would be walking and "were on the way," we were told. The local villagers continued their singing and dancing. We were served the typical African style, hot tea which is very sweet and milky; along with boiled eggs in a small bowl.

More than two hours passed before we heard sounds in the distance. Mwakalosi told us that the bride and her entourage were near. The intensity of the chanting and dancing increased. A huge dust cloud could be seen off in the distance.

Several minutes later we could see the bridal party approaching with much pomp and celebration. Her head and torso were covered completely with a bright colored khanga while she was led by dozens of young girls and women, many of whom were dancing around her. Some were bearing part of the bride's dowry; blankets, sleeping mats, and clothing, cooking pots, pans, food and a large wooden mortise for pounding corn. The groom had already paid for several cattle as a bridal price.

A huge crowd of more than a hundred, singing and dancing around the party, made it difficult to see through the dust filled air. The drums and singing intensified to a deafening crescendo.

Shortly, the group filed in and led the covered bride to a chair in the middle of the courtyard. The bridegroom came to sit next to her. Family and attendants sat in a line extending from each of them. When a large basket was put on a low stool in front of them, the crowd started passing by to drop in money or gifts (unwrapped) for the couple.

The crowd was quieted by the groom's father and the drumming and dancing stopped. The Christian ceremony was then performed, bonding them in the Spirit of the Lord.

At this point, the bride's covering was removed from her head. Mwakalosi could witness who his bride was for the first time. His family had made all the arrangements and he had not even met her previously, according to their tradition.

She was a lovely, shy bride that kept her head down much of the time. Then the dancing and singing began again with full enjoyment. Large baskets of roasted meat and rice were passed around.

After enjoying all the activities, we congratulated the groom, bride and families. Then, following the custom, we left our gift in the nearly full basket, congratulated the couple and family, and excused ourselves to leave the party which would continue celebrating for the rest of the night. The drums continuously resounded throughout the countryside for all to know the joy of a wedding.

"When someone invites you to a wedding feast..." Lk 14:8a

M: Dividing Time

Climbing into the old, open, short-wheel based Land Rover, I bounced home thinking of my tremendous responsibility at the hospital. I had accepted the old vehicle for transportation and to carry supplies for the new hospital nearing completion.

Everything on that Land Rover shook. It made so much noise that it was impossible to even hear another person in the vehicle. It had no windows and the canvas top flapped. Although some stabilizing parts were missing, it was faithful to get me where I needed to go. I was always fearful that it would give up the ghost at almost any time. It hauled hundreds of pounds of supplies.

I spent those first days organizing the staff and procedures, floor setup, nurses' stations, meal preparation and laundry for the patients. All the nursing and patient care would be under my jurisdiction. It was an awesome task.

My little girls now had an ayah (AH-yah) who would care for them while I was taking care of hospital needs. I needed every spare minute to have our new hospital ready for patients. Nursing set-up was familiar to me; putting procedure books in order, seeing that the necessary equipment was placed in the right area, and placing of beds and supplies. The doctors were assisting in finding personnel.

I soon discovered that the great adventure was locating basic food supplies and setting up daily menus for patients. There were no large stores in which to find supplies. Going into small Indian shops amazed me because I could find only certain things in one shop and look for other things in another. The strong unexpected smells of strange spices and foods were really deterring me in making good decisions. Choosing the spices with which African patients would be familiar, really added to my choices and long discussions with the shop keepers. The shops had strange laundry detergent and soap from different countries. I could not even read the labels. All the supplies were shipped from many areas of the world since few were processed in Tanganyika.

I didn't let my hospital activities or exhaustion take away from the special time with our family in the late afternoons and evenings. There was a job to be done. I wanted to be equal to the task at home; preparing meals, entertaining guests, supervising my helper and preparing to teach Bible studies at church. Health issues sometimes interrupted, particularly cases of malaria and tonsillitis.

Then Janice broke an arm when she fell off the Post Office steps. I felt so close to my children that I felt as badly as she did that first evening. These were times I leaned on the Lord's guiding hand and wisdom to perform the duties required of me. Through it all, even in mundane chores, I felt I was serving Him joyfully. The Lord was my strength.

"Whatever you do, work at it with all your heart, as working for the Lord, not for men" Col. 3:23

C: When Roosters Crow

The Mwankenja church was thriving. Anosisye's dream had begun to be fulfilled. People were saved and professions were made at most services. Anosisye earned the respect of the people and became an effective pastor and leader. We would go there as often as possible along with starting work in other places.

I noticed that an old man, whom I had baptized, always arrived at about the time for the preaching to begin. I inquired of Anosisye about him and found that his name was Andulile (Ahn-do-LEE-lay). I approached him following one service and asked, "Andulile, I notice that you only get here in time for the preaching. Why don't you come in time for the singing? You would enjoy the songs."

"I come from far away. I walk slowly and can't get here any sooner."

"Where do you live?"

He told me the name of the village. I had not heard the name so asked where his village was and he pointed, simply indicating the direction of his village.

His not having a watch or knowing much about time, Andulile could not tell me how far his village was from the church. When I continued prying to find out exactly how far away he lived he told me that he had learned to be on his way when the roosters began crowing in order to be at church by the time the preacher began preaching

I asked about the possibility of our coming to his village so that he would not have to walk so far. He showed considerable excitement in the possibility of our doing that. After talking with Anosisye, we told Andulile that we would come to his village on a certain day to have a service with his village.

On the appointed day I drove from Mbeya to Mwankenja for Anosisye and then we continued driving, over the extremely rugged terrain, to Andulile's village.

When we arrived we found that Andulile had gathered many people in an open place near his house. Most of them knew little about Jesus or about churches. Anosisye first spoke, telling them about us and our work.

I preached and, to our pleasant surprise, most of those present indicated that if we were to have a church in their village they would be a part of it. Their hearts and minds were ready for true life changing decisions.

Elderly Andulile had prepared the way. Now, Andulile would no longer have to walk over six hours to reach the other church for worship.

Not too long following this first visit to Andudile's village, we left for our first furlough in the USA. One missionary family came to replace us in Mbeya to strengthen the five new churches and establish more. Another family was appointed to live in Tukuyu (Too-KOO-you) to lead the five new churches there and in planting and developing more churches in the Rungwe District.

We felt so pleased that the Lord had opened these doors for a firm foundation of the churches in the Southern Highlands in the 27 months we served there. The future in this area had consequently led to an outpouring of the Holy Spirit in reaching hundreds and thousands in baptisms and unnumbered churches.

"They preached the good news in the city
And won a large number of disciples." Ac 14:21

M: Dancing Over a Grave

Drums were rhythmically beating loud and strong in these morning hours. I had never heard them in the daytime; only in the night. They sounded so near they really perked my interest.

As I was preparing the wards for our new hospital's opening, I asked one of my helpers about them. "What's happening that we have drums beating in the daytime?" I inquired of her.

"The headman of the village next to the hospital died last night and they are calling people to his burial," she responded. "He was a very important man and well liked. I really should go to show my respects," she asked in a coy way for my permission.

"Since we are just next door, I feel like it would be a kind gesture for both of us to go. It would make for good public relations and let the village know that we care about them," I responded. I was really eager also to see the method and ceremony of the burial.

We went out one of the side doors, across the field to the edge of the village. Mud houses with grass roofs filled the area with banana palms spaced around them. Cleared ground and no other vegetation were seen through the village.

As we approached, we saw hundreds of villagers who had already gathered. My helper mentioned that we really needed to go into the widow's house first and express our sympathy.

We crossed over to a large, round hut near the center of the village. Since the door was very small, we left our shoes outside and bent low to enter. The room was filled solidly; women crunched closely to other women with many wailing and trilling with their tongues to express deeper grief.

It was so dark in the room that it took my eyes a time to adjust. The despair of this agonizing sound pierced my heart. We edged in, on our knees, while others shifted for us to approach the widow. It was a tight squeeze to get through.

We expressed our deep sympathy by holding the widow's hands. The loud sounds of wailing made it nearly impossible to pray. Then I assured her of my prayers for the Heavenly Father to bring her comfort. She continued to weep. We knew she most likely did not know our Father in heaven. We sat a short time by her when the drums seemed to get louder and stronger.

When we arrived we had seen four young men beating on very large drums. A fire nearby was being used by one of them; holding the top of the drum near the fire, to soften the skin making the sound even more resonant.

My helper whispered to me that they were ready to put the body into the grave. We quietly moved outside. The body, wrapped in blankets, was slowly lowered to the bottom of the open grave. Then two men went into the grave and placed the body on an indented shelf that had been dug out into one side of the grave.

"Why are they doing that?" I inquired softly.

"They place the body to the side of the grave so that the 'evil one' cannot find him at the bottom of the grave."

Immediately, many men began to fill the grave with dirt and mounded it up slightly. It was patted down by the backs of shovels. Then all moved back and away from it.

Drums seemed to change their beat. Surprisingly, a handsome and very muscular man appeared, dressed only in a loin cloth; his body shining with fresh oil rubbed all over him. With a large spear in his hand, he began to gracefully dance about and over the grave. His dance intensified as he appeared to be fighting an unknown enemy; running, jumping, mocking with his spear. He twirled, whirled, and gracefully jumped all around and over the grave, like a magnificent ballet.

Again, I was dumbfounded. "Please tell me the meaning of this dance."

"The man is fighting the evil one and chasing him away so he will not take the spirit of this dead man."

"If they only knew that Jesus has already become victorious over the evil one, they would not have so many fears. We have come here to help your people know the way to peace and everlasting life. We hope we can soon begin to share the Good News in this village," I told her.

> *"Death has been swallowed up in victory." "Where,*
> *O death is your victory? Where, O death is your sting?'*
> *The sting of death is sin, and the power of sin is the*
> *law. But thanks be to God! He gives us the victory*
> *through our Lord Jesus Christ." I Co 15:54b-57*

M: Milk in the Face

After the drowning of our fellow missionary in Dar es Salaam, Sam moved to Dar to take over his work. This meant we were now responsible for the Mbeya town work as well as developing the work in surrounding areas. The first, small church in Mbeya town was not yet organized, even though they were meeting regularly and had baptized converts. The field was really ripe for harvest! Great plans were in the making for our first Sunday's service in this small church.

On Saturday, we walked through the neighborhood inviting everyone we could find to attend. People were friendly and appeared to enjoy talking with us. Carlos, anxious to do a good job, had spent long hours going over his first Swahili sermon for this new group. It was an expectant and exciting time; to begin digging our toes into the local work.

Extra benches were brought in to fill the one, small room of the rented, mud wall building. A simple, wooden speaker's stand was in front. We brought our portable, pump organ; angling it in the corner so I could see everything going on in the room. Janice was sitting with one of the African ladies who loved her and was enthralled with this white child. Tiny little Ruth was dozing in her little, grass basket right beside me.

The crowd kept coming in; filling every seat. We moved benches closer to the front; to right in front of the pulpit. Many stood in the back, next to the wall. Some stood outside the door. Others sat in any small spot into which they could squeeze, making the room utterly packed.

The service started off excitedly. People were warm and responsive to learning hymns and to Carlos's leadership.

As he confidently started his sermon, I noticed a lady right in front of the pulpit holding twins, about fifteen months old. Since she was nursing them, she had no clothing above the waist. As Carlos proceeded into the sermon, I noticed one of the twins began twisting his milk source. The mother appeared greatly endowed and with an adequate supply for the twins. She was oblivious to the baby's actions.

All of a sudden, the little child turned loose of the breast and milk flew through the air; striking this straight-laced, West Tennessee preacher right in the face. He became bright red with embarrassment, took out a handkerchief to wipe his face, his train of thought absolutely lost. He turned to me and said, "Let's sing another hymn."

I'm afraid I nearly choked trying to hide my laughter. After the hymn, he got his composure and had a great service when many were saved. Afterwards, he learned not to be disconcerted by such experiences.

"Never be lacking in zeal, but keep your spiritual fervor, serving the Lord. Be joyful in hope, patient in affliction, faithful in prayer." Ro 12:11-12

C: Battle with Witchcraft

We heard a call at the side door. It was a woman's voice which I did not recognize. Going to the door, I saw Maria's daughter, Marta, standing there weeping.

"What is wrong, Marta?"

"My mother is very sick. I fear that she will die."

"Mama Owens is at the women's Bible study. She will be here soon and I will tell her. She will be there in no time."

I asked that we pray for her mother. After we prayed, she left, still in tears.

When Myrtice arrived, I told her about Maria and, without coming into the house, she got back into the Land Rover and immediately drove away. Only having been gone a short time, she came back. She said that she felt that witchcraft was involved and that I should go. I went straight away.

Upon arriving at Maria's house, I found many people standing around outside and others crowded inside where Maria lay on a low bed. I called her daughter aside and asked her to tell me what had happened.

I listened patiently as she told her story.

"Before we came to Mbeya my mother was a sorceress. She worked with and for a very prestigious and powerful witchdoctor. We were very unhappy and wanted something different. We wanted a better kind of life, so we, without telling the witchdoctor, left and came to Mbeya. When we got to Mbeya, we found your church. We were so happy to accept Jesus and your baptism. We loved our church.

"My mother was so pleased when Mama Owens asked her to be the leader of the women. We both were so happy."

"Go on."

Then Marta told me that, four days before, the witchdoctor showed up at their house.

"He was so angry. He said that my mother had done a very bad thing by leaving him and becoming a Christian. He said that he would do something to her that everyone would never forget. He told my mother that she would lie down and go to sleep, that she would sleep for three days and die."

After a short break and with heavy tears she continued, "This is the third day. She has been asleep for three days. I fear that she will die."

I asked those in the room to leave. I also asked that Marta leave.

Alone in the room with Maria, I spoke to her but saw no response. She did not move. Her eyes showed no evidence of life. She lay as if in a coma. I prayed silently first and again sought a response but got none. After several minutes of effort I still got no response from Maria.

I then knelt by her low bed and put my hand on her shoulder and beseeched the Lord on her behalf. In my prayer I iterated that, if Maria were to die, witchcraft would win out in Mbeya. It would be a victory for the witchdoctor. I said with urgency, "Please, please Lord, do not let Maria die." I said this several times.

Then I prayed with my hand on Maria's head, "The devil has Maria in his clutches. If she can't break loose from him she is going to die. Please, Lord, do not let Maria die."

When I had said this, I felt Maria move. I opened my eyes.

Maria's eyes were open and she said, "I do not belong to the devil. Please do not say that I belong to the devil. I belong to Jesus."

I took Maria by the hand and she slowly sat up on the side of the bed. Still holding to my hand she stood up and I slowly led her out of the room.

When the people saw Maria, there was considerable commotion. Some screamed in disbelief and ran away. Others laughed and cried at the same time, lifting out their hands to Maria saying, "Thank you, thank you, thank you." Marta hugged her mother and they both cried with joy.

Many accepted Christ because of what happened with Maria that evening. On the other hand there was one, somewhat disconcerting result. Many believed that if a witchdoctor placed a curse on someone it took a bigger witchdoctor to remove the curse.

In the days that followed several people came to me, the "bigger witchdoctor," asking that I remove curses, which other witchdoctors had put on them or on their families. This did give me an opportunity to witness. I could tell them that Jesus was greater than any witchdoctor.

Jesus ...said "All Authority in heaven and
on earth has been given to me" Mt. 28:18

M: Anna Teaches Sunday school

"I really need some help with teaching. Who in the world can we get to help when we only have young Christians?" I asked my husband.

Bible study was needed to build a strong foundation of the faith. Carlos began teaching a men's class. When I began a women's group, I realized that we had a large number of children attending also. No one was available to teach this group. So the children sat with the mothers in their class. We had more children than women.

After a few weeks, I asked if one of the new Christian ladies would be able to help teach the women or children.

Faithful Anna, who had never missed a study, nodded her head. She said "I don't know much but I would love to teach the ladies. There is a problem though because I don't know how to read."

Quickly trying to think what I could do, knowing there was no time to teach her to read, I asked her, "If I teach you the Bible lesson on Saturday, do you think you could teach Sunday?"

'Yes, I would love to try to do that."

With some doubts that this would work, I began to teach Anna every Saturday; the full Sunday school lesson. She was so attentive and asked me to repeat many things. I was anxious to see how she would manage.

So, on the following Sunday, I stayed in the class for a short time before taking the children to their class, on a grass mat, outside. To my amazement and pleasure, I heard her nearly repeating word for word the lesson I had taught her. She had a tremendous mind to remember. Her enthusiasm and joy in the Lord flowed through her teaching. Being illiterate didn't affect her learning to serve the Lord in a very effective way.

"The Lord will reward everyone for whatever good he does." Eph 6:8b

C: Straws in Beer Pot

We had spent the best of one day at Mwankenja. There were more than seventy who had made professions of faith and we wanted to be sure that they understood and had been born again before I baptized them. We, along with Anosisye, agreed that twenty seven of these were ready for baptism.

On Sunday, we came with considerable excitement, expecting to baptize twenty seven new converts. Upon arrival, I greeted Anosisye and asked him if all were well for the baptizing.

"All but Ambindwile!"

"Ambindwile can't be baptized?"

Anosisye explained that Ambindwile, on the day after we were there, got drunk and that they felt that he should not be baptized.

About that time Ambindwile walked up. He was evidently very sad. He was shaking his head as he spoke, "Please, brother missionary, I want to be baptized. Please let me be baptized."

"What happened, Ambindwile? What have you done?"

Ambindwile began to tell his story; "I was singing as I walked down the path. I was so happy that I had been saved and would be baptized. As I walked along, one of my old friends met me. He was one of the men with whom I used to drink from the beer pot. I had not seen him since I started going to church. He wanted to know why I was so happy. I told him what I had done and about the baptizing."

Ambindwile told us how his friend took him by the hand and led him to the place where men were drinking native beer. He said that they all got up, greeted him happily and pulled him down beside them on the ground around the big beer pot.

"Before I realized what was happening, one of the

men placed one end of a long straw into my hand and the other end in the pot. Before I knew it, I was drinking with them. Soon I was drunk. I will not do it any more. Please let me baptized."

With his obvious sincere repentance, both Anosisye and I agreed that I must baptize him. From that day, he was faithful in the church and soon began assisting Anosisye by preaching in neighboring villages. In less than a year be became pastor of one of the new churches and has since been a faithful leader, not only in his home area but also in the Convention. He had learned a powerful lesson of the persuasive nature of unsaved friends.

"The Almighty One, God, the Lord!
He knows." Jos 22:22a

C: Andulile's Shoes

We left for furlough after Andulile was effectively leading his church as pastor. The new missionary took over the work in the area including Andulile's church. As time went on, more accepted Jesus as Savior and the missionary baptized them. The church grew under Andulile's leadership and the missionary was anxious to give him whatever he needed to do his work better.

After a time the missionary wrote us that he wanted to assist Andulile by providing a bicycle to help him in his pastoral visitation, but Andulile told him that he was too old to learn to ride a bicycle. He said that the hills were so steep and rough that he would fall and hurt himself. He did not want a bicycle.

The missionary asked if there were anything else he wanted or needed.

Andulile's quick reply was. "My feet hurt when I walk and I have never owned a pair of shoes. I have often thought that if I had shoes my feet would not hurt so much when I walk."

The missionary was pleased to get shoes for him and reported that Andulile walked proudly in his new shoes.

We followed Andulile's ministry over the years. He, even though old, became one of the best pastors in the area. He and his church led other villages in having churches.

"He grew and the Lord blessed him." Jud 13:24b

M: Bark Belts/Ivory Bracelets

The exciting response to the Gospel message in Rungwe challenged us to look further for opportunities to spread the work. We drove further south until we came to Kyela (KYEA-la) on the shores of Lake Malawi. The heavy, green, plant growth showed the richness of the region. Many of the people were drying fish nearby to sell at inland markets.

Taking a break from the stressful work, we stayed overnight in another mission's rugged guesthouse which they had built as a retreat for their missionaries from other areas.

As we walked on the dark-colored sandy beach, we paused to watch the many people who were passing with their fish traps. Our girls immediately sat down to play in the warm sand. We were quite surprised to see some of the women who were of the old tradition; wearing brown bark belts—one piece around the waist with one piece connecting between the legs. This was all they wore. This tradition was passing and was rarely seen.

In the earlier days, all women wore these belts. They were hand made from the bark of a special tree. Later, when money was more available women abandoned the bark belts for the colorful 'khanga,' (KAH-nga) two piece identical cloth sold in most shops and African markets. Arab traders on bicycles also sold them from village to village. Old traditions were beginning to pass away.

Edwardi, one of new converts in Mbeya town, went with us to visit Masoko Chini (Mah-SO-koe CHEE-nee) for a preaching service. He was originally from the area so the people received him and us fondly. A large crowd soon gathered around on that day.

We noticed that many of the women wore beautiful, heavy, ivory bracelets on their arms which looked like an inch or more slice of an ivory tusk; smoothed beautifully. As I sat with the women on fresh cut banana leaves on the ground during the service, they were very friendly and enjoyed playing with our young daughters.

I was deeply concerned with the physical problems that I was seeing among them. One woman had one huge, swollen leg; elephantiasis, caused by a parasite blocking the lymph system. The name comes from the fact that the legs become to look like legs of an elephant. I begged her to go to our hospital in Mbeya where she could receive treatment. I assured her that I would be on the lookout for her and see that she received proper care. She shrugged her shoulders as if to doubt anything could help. I quickly wrote a note on a paper I had in my purse to refer her to one of our doctors.

"Just take this with you. I assure you they will take care of you. I will also be there to help you if you need me."

Later, she did appear at the hospital for treatment. I was so thankful that she followed through from my suggestions.

When we were back in Kyela several months later for services, she walked up to me recalling to me who she was. Her leg was greatly improved and she was able to walk better. I told her that I just thanked God for her healing. She then took a beautiful, ivory bracelet off her arm and took my arm and put it on me.

"Oh, you can't give that to me. It's very valuable. It must be so special to you and you have worn it most of your life," I said, remembering that she said her father had given it to her as a little child.

"No, you must keep it. You have given me help with all my pain. I want to thank you for helping me find medical care. Please remember me by this gift."

I felt so undeserving of this beautiful gift and so humbled by her generosity. We had learned that we should never refuse a gift of appreciation as this was an important part of their culture.

To this day, when seeing the bracelet in our collection of African artifacts, I am so very proud of such a valuable gift, which came with such love and appreciation. I will remember with humility this dear woman, who not only found help for her condition, but also found the love of Christ.

"For if the willingness is there, the gift is acceptable according to what one has, not according to what he does not have." 2Co 8:12

C: Buttermilk

Following a service at Mwankenja one Sunday, Anosisye asked that I go with him to visit one of the church members, an old man who was sick. He explained that this was a new member who had cut his leg with a machete while cutting firewood.

We left the church and walked quite a long way, passing through banana trees and some patches of coffee. Along the way we greeted many people who were sitting near or standing around their huts. There were always many fond greetings.

Soon, we arrived at the hut of the man who had injured his leg. He was sitting on a low stool near the door in front of his hut and his leg was bound with some not-too-clean rags. With difficulty he stood to greet us.

Dragging his bad leg, he hobbled into the hut and brought out more stools; about a foot high, hand carved, and round, for us. Then he returned and brought out a blackened, clay pot which was covered with a board. On his removing the board, I could recognize that the pot was filled with buttermilk.

The old man, seeing that there was trash floating on the milk, looked around and, finding a stick nearby, took it and proceeded to remove the trash from the pot. After some of the trash was removed, he stirred the milk vigorously with the same stick. Then he returned to the hut and brought joints of bamboo and began filling them and handing them to us; his guests.

I sat there and recalled stories I had heard about the African cows' having tuberculosis. I had read that one could get the disease by drinking the affected milk. I did not want to hurt the old man's feelings but I certainly did not want to drink his milk.

Holding a large cup of buttermilk with both hands, I was thinking of things about which I could talk. I talked and talked, holding the cup tightly in my hands. As long as I was talking I did not have to drink the buttermilk. Time seemed to be running out.

When I was beginning to think that I would have to drink some of the milk, the old man got up and went into the hut again. For what? I did not know.

Seeing that Anosisye had finished his milk, I reached over and poured my milk into his cup. He was happy about this as he loved the milk, so it seemed that I had made a good move.

The old man returned and seeing that my cup was empty, had a very pleased look on his face as he asked, "May I refill your cup?"

My reply was, "No thank you. One cup is enough."

After praying and assuring the man of our concern and prayers we left. As we walked through the village and back to the road I was grateful that I did not have to drink the buttermilk. I did not know how it would be the next time.

*"The kingdom of God is not a matter of
eating and drinking." Ro 14:17a*

M: Duck in Briefcase

One afternoon when we had been in Mbeya for several months and had assisted in the beginning of several churches in both the Rungwe and Mbeya Districts we had an unexpected visitor. He was well dressed, spoke beautiful English and carried a fine leather briefcase. He introduced himself as Mwankenja and explained that he was a part of our new member's family in Tukuyu. He had been in England studying to be a doctor. We were so pleased to see this bright young man to have such a marvelous opportunity. We recalled our reading about him in the local paper.

A reporter in England had interviewed him and sent the report back to our daily paper. The reporter asked about the thing he missed most by being away from his home in Tanganyika.

He had answered, "The smell of cows in my father's hut." By custom, the cattle were housed in a structure adjoining the hut for protection against thieves and wild animals.

While still standing outside at the door he said, "I wanted to come by and greet you and thank you for teaching my people about Christ. I became a Christian while in England. We are so happy that you have come to Rungwe."

We invited him inside, served him the traditional tea and had an enjoyable visit with this brilliant and caring young man. We were so pleased that he was preparing to care for the medical needs of his fellow countrymen. We had a very lengthy conversation, hearing about his adjustments to the British way of life and to the strenuous studies in medical school. As he got ready to leave he said he had a gift for us.

Opening his leather briefcase, he slowly reached in, bringing out a live duck; flapping and fluttering! He held it, by the wings, in midair for a moment, as it tried to get away, and then handed it over to us. We were so surprised that we could hardly answer for a moment. We grasped the wings while it was squirming trying to get loose, and tried to think of a place to put it. Thanking him profusely we accepted this 'thoughtful' and generous gift graciously.

Now we were wondering what the duck had done to his beautiful leather briefcase. He must have kept him inside it for all those hours while he traveled from Tukuyu to Mbeya and to our house plus the time of our visit with him. His hiding the duck was his act of a new found etiquette in the world beyond the normal life in Africa; utterly spoiling a beautiful briefcase.

"It is more blessed to give than to receive." Ac 20:35b

C: Leaning Door

Mwaijande (Mm-wah-ee-JOHN-day) accepted Christ in Mbeya and invited us to his village, Lupando (Loo-PA-nn-doe), in the Rungwe District. Most of the local people called the place Masoko (Ma-SOW-koe) Juu (JEW), the market place at the top of the hill. We started our services in a grove of banana trees near the market. Some brought low, handmade stools on which they would sit, while the rest sat on grass mats spread all over the ground.

The people of Lupando responded well to our ministry and soon there were converts, a baptism and a church. They met first under a makeshift structure but soon wanted a more permanent building.

Church members burned sun-dried mud bricks and we provided doors, windows and corrugated metal for the roof. Church members did the construction under my supervision.

I sensed from the beginning that there would be some problem in getting things "right." I felt considerable concern when I needed to be away for two weeks and the walls were high enough that they would put in door and window frames. However, I did leave them with their work.

Upon my returning and driving down the grade towards the church, I could see from quite a distance that the front door frame was leaning. On checking I found that it was six inches out of plumb. I took Mwaijande a ways from the church where we stood looking back at the church.

"Do you see anything wrong?"

"No. It looks fine to me."

I prayed for patience as I knew that we were dealing with people who had little schooling and most knew little about straight or plumb lines. They were very keen thinkers and knew much about common and everyday things, but straight and plumb lines were not in their vocabulary and understanding.

The church was finished and dedicated to the glory of the Lord. The Lord added to the church those who were saved. There were many. One church's leaning door certainly didn't deter its ministry.

Lord added to their number daily
those who were being saved." Ac 2:47b

C: Praying for Rain

The rainy season had begun and the villagers had planted, but the rains stopped and the plants were drying up.

Without rain, there would be no harvest. Without a harvest, there would be mass hunger. The villagers were desperate. These elders had called on the witchdoctors to lead them in praying to the ancestral spirits for rain.

On the edge of the Sinsitila village, every man present bit a piece from his stick and spit it out. We had not witnessed that before. Neither had we heard such groaning, moaning and chanting nor seen the witchdoctors dancing in this fashion. Having been in the area for only a short time this was all new to us.

Back at our house that morning Roberti had said, "There will be a special meeting this afternoon at Sinsitila. The elders have called the village out to pray for rain. They will be led by the witchdoctor. You can come if you wish." I was pleased to go.

It was widely believed that, for some reason, the spirits were angry because of something which someone in the village had done. The spirits had stopped the rains and only such a meeting could appease them and cause them to send rain.

The meeting had carried on for more than two hours when the chief witchdoctor raised his hands. The entire crowd became silent, apparently awaiting an announcement or some kind of proclamation by the witchdoctor.

The witchdoctor mumbled something in a language, which we could not understand. He then moved both hands rapidly from side to side and put them quickly to his sides. This apparently was a sign to the people as they began moving around and leaving the meeting. We also bade farewell and went away.

Several days passed and there still was no rain. The witchdoctor's efforts had failed.

We all prayed for rain and the rain came after eight days. The crops grew and there was a good harvest. God was good and sent rain but we do not feel that what went on that afternoon at Sinsitila had any thing to do with it.

Roberti led in the beginning of a church at Sinsitila. They built right near where the elders and witchdoctors had prayed

for rain. Roberti became the pastor. His father, a polygamist
with four wives, was saved and became active in the church
though he was not baptized due to his having four wives.
Three of the wives accepted Christ.

Roberti and his wife went to the seminary and after
graduating, he returned to be pastor of his home church. He
became a leader in his local association and in the national
convention. From paganism to proclaiming the Gospel is
surely God's way.

They "became guilty of Baal worship." Hos 13:1b

C: Mwaijande's First Funeral

Mwaijande continued living in Mbeya and kept his job.
He would travel to the Rungwe District on weekends where
he would lead the church in his home village, Masoko Juu or
Lupando.

On one Sunday following the service at Lupando,
someone came to tell Mwaijande that a child had just died in
the village. The family had called for him to come to assist in
the child's funeral and burial. As it is the custom in the
tropics, families bury those who die within a few hours, so
Mwaijande knew that his time was short. When he got back
to Mbeya he came to our house to tell us about the service
and the funeral.

"I got on my bicycle and started down the mountain
towards where the family with the dead child lived. I was
nervous and all of a sudden I realized that the missionary had
taught us many things but had not taught us about how to
have a funeral. I did not know what to do when I got to the
house where the child had died."

"Tell me. What did you do?"

"Well, I began to think. We always read the Bible, sing
and pray in every service that we have so I decided that I
would do that. I would have the people sing and I would read
from the Bible and pray."

"What did you read?"

"Not knowing what to read I just opened the Bible and read from where it opened."

"How did it turn out?"

"Everyone seemed to be happy so I guess it turned out fine."

When he told me what he read I did not see any relationship with the verses and a funeral but feeling that he had comforted the family by being there, singing, reading from the Bible and praying, I made no further comment, thanked him and remembered to talk about funerals in our next preachers' meeting.

> *"For the Lord gives wisdom, and from his mouth comes knowledge and understanding." Pr 2:6*

C: Roosters do not Survive

We had seven men serving churches as pastors in both Mbeya and Tukuyu. I gave them bus money once a month to come to our house for Bible, pastoral and homiletics study. The meetings were rewarding and I looked forward to them. We had a place in the town where they could sleep over, so I had two days with them each month.

Along with their pastoral needs we were concerned in other ways to assist them. Most African families had chickens but they were small and their eggs were also small. When I ordered day-old Rhode Island Red cockerels from Nairobi for our own use, we decided that we could help the pastors by giving each of them two young cockerels, assisting in upgrading what chickens they had.

When the new roosters were old enough for breeding they would either eat or sell all the other roosters they had. Then the new ones would fertilize the eggs that they would use for settings. We would ask them to promise to do the same with a neighbor when they had upgraded stock and ask the neighbor to follow suit. They seemed to be delighted and promised to do what I had asked them to do.

When the roosters were two months old, the pastors came for their monthly study. On leaving, each pastor took with him two of those healthy, red birds. I had tied their legs and put them in burlap bags to make carrying them easier. During the ensuing month, both Myrtice and I wondered daily about how they would fare and took pleasure in our having done something, which would benefit each pastor's family and in turn help many African families. The pastors came again after a month and we were anxious to hear about our chicken project.

"How did it go with your chickens?" I asked before beginning the normal studies.

One said, "After about ten days one of mine got sick and died and fearing that the other would also get sick and die we went ahead and ate him."

The second pastor said, "One night, a weasel came and killed one of mine and fearing that he would come back the next night for the other, we went ahead and killed him and ate him."

The third preacher said, "While we were away one day, someone came and stole both of mine."

The fourth said, "Last week we had company and with nothing else to cook, my wife killed both of mine and we served them to our company."

The fifth man said, "Mine are doing just fine. They have grown and soon we will eat or sell the other roosters. We are looking forward to getting eggs and new chickens which we can share with other families in the village."

Even though some of our endeavors do not accomplish what we desire we do not lose heart but continue looking for ways to help.

"Through patience a ruler can be persuaded." Pr 25:15

M: Food for Journey

Time for our first furlough seemed to come so quickly. We had seen such marvelous growth of the Lord's work. We knew that many great things would continue to happen in the days ahead. God was moving and blessing all the churches and Christians after less than three years.

The time was ready to say our goodbyes to our dear churches and wonderful Christian people. We felt like they were family to us. We began to make our rounds to say goodbye to each group. Very unexpectedly, they began to give us farewell gifts.

One church wanted us to have clothing like they had. One church, in Rungwe, gave Carlos an elders' long, orange gown with a blanket to put over one shoulder. Others presented him with walking sticks and drums. Women of the churches gave me colorful cloths like those that they wore. We were so grateful for such a loving people.

The Safwa (SAH-fwa) tribes' people of our church at Njia (Nn-GEE-ah) Panda (PAHN-dah), higher in the Poroto (Poe-ROW-toe) Mountains, wanted to be sure that we had food for the journey. They, one of the more primitive tribes in the region, had been responsive to the gospel.

When they travel, they have to take enough food to eat on the way since most trips are long distances and there is no food available. When they presented us with a live goat and stalks of bananas on the day before we were to fly out of the country, we were stunned to know what to do. Graciously, we received the gifts offered.

We laughed on the way home, with our goat in the back of the Land Rover, thinking of what the response of the airline's flight attendants would be to the food we had for our journey! Wisely, we gave the goat to one of our helpers, as a gift of appreciation for his faithfulness. We felt so blessed and loved by all these dear people who received the Word of God and became faithful followers in the Kingdom.

"Consequently, faith comes from hearing the message, and the message is heard through the word of Christ." Ro 10:17

M. Furlough

Returning to America on an airplane, we were filled with anticipation of seeing family and friends again. We attended family reunions and spoke in our home churches with much joy. Being back with loved ones was great. We rented an old, furnished house, which had not been lived in for some time. It became our home for the year. Getting back to living in America with the fantastic grocery stores and clothing shops made life delightful.

From the very beginning, the phone kept ringing as churches invited us to speak. This special time of sharing helped the people have knowledge as well as a heart and concern for the African work and encouraged us. Since our support was a cooperative effort of many churches, we were able to thank them for the support through these years. There was no need to beg for assistance. They were already providing it.

Days were filled with traveling, speaking, visiting and sharing in churches, camps, small groups and civic clubs. In our busy-ness, my pregnancy became evident. It was a joyous time to invite another daughter into our home.

Debra Ann, with a full head of hair, was born on a cold, February night. In fact, the doctor wasn't expecting a fast birth and had invited Carlos to go home with him for a cup of hot chocolate while they waited. As Debra did not want to wait, they missed drinking all their chocolate!

When Debra was five weeks old, we took her with us to North Carolina for a state-wide meeting where hundreds of ladies listened while I shared about our mission work.

Though she was left in the nursery, to our surprise the director had someone bring Debra to the stage and introduced the audience to our newest member. The ooohs and aaaahs were heard throughout the auditorium. She was dedicated on that occasion to the Lord's service, which became a significant factor in her life.

As the year quickly passed, we were even more eager to return to our mission to carry on the work we had begun. Since other missionaries had come to fill in our vacancy, we were asked to open up new work in the remote part of Tanganyika, on the western border, on Lake Tanganyika. Many new challenges awaited us!

> *"Open your eyes and look on the fields!*
> *They are ripe for harvest."* Jn 4:35b

Chapter Five

Far in the Bush

Lord Twinning, Governor of Tanganyika, in 1956, told three missionaries from Nigeria that Kigoma was one of the neediest places in the country. He said, "The people there have only recently lost their tails." We felt that his was an unfair statement but the people were definitely primitive and backward in many respects.

When we arrived, we found men walking the streets wearing upturned burlap sacks given to them by the Port Authority. The head could slip through a large hole in the bottom. There were holes in the sides for the arms. These men had come from upcountry, many without clothing, to work in the port, loading and offloading 100-kilo (220 lbs) bags of grain or other commodities. Two men could pick up a bag and place it over the stooped shoulders of a man half the bag's weight. Braced under the load he would take it onto or off a ship and drop it at a designated place.

These men chewed hashish to numb their bodies, giving them the ability to handle the heavy loads.

Fish was plentiful in the early mornings when the fishing vessels returned from their over night fishing on the lake. Tilapia was one of the main catches. Light from the boats' large lanterns attracted thousands of tiny fish, dagaa, to the surface and the tilapia came from the depths to feed on them. Large nets pulled in hundreds of pounds of fish in this manner each night.

Many people came to the docks each morning to buy these fish, which did not cost very much. Some of the fish were very big. One morning, I saw a man walking in the town holding one by its mouth. With the fish's hanging over his shoulder, its tail dragged on the ground. Some of the fish were brought up from the so deep - Lake Tanganyika being the deepest lakes in the world - that the change of pressure caused the floater to burst through the fish's mouth looking like a huge tongue. A Ha tribesman was not very large but these fish were tremendously big to me.

Kigoma, on the shores of Lake Tanganyika, is the eastern gateway to the Congo. The Kigoma Region, the home of the small in stature Ha people, also had many of the Tutsi tribe, some of the world's tallest people from Burundi, 35 miles to the north.

Ujiji, five miles south of Kigoma, is the famous meeting place of Henry Stanley and Dr. David Livingston. A large monument marks the place of their meeting under a great mango tree just a few yards from the shore of the lake. John Glenn visited the area in 1967 documenting Stanley's venture. The town of Ujiji with 30,000 people when we were there, was 99%+ Muslim.

Gombe Stream, where Jane Goodall did her monumental work with the chimpanzees, is 17 miles north of Kigoma, on the Lake. We would live in Kigoma.

C: Breakfast at the Livingstone

With the family, we drove three long days from Dar es Salaam to reach Kigoma. Having eaten cold travel food most the way we talked of how nice it would be to have some warm food.

Late in the afternoon of the third day, when we were less than 100 miles from Kigoma, we came upon a large crowd of people in the road ahead of us. In great jubilation, the people chanted and danced as they moved along. When we came near the crowd, they moved to the side of the road to let up pass. We saw that two men were carrying a very large leopard, its legs tied to a pole. We stopped and got out of the Land Rover. The people continued their chanting and dancing but without moving forward. They seemed to be pleased that we had stopped.

A very pleasant young man told us that this leopard had been killing their goats and young cattle. Early that morning the men of the village had come together with their spears to hunt down and kill the leopard. They were successful in finding it, surrounding and killing it with their spears. They were on their way back to the village where there would be celebrations into the night.

Noting that the leopard had large claws, I said to the young man, "I would love to have one of those."

Somewhat to my surprise, he, without comment, took his machete and cut off one of the leopard's toes. As he and the crowd cheered and laughed, he handed it to me and said, "Take it. We don't need his claws."

We arrived in Kigoma after dark and checked in at the Livingstone Hotel. I had been there alone on three occasions looking for a house. I had found one of sorts, in a courtyard behind an Asian shop on the main street.

The accommodations at the Livingstone were clean and reasonable in price. We were pleased to get baths and to bed enclosed with mosquito netting.

In the morning, we went to the dining room and were delighted to see coffee, eggs, sausages, toast and jelly on the menu. The waiter appeared in his white robe and red fez.

I first asked him to bring coffee for Myrtice and me.

"I am sorry, Sir. We do not have any coffee."

"May we have eggs, sausage and toast and some water?"

"I am sorry, Sir. We do not have sausage."

"Then bring some eggs and toast?'

"I am sorry, Sir. We do not have eggs."

"Well, what do you have?"

"We have bread and sardines."

We sat and ate toast with sardines and drank water.

At 8:00 we saw the waiter go out the front door and across the street to a grocery store which had just opened its doors. He came back with a package in his arms.

After a time in the kitchen, he came out with a nice breakfast—eggs, bacon, toast, coffee and milk for the children. We ate our fill with gratitude.

We spent the next two days at the Livingstone while cleaning out the rooms where we would live. On the third day in the early morning the train arrived from Dar es Salaam with our crates. We had hired a truck which brought them up the hill to our place. Immediately, we began unpacking things for sleeping that night. We spent the next few days settling in and getting acquainted with our neighbors and the town. It was such a good feeling to finally have a place to call home after over three months of waiting for a place to live.

"Be content with what you have." Heb 13:5

M: Four Rooms in a Row

"Where are my dolls and toys?" cried Janice, our little five year old. "I want my toys!" she impatiently demanded.

"We are sorry but they are in the crates. You will have to wait until we can unpack in our new home." I tried to assure her. All of our things had been packed up from the Mbeya station, and new crates that we sent to the field from home were still sitting in storage. It became a familiar and daily answer, "It's in the crates."

We had returned with the three daughters now. Debra Ann was born while we were stateside—now more than six months old. Ruth Ellen had grown to three years and Janice nearly five. Trying to keep children happy while waiting for a place to live, challenges the mind and emotions. Luckily they could be contented with the simplest of projects. Even the sand in the courtyard was a great place to play though so very dirty.

It certainly wasn't the most desirable place to live; enclosed in this small, hot area with four rooms opening to a concrete porch. The metal roof put the inside temperature up to unbearable temperatures each day. We did most of our living on the small open porch in front of the rooms to catch the slightest air movement.

The small sandy courtyard completed our new living area. Tucked behind the shops so snuggly and enclosed by high walls with glass shards embedded in concrete at the top, we felt that our new home was a gift from God until we could get a house built.

Our neighbors were the shopkeepers, also living behind their shop, in the same courtyard as ours, but separated by a block wall. The neighbors' radios, blasting the whine of

Indian music, were so loud that sometimes talking or sleeping was difficult. In a completely open place without air conditioning, the smells of Indian cooking, or rotting trash were bothersome, but they did not take away the joy of having a temporary place to live. With our small children, just to get settled after all these months was our greatest need

When the crates were delivered from the train, we hastened to place the necessary items; beds in two rooms, dining table in one, and a little sitting room furniture in the other. The most basic furniture filled the tiny rooms.

It was always a problem at night when the children would awaken crying, since we had to go outside to enter their room. Even going to the bathroom meant going, in the dark, across the courtyard. We had a floor-level toilet of the Indian style but thankfully it did flush with water. The shower was in the same small building but with only cold water.

Before we knew it, we had basic needs met, though several crates had to be left unopened on the porch. There just wasn't room for them. Some boards on the top were loosened to pull out an item or two. This later became a problem when a helper decided she could remove clothing, paper goods, etc. from them without our knowing it.

Being on the shores of Lake Tanganyika, we enjoyed the beauty of the place. The market place had an abundance of tropical fruit but limited vegetables. Fish was always available. Beef was slaughtered daily but was very old, tough, and covered with dirt and flies. Since foods were limited, we cooked all meals from scratch in our home.

The kitchen was only a 6 ft. by 8 ft. size, across the courtyard facing the porch. We squeezed our stove and cooking utensils in the small space. I was kept busy running back and forth to see about the cooking, teaching school to my children, or doing other necessary chores.

Our dishes had to be washed in a small sink on the porch. The only time that we had big problems was during the heavy rainy season. I would always try to dash to the kitchen before I got wet, but that didn't happen. Since it was always very hot, being a little wet was no problem!

We did find some loaf bread in one of the shops; unwrapped, so tried to use it. When we cut it, we were shocked to find pieces of flies and bugs inside.

Carlos decided to make friends with a baker to see how it was made. The very cordial Indian baker was happy to show his kitchen. To his surprise, Carlos saw a worker kneading the dough, on a cement floor, with his knees and sweat dripping off his body. Without doubt, we never bought bread again. After that, every morsel of bread came from my own kitchen.

Since basic salad or green vegetables were hard to find, we began a small garden in the corner of the sandy courtyard. We had brought seeds with us, so we dug up the area, fertilized it and planted the seeds. An agricultural friend had sent sweet potato seeds with us which had been newly developed at that time in Louisiana. We were so thankful because the local sweet potatoes were white and became grey colored when we cooked them.

With the humidity, heat and hard work, we soon were harvesting some delightful extras for our meals. The sweet potatoes were one of our biggest accomplishments in gardening, not only in size but taste. Later, these same sweet potatoes, propagated by shoots from the vines, were given to pastors and many fellow missionaries, since potatoes were not allowed to be imported because of disease.

One day, someone came to the gate selling a small duiker, a very small antelope, which he had found in the bush. Our children were so excited that they wouldn't take no for an answer. So we ended up with a darling animal making antics all over the yard and on the waxed floor front porch of our four rooms. He would chase the children and slide up and down the porch. Fun was had by all. His favorite spot was resting under the sweet potato vines and chewing their leaves. Soon the rains came and he became sick. Unfortunately we lost him.

Again, a national appeared with a small monkey on his shoulder. The children thought they really needed some entertainment, so we took him under our wings. We made a cage for him to use when he needed to be confined but he enjoyed the home and playing with the children for a short time. Then he began to get excited when the kids did, and would bite them. He only would stay with me and not bite me since I was the one who usually fed him. After several episodes of biting, we felt that he needed to go, so we passed him on to a good family who had older children to care for him. He was delightful and playful but very temperamental.

It wasn't long before we began experiencing the problems of living here. Malaria became a big problem with the children. It seemed like every time they were sick with one thing, malaria popped up also. It was a constant effort to keep the family on prophylactic malaria drugs to help but, in spite of this, we all had malaria many times.

Mango worms became a big hassle too. We soon learned that the mango fly lays its eggs in elastic of garments drying on the line. Soon we would have raised itchy, red areas on the skin. After a time 'when they were ripe' we could squeeze a little worm out of the skin.

Barefooted children and sandaled feet were open for the small jiggers in the soil to lay their eggs on the edge of the toe nails. Again, we had to endure swelling and itching of the skin in that area until it was ready for the worm to be squeezed out.

Parasites continued to be problems all our time in Africa. We soon learned how to handle them and carry on with life.

We tried to take at least one afternoon in a week to go to the lake edge, which had a rather rocky shore with only a small amount of sand. Not far from the shore the water became extremely deep as the bottom dropped off to one of the deepest lakes in the world. The children could swim or play on the beach with our constant attention for their safety.

Even so, this was a special time of relaxing, watching the placid water, having a picnic and to watch the fishermen, going out in their canoes with lanterns already lit for their night of fishing. Most enjoyable were the beautiful sunsets over the lake with the Congo Mountains on the other side.

In this very remote place, God had provided a beautiful oasis for us.

"Trust in the Lord and do good; dwell in the land and enjoy safe pasture." Ps 37:3

M: Market Opens Door

Stares came from every direction as our family climbed out of the Land Rover and went into the market place in Gungu; one of the nearest villages to the town. We were the only white faces around with swarms of Africans bartering and visiting in this local market.

Smiling at all that looked our way, we saw the response soon as some men came over to speak to us. Carlos, being a very friendly man, struck a conversation and began chatting with these men, in their language. They acknowledged the family by smiling at our children and me, pleased to see his family. He explained that we were new in the area and wanted to meet some of the people here.

After some time, Carlos broached the question of what these men would like to learn.

"We know you speak English being from America, and we want to speak English." They all agreed.

We found out later that these men were the leaders of the local Political party.

Knowing that they were Muslim in faith, by their white gowns and caps, Carlos immediately agreed to teach them. They arranged to meet in a nearby school (simple, open rooms) after classes were out in the afternoon. All were excited and said they would bring some of their friends.

While he continued his talking with them, I noticed that some women nearby were selling dried beans—piles neatly arranged on a grass mat. They had measured out their produce with a small tin can.

Our small, blond children amused the women and as we came near, they reached out to touch them and to talk with us. They were amazed that we, even the children, spoke their language. We enjoyed sharing with them and buying some of their produce. Shortly, I asked them if there were something they would like to learn to do.

"We've never been to school. We would love to learn to read our language," they answered. After reaching to touch our children's clothing, one added, "Did you make these dresses for your girls?"

"Yes, I did. Would you like to learn to hand sew for your children?"

All the women responded enthusiastically, "Please teach us!"

After some time, to organize and prepare our classes, we gained permission to meet regularly in one of the school's classrooms. We took alternate days for teaching.

Carlos was so pleased to see a large group of men arrive to learn English. Materials were in short supply but, with a homemade blackboard, he began his class with the basics in conversational English. As they approached reading time, he stated that all the books we had for reading was the Bible. At first the men just refused.

"Sorry, we need to use these books to read or I can't teach you."

Discussing the issue a long time among themselves, a spokesperson announced, "We will agree to use the Bible if you will continue to teach us to read."

This was a tremendous decision for them for their Islam religion did not allow reading of the Bible. This would be a sin for them.

Without doubt, God had touched them to agree. The use of the Bible opened the way for these firm Muslims to learn of Jesus. Their agreeing would have tremendous impact on their future.

"For the word of God is living and active.
Sharper than any double-edged sword," Heb 4:12

C: They Came by Night

There was a call at the courtyard gate quite late one night. I went to the gate but could not tell right away who was there, as the gate was a solid door.

I opened the gate to five of the men who had been studying at Gungu.

The men pushed inside quickly.

"Let us come in. Close the gate. We do not want anyone to see us here. If they do, they will want to know why we have come. We don't want them to know."

"Why have you come?"

"You have been teaching us. We have been reading the Bible. We like what we read in the Bible. Never having read the Bible before we did not know what it said."

"What do you want to do?"

"We want to accept Jesus as our Savior."

I wanted to shout. We had prayed. God had been at work.

We spent the next hour reading the Bible and explaining how a person accepts Jesus. Each of the men prayed to accept Him as Savior.

They all were concerned about what would happen to them when the Muslim community found out what they had done. We agreed that, for the time being, they would tell no one what they had done. I told them that I believed that God would let them know when they could tell others. They went away into the night rejoicing yet cautious.

At the next English lessons, things were different. The men asked to read more from the Bible. They wanted to know more about Jesus.

Several weeks passed and, at one class session, all five men said that they were ready to confess Jesus publicly. They said that they were ready to face any opposition which might come.

Word spread rapidly. Two of the men dropped out of the classes and we did not see them again. Persecution had been intense. Yusufu, Kin'gombe and Omari took the brunt of the opposition and remained faithful after baptism. Omari dropped away after about a year. Kin'gombe turned away after about two years and returned to Islam. Yusufu remained faithful. He never turned back.

"He came to Jesus at night." Jn 3:2a

M: Jane Goodall and the Chimps

When we had been in Kigoma for only two weeks, we heard someone at our gate. To our surprise, there were two lovely English women with a black helper.

One introduced herself as Jane Goodall.

"This is my mother who has come from England to visit me and this is my personal assistant"

She told us that she had not been at the chimpanzee reserve very long and had come to town to buy some supplies. She had heard about us from one of the shop keepers and decided to come by to see us.

They were such delightful and dedicated women. Jane was so pleased to have her mother visit for several months while she was studying the chimpanzees.

After sharing some hot tea, sandwiches and cookies with them, we asked if we could be of any help. We knew that Jane did not want to leave the reserve, for she had begun to follow the chimps and needed to know where they were resting at night in order to find and follow them the next day. Jane looked so thin that I asked about how she managed her food.

"I don't have any refrigeration, so my food, such as meats or chicken, can only last a day. I really need some way to have extra food. There just aren't enough tin goods in the shops."

"Perhaps we could freeze some of these things, pack them well, and you could have meat or chicken for several more days."

"Oh, I would be so grateful. I could send my helper to town each week if you could have something ready for me." We made a permanent agreement.

I kept a regular supply of frozen chicken and meat ready for Jane. She began eating better and looked better when we visited the reserve a few months later. She was so appreciative of our help that she let us observe the chimps in her first phase of getting them to come into camp by putting out stalks of bananas. Though we had to stay inside a tent, we got some of the very first pictures of these charming and fascinating chimpanzees at first hand in the Gombe Game Reserve. We often took our visitors to visit Jane and the chimps.

Our encounters with this research scientist, Jane Goodall, proved to us that if only most Christians had as much dedication to their task of sharing the love of Jesus as Jane did in researching the chimps, this world would soon be truly evangelized.

Since Jane was so committed to her project, we would see her in town only a few times more, but we did go to see her many times on the reserve. From that time on, we got very involved with all the official visitors coming to visit Jane from National Geographic or from the Leakey Foundation; mainly members of the Leakey family, who were sponsoring Jane's work.

Frequently, we met their small planes in our simple airport, which is only a field, because they would buzz our house to let us know they were arriving. When Richard Leakey arrived by plane one day, he brought a monster of a snake in a gunny sack. We asked him to please just leave it outside. Then we entertained him, and his party, fed them and helped arrange boat passage to the reserve. He did take his snake with him.

When some of them became ill, our home became their hospital. One lady, who arranged National Geographic lecture circuits, came to visit Jane for a time. Unfortunately, she developed a terrible infection on her leg. After taking her to the main regional medical officer, he recommended bed rest and daily injections of penicillin. Since the hospital was unacceptable for her, we cared for her in our home for over a week. We enjoyed a fresh perspective from the outside world.

One morning we had pancakes. We shared with her that we couldn't buy syrup so we made our own and used maple flavoring. We told her that it tasted just as good as real maple syrup.

She answered very firmly, "You definitely have been in Africa too long!"

"Each one should use whatever gift he has received to serve others" 1 Pe 4:10a

C: Sometimes Baptism Hurts

Yusufu, one of the men who had come to study English with me, had been Muslin and a leader in his village. His having converted to Christianity caused considerable stir in the Muslim community. We expected the worst but were surprised in what happened on the day I baptized him.

After the preaching service, the entire congregation walked the two miles to the shore of Lake Tanganyika. As I baptized seven, the first converts in the area, there was much rejoicing. On the edge of the crowd were several Muslims, who had come in order to report to their community, who was extremely unhappy about what was going on.

After the baptism was over we walked back to the church and Yusufu went to his house, which was next door. He found that his wife, Mariamu, who had not gone to the lake with their three small children, was gone.

He came to me and said, "Her father has taken them."

"Why would they do that?"

"Now that I am no longer a Muslim, he will say that she is no longer married to me. He will say that she and our children must come back to him."

"Can he really do that?"

"Yes, that is according to Muslim law."

In the days and weeks to follow, we did a lot of praying with and for Yusufu. He was firm in his decision to follow Jesus but had much concern about his family. He went daily to see them and Mariamu's father, pleading with him to allow his family to return to his house. We continued praying.

After just over five weeks, Yusufu came to our house early one morning.

"Her father has agreed to let her and the children come home."

"How did you get him to do that?"

With a smile on his face Yusufu said, "I believe that he became tired of my coming to his hut every day!" jokingly saying. "After much praying, I know God has his hand on my family."

We rejoiced and thanked God in prayer with Yusufu. He went back to his house in Gungu a very happy man.

> *"Be alert and always keep on praying for all the saints." Eph 6:18b*

M: Land Rover in a Hole

Crying babies, toddlers crawling about, and small children running around playing, did not interfere with these mothers learning to read. They were so intent on learning that they were not even noticing the havoc. The little classroom was absolutely full each time that I went to teach the women. This was the first time in their lives they ever had the opportunity to learn to read their own language.

I knew that most of them were Muslim, since they wore their black 'buibui' (spider) dress that covered their entire body with only a small area open for their eyes. Regardless of their faith, I included simple Bible lessons in each class period. It was a real challenge to teach these forty five women.

Some had a hard time but the majority was very quick to learn, soon reading simple sentences. One of the best students was Hadija, a young girl about sixteen years old. She comprehended reading well ahead of the rest and even began to assist me in teaching other students.

Hadija had asked me to come to her home, because her father wanted to see me. I had sent the Book of John in Swahili home with her. Since he was a Muslim, I was scared that he would be angry with me, but I felt that I should go anyway.

Driving through the village, following her directions, suddenly I saw the big hole dug for trash right in the middle of the road. I couldn't stop fast enough. Land Rover and I ended right in the hole while the rear wheels were off ground.

Men who were sitting all around their huts just looked at me while talking or playing bao (BAH-o), a favorite board game for men. When I got out and asked if I could find some help, they all got up, came directly to the truck, and surrounded it. They had asked that I get in and put it into 4-wheel drive and reverse.

When I climbed in and doing as they had asked, I was startled. All at once, these twenty plus men just picked it up out of the hole. 'Wow," I thought. It was like being lifted right up and on firm ground again. I pulled ahead a short distance very relieved, and expressed a prayer of thanksgiving to the Lord.

As they returned to their sitting places on the ground or little stools, I got out and went over to them. "Thank you so very much. You are so kind to me." I told them in Swahili as I went to each man and gave him a bow of respect and expressed my gratitude.

Shortly afterwards, when I arrived at Hadija's home, I felt really shaken up. Maybe I should not have come after all since I had no way to contact Carlos out here in the village if something went wrong.

Braving the situation, I began calling out "Hodi, Hodi," (hello, hello) outside her house. I was instantly greeted by my friend with words of "Karibu" (welcome). She was so pleased that I had come. She led me into the courtyard to an old man sitting on a grass mat on the ground by his hut.

"This is my father, Mama Owensi," Hadija said, introducing me to her Muslim father.

I bowed and greeted him. He smiled and nodded his welcome to me. I was still frightened at what he might say to me since I had been teaching her about Christianity.

"I want to thank you for teaching my daughter how to read. She has been reading to me from this little book which you gave her. I wanted you to come and explain some of it to me."

My heart swelled up with joy when I realized that he really wanted me to share the Gospel with him. There was nothing to fear! Hadija gave me a short stool about a foot off the ground. Then I sat with him, face to face, sharing the Good News. He seemed very pleased and listened intently. After questions and much discussion I asked if I could lead in prayer. He had no objections.

I was able to continue with friendly family conversation while Hadija prepared the traditional tea time for us. I was so grateful for this special time in the non-Christian home. As I said my farewell the old man stated, "I am very impressed with your words. I would like to learn more of this one called Jesus Christ."

How thankful I was that I went to see him in spite of my fears and mishaps. I was assured that, with the Lord's guidance, some Muslims are teachable about the real truths of God's Word.

> ". . whoever hears my word and believes on him who sent me has eternal life and will not be condemned; he has crossed over from death to life." Jn 5:24

C: More Time to Find Food

Yusufu came by one morning to tell us that the Gungu church had voted to move the 10:00 Sunday school back to 8:00.

"You cannot do that. That is too early. We would not likely be able to get there by 8:00. Why have you decided to do that?"

"Most of our members come to church without having eaten anything as they have no food in their huts. They have to search for food for their families each day. We decided that if we were to start Sunday school at 8:00 and worship at 9:00, we would have more time to look for our food for the day."

My heart sank and I felt humbled. I knew that most of the Gungu members were poor but I had not realized that most of the families had no idea what they would eat when getting up each morning. I felt ashamed and apologized to Yusufu.

"Yusufu, whenever you want to have Sunday school, let us know and we will be there."

"And Moses listened." Ex 18:24a

M: Facing Village Elders

"Mama, come quickly. The tribal council of our village is meeting right now. They are going to decide if you missionaries can stay and teach us in our village." Yusufu anxiously spoke to me while I was in my women's Swahili class.

"Sorry, I'm not the one to go. You must go get Mwalimu (teacher) Owens. I am only a woman and they would not respect anything I have to say."

"There isn't time to go to your house. You must come now!" he insisted. "If you don't come, you most likely will be refused permission to work here."

I was unsure of what to do. I knew all the elders were Muslim men who had no respect for women. Wives were considered only as property they had bought with a bride price and they were like personal slaves. The men were the firm rulers in their homes.

Yusufu insisted again that I go immediately with him.

Explaining to the women that I must go for a while, I left them to continue an assignment with Hadija, my gracious helper, who had quickly learned to read. She was a very intelligent young woman.

As Yusufu and I hurried, we arrived at the meeting of village elders gathered under tall palm trees. My heart was beating hard. I prayed as hard as I had ever prayed knowing this was such a critical situation concerning our work.

Nearly fifty men, all Muslim, were seated, discussing many things. They spoke so quickly and firmly that I couldn't follow all they were saying. I kept looking at Yusufu for clues but he was stoic. After nearly an hour, the discussion stopped.

The leader stood up and announced clearly,

"We have seen these people working with our families and friends. They are doing good and no harm to us. We have agreed that they can continue their work here."

I wanted to shout for joy. As I looked more closely at most of the faces of the group I then realized that many of them were the very men who had helped pick up my Land Rover out of the hole in the road.

All I could think was, "Lord, you knew why I needed to fall in that hole; to meet these men. I thank you, Lord, for preparing the way."

I did not delay in going from man to man; curtsying, bowing, and thanking them for their help. God certainly demonstrated his power in touching the thoughts of these leaders to allow our Christian witness to continue in this Muslim village.

> *"I know your deeds: See, I have placed before you an open door that no one can shut. I know that you have little strength, yet you have kept my word and have not denied my name." Rev. 3:8*

M: Women and Eggs

One woman said, "We want to learn to cook some of the things that you cook. If you would teach us, we could make and sell things in the market. That would make us very happy!"

The women had completed their basic course in reading Swahili. They were now anxious to learn some new skills. Food for them was ugali, a mush cooked firm in a pot by adding corn meal to boiling water and stirring constantly until it was thick enough to eat with the fingers. This was their staple diet, served with a sauce made from whatever they could find; wild greens, an onion, beans, or occasionally fish or meat. I was eager to improve their diet, since many of the children were malnourished.

"Let's start with basics. How about some eggs cooked in several ways? They are so very good for you and your children."

"Oh, no, Mama (which they called me, a term of respect), we are forbidden to eat eggs. If women eat eggs they will not have children!" they said regretfully.

I couldn't resist. "Your men are trying to fool you. They want all the eggs themselves. Look at me, I eat eggs regularly and I have three children!"

They had all seen my children and started whispering among themselves.

One raised her hand and said, "Please teach us many ways to fix eggs. We think what you say is true." Laughs and giggles ensued.

At our next class the women learned how to boil, scramble, and fry eggs as well as make an omelet or a healthy milkshake with eggs and milk. They were very attentive and excited as we all tasted the foods prepared in different ways. Each one was given an opportunity to prepare them as I had demonstrated. Not an egg was left and no women failed to eat them.

"These eggs are so good and so easy to prepare. Yes, we will now fix eggs for our children". They giggled and laughed as they continued to eat until everything was finished.

They also learned that day to make basic pancakes (flapjacks) with their corn meal and also with flour. I helped them understand the needs of the children for more protein, especially beans in their diets. They could be made easily and were healthy food for them. Often I had seen little ones even around one year old or less trying to eat the hard roasted corn on a cob. They were limited in knowing what they could use. They loved milk but were unable to buy it and had no way to keep it from going bad.

Later I was able to bring them small papaya plants to plant around their homes in order to have this fruit, rich in vitamin C, for their families. They grow quickly and have delicious fruit, usually within a year. We had planted several trees at our house and had started the plants ourselves for this project. I taught them to throw their dirty water on the plants to keep them growing. In less than a year many of them had trees loaded with large, healthy papayas.

Still they wanted to fix something they could sell in

the market place. Seeing so many peanuts in the market at that time I began to think that peanut brittle would be a great product to sell to those coming to the market. Since making it was such a simple cooking task, they all learned very quickly and were successful in making wonderful peanut brittle, also sugared peanuts. It was my great delight to later meet some of these same women in the market, smiling because of their booming business.

Many of these became very devoted Christians because of hearing the Word taught in my Bible studies or devotionals in every class. Some began to attend the Sunday worship services held in the same building as our classes but became secret Christians because of fear of their husbands. God opened hearts of these women to His eternal kingdom.

"Whoever gives heed to instruction prospers, And blessed is he who trusts in the Lord." Pr 16:20

C: Independence

Tanganyika became an independent nation from England in December 1961, becoming the Republic of Tanganyika. Not too long afterwards Tanganyika and the island country

Zanzibar, forty five miles offshore, united under the name of The United Republic of Tanzania and Zanzibar. Not long after that the name was changed to Tanzania: Tan- (the first three letters of Tanganyika), -zan- (the first three letters of Zanzibar) and -ia (making the word Swahili). It is pronounced Tahn-za-NEE-ah. Independence brought much celebrating. We rejoiced with the people. Then the unexpected happened.

Our house on the lake was finished and we had moved in. Wanting to let the people know that we were happy with their yet new independence, I went into town, purchased one of the country's new flags, and put it on a pole at our driveway entrance.

About mid morning of the same day, a Police Land Rover drove down our driveway. I went out and greeted the two policemen as they were getting out of their vehicle.

"Why have you put our flag at your driveway?"

"We know that you are happy that you have independence and we want to show that we are happy too."

"You are a foreigner. You are not one of us. You are not allowed to fly our flag."

We were disappointed, but realized that they had laws and rules. We were foreigners so I took the flag down and apologized to the police.

For eighteen months, we had lived in those four rooms in town behind the shops. It was not the best of arrangements but had served its purpose, giving us a roof over our heads. When the local authorities approved our request for the building site overlooking the lake, we were thrilled to move in after eighteen months of waiting and building. It had been a big task; overseeing the construction.

When we had been in our new house for only a short time, we read something in the national newspaper, which astounded us. We saw that, without contacting us, the government had taken over our house. What a shock! What would we do? The paper was full of businesses, buildings, coffee plantations, and sisal farms that they were confiscating. Only by God's grace did we even see our house listed.

After numerous visits to local government offices and several trips to Dar es Salaam, we were informed that we could retain the house by paying the Government 10,000 shillings. That was $1,223.00 in U.S. currency at that time. Our mission and board agreed and we paid the money to keep our house. They never asked for it again. With daily gratitude to God we appreciated our home more than ever.

"Give to Caesar that which is Caesar's. . ." Matthew 22:21a

M: Clinics and Home Schooling

Halima sat next to me every Sunday when we began our services in the same school building where we had our classes. Like me, she had three small children and she had been learning to read in the class. She was gracious and responsive.

"Halima, your baby has a bad eye infection. You need to take him to the hospital for some medicine," I told her one Sunday.

I had not thought of doing any medical work here at that time. I had been very involved in home schooling our children, caring for many visitors who passed through the area, working with the women's classes, and writing Sunday school lessons to use in our young mission.

When the following Sunday came, I noticed Halima did not have her baby with her.

"Where is your baby? I hope you were able to get some medicine for his eyes"

Suddenly she broke down crying. "My baby is dead. I did take him to the hospital but they said they were out of medicine. In the next two days he began coughing badly and passed away that night. We buried him early the next morning."

I put my arms around her. "I am so sorry." Not only feeling very sad for her I also felt very ashamed for I knew that I could have helped her. At that moment I knew that I must start a ministry with primary care clinics to help these dear people who were coming to the church. If the local hospital could not provide any care, I felt God wanted me to step in and do my part. This child could have been saved with antibiotic eye ointment. Undoubtedly the infection had spread to his lungs, causing a pneumonia which could have been prevented.

That very week I was able to get permission from the regional medical officer. He shared with me that the hospital had very few medicines and few trained workers.

"Anything that you can do to help the health of my people would be greatly appreciated."

Also our mission gave me a go ahead to do the clinics, since I was already registered in the country and had worked at our hospital in Mbeya.

One of our doctors assisted in procuring medicines and giving some helpful guidance. In no time at all, I began regular clinics in the morning hours in the small room behind our house.

Daily, I also had to teach Janice and Ruth. Debra, not yet old enough for school, participated. After teaching them for a short lesson, I would give them an assignment to complete. They could play when this was finished. During this time I would see several patients. As soon as I could, I would whistle for the children to come inside to continue with lessons. This went on most of the day.

The popularity of the clinic grew so much that we would have well over one hundred patients waiting every morning before 8:00 a.m. I finally had to decide to see only those and their families who were attending church or our classes.

Our church services really grew quickly in numbers. Some surely came in order to be able to come to the clinics, but I believed firmly that God's Word would begin to touch their hearts. I was so thankful that I could help spare a few lives that otherwise would not have had any help at all, and touch hearts for the Lord. And in spite of the busy days, our children did excellent in their schooling.

The Lord provided the strength and help that I needed, and many hurting patients had the appropriate medical care. The other activities fell successfully into place.

> *"He gives strength to the weary and increases the power of the weak." Isa 40:29*

C: Leopard Man

The group of young boys, who were coming regularly two mornings a week from Bangwe (BAH-ngway), to learn to read and to hear Bible stories, did not show up. Since this was the first time in nearly three months they had missed coming, we were concerned. We made some inquiries but learned nothing.

After three days two of the older boys came to the house late one morning. Both showed evidence of fear.

"What has happened? Why did you not come for your class?"

"The leopard man has been in our village. We are afraid to go out."

"Tell me about the leopard man."

One boy said, "From time to time the leopard man comes into our village at night. He goes from hut to hut frightening the people. Sometimes people die after he has passed by their hut. We fear that we will die, so we hide."

The other boy continued, "We wanted to come to the class but feared to come as people say that the leopard man hides along the road from our village to Kigoma. If we come to Kigoma and to your house, we fear that he will see us and pass by our hut that night. So, we have stayed at home. Today we went into the bush and came by another route. Maybe he did not see us."

The first boy said, "The other boys were too afraid to come with us. They said that if we were to come we all would likely die because of the leopard man."

I told the boys that I had heard of the leopard man, that he was a witchdoctor sort of man who dressed in a leopard skin to spread fear among the people. I counseled them that they should try hard not to fear the leopard man because he was only a man but a bad one who wants to hurt people.

They said that they wanted to come to the classes and would see if they could get the other boys to come with them.

The boys never came back. We were sad as we knew that their fear grew out of something which was not real. Unfortunately, their parents believed in the powers of witchdoctors and of the leopard man and had little interest in their boys' learning to read and to hear Bible stories.

On numerous occasions we witnessed the terrific power a witchdoctor could hold over a person. Because of extreme fear some would actually get sick and die. We learned, moreover, that God and Jesus are more powerful than any witchdoctor and that, by trusting in God and Jesus, a person could overcome the power of the witchdoctor.

"The evil man brings evil things out of the evil stored up in him." Mt 12:35b

M: Ashes around Church

As we drove up to the new Gungu church the whole congregation was standing outside looking very disturbed. Persecutions from the Muslim community had hit several of the converts and we were very concerned that someone else had been threatened or attacked.

As we got out, Yusufu, our pastor leader, walked slowly to us.

"They are trying to use witchcraft on us now. Just look at the ring of ashes around the church building."

We slowly walked all around the building to see that someone had thoroughly spread ashes completely around the building, not missing a spot.

"What does this signify, Yusufu?"

"It means that if anyone passes over the ashes, they will see disaster, most likely through some kind of fire. They want to bring fear so no one will worship here anymore."

Carlos said, "We don't fear the power of witchcraft. We know our Lord is victorious over evil. Let's go in," as he motioned to the congregation.

Everyone stood back as he walked through the door and our family followed without any hesitation. They waited a few minutes to see if anything would happen. Seeing we had no problems, they slowly entered the building.

We began our service with a prayer of thanksgiving and praise for the Lord's protecting us and proving His power over the witchcraft. Soon the joyous singing of victory rang out. The service was filled with the Spirit of the Lord and the people committed themselves anew to the powerful, living Lord.

Satan had no control on this congregation. We would have loved to have seen the faces and heard the words of those who had tried their witchcraft on a church of our loving Savior.

"I have told you these things, so that in me
you may have peace. In this world you will have trouble.
But take heart! I have overcome the world." Jn 16:33

C: Search for Missionaries

We were having a service in a small, rented building at Gungu, a village not far from the shores of Lake Tanganyika. We were well along in the service when two men appeared and stood at the door. After a while they came in and sat at the rear of the church. We finished the service and spoke to the men who told us their story.

A young man from their village had gone to the capitol city, Dar es Salaam, looking for work. One Sunday he attended a church near where he was staying. The missionary witnessed to him and gave him a tract. He found no work and, after a time, returned to his village more than nine hundred miles away.

He read the tract repeatedly and, according to his testimony, the message in it tugged at his heart. He took the tract home with him and shared it with a number of people in his village. Two men, also impressed with the message in the tract, decided to see if they could find out more about what they had learned.

Danieli (Dan-ee-AA-lee) Bihali (Bee-HA-lee), one of the men, wrote a letter to the address on the back of the tract. A letter came in response telling them about us in Kigoma, less than one hundred miles from their village. Danieli and a friend, Samweli (Sa-mm-WAY-lee), walked several miles to a main road and took a bus to Kasulu, some 35 miles from their village. In Kasulu, they found another bus and came to Kigoma looking for the missionaries.

Arriving in Kigoma, they made inquires about missionaries. Different people told them that there were no such missionaries in Kigoma. Those who told them this were Muslims who knew that we were there. They would not accommodate these men by telling them about us. The search went on for three days.

On the afternoon of the third day, weary and disappointed, Danieli and Samweli were walking from the town towards the main road where they hoped to find a bus to take them back to Kasulu (Ka-SUE-loo) and in turn to their village.

Nearing the main road, the men heard singing not too far away in the village. Believing the singing to be Christian, they walked into the village and found us.

After the service we spent time with the two men, after which they came back into town with us and spent the night. On the following morning, we took them to the main road after having made plans to visit Kibanga (Kee-bah-NN-gah), their home village. The months which followed were exciting and fruitful.

The more than seventy five miles from Kigoma to Kasulu and on to Kibanga were stressful. During the rainy season, we would slip and slide even with the four wheel drive Land Rover. During the dry season, the red dust covered everything and the deep ruts and pot holes made for difficult travel. We got used to those roads in time.

Travel through the forest was fascinating. The blood red, fireball plants were numerous at the beginning of the rains. In addition, about the same time, we could harvest edible, orange mushrooms that were usually plentiful. Cooked in a butter and lemon juice sauce, they were exceptionally delicious served on toast, a special treat for us.

Kibanga was twenty-two miles beyond Kasulu. If it were dry, we could drive through the creek bed and on to the church. If it were raining and the creek was up we would leave the Land Rover at the creek, wade through, and walk on to the church. On occasions, if I were alone, I would remove most of my clothes, bundle them up with my Bible and other materials, place them my head, and wade across the creek. On the other side I would put my clothes back on and go on to the church.

Getting to the church and greeting the people was always exciting. They were extremely poor but usually very happy.

Their offerings consisted of little money; maybe a few coins. Most brought produce which they placed at the altar in front of the pulpit; ears of corn, dried beans, and hands or sometimes stalks of bananas and the occasional chicken or a rooster would be offered. Occasionally there would be a goat. Church leaders auctioned these items outside following the service. They took the items which members did not buy and offered them for sale in the local market on Monday. Money from sales went into the church treasury.

"I am the Way and the truth and the life. No one comes to the Father except through me." Jn 14:6

M: White and Black Twins

Working with people steeped in primitive customs and fears, we saw the irony in their dealing with their fears. In one regular daily primary care clinic, a patient arrived visibly heavy with child. Upon checking, I found that there were two hearts beating and exclaimed, "You are going to have twins!"

She immediately broke down in tears.

I asked why she was crying. "You should be so happy to be blessed with two babies."

She, still weeping, exclaimed, "We are taught that having twins is a curse. One or both will die. I do not want to lose my babies."

I attempted to persuade her that God had blessed her in an extra way by giving her twins. "The Lord will help you and care for you. I will also do all I can to help. Please do not fear. Let God help you," I stressed.

After receiving her medications, she left the clinic still in tears and without further response.

Around two or three weeks later she returned. Seeing the two little bundles in her arms excited me. When her turn came to come into the examination room, she was all smiles. I congratulated her and asked to see her little ones. She removed the cloth covering the baby in her right arm. He was beautiful; small but healthy. Then she took the cloth off the second baby. What I saw startled me. The child was as white as a ghost. She had greased the baby from head to toe and sprinkled him with flour. He was solid white.

"What does this mean?"

"The evil spirit won't get my babies now as I do not have twins. I have a white baby and a black baby, not twins!"

Her reasoning gave me an inside chuckle. After treating her and the babies, I promised that we would do all we could to help her have healthy babies. I spent extra time, sharing with her how the Heavenly Father would also help her as she trusted and believed in his love and power.

*"You are my hiding place; you will protect me from trouble
and surround me with songs of deliverance." Ps 32:7*

M: Unusual Means

We rode high in our Land Rover poised on the flat car of the railroad line. Our Land Rover was sitting on it, riding on this dangerous rail track through the flood-covered region. The girls were asleep on the makeshift bed in the back. Carlos and I sat in the front seat trying to doze, but seeing how deep the water was, we began to feel real anxiety. Our thoughts were on what if the track gives way in the flooded area? What if the train turns over, or gets stuck in an area where tracks have disappeared?

For two weeks our whole area had been in one of the worst floods for years. All roads were closed and all transportation had been shut down. The area was in desperate need of basic food supplies. Beside that, we were scheduled to go to Kenya to lead the large conference for pastors and leaders in preparations for the all Kenya-Tanzania Revival Campaigns that would have American pastors coming to lead. Tremendous preparations had been made and it was absolutely necessary to bring all the plans together to make the crusade successful.

Finally, one of our friends told us that the rail line was going to attempt to send one freight train through the flood waters to bring supplies into the area. Carlos rushed down to see the station master praying that we could go back on the return train. Otherwise, we were completely stranded, for there was no air service at this time.

"If you are willing to chance the dangers of a washed-out line, I will provide a flat car for your vehicle to ride on. Then you can proceed from Tabora by road to Kenya," the station master hesitantly stated.

"If your train made it okay coming in, we feel it is worth the chance to try to return with it. We have no other way to go and I must be at the meeting to lead this program," Carlos stated with assurance and determination.

He knew that the workers on the line had gone very slowly checking the track all the way. He knew they would not chance their precious train engines and cars.

We left late one evening, bedding down in the Land Rover, as the engines huffed and puffed out of the station. We felt quite exposed by being open to all around us on the top of this flat car. All night long it seemed to slowly move. Early the next morning we got out to see where we were. Then we realized we were only ten miles out of town. The train was now returning to town. The heavy train was too much for this engine on the upgrade out of town.

They added another engine and began the trip again by noon. We could see the villages near the tracks and all the people who were outside watching. Our three little girls sat on top of the hood waving vigorously.

We slowly moved on past the village that had stumped the first train. We ate our food while standing outside the Land Rover and enjoyed the countryside as the train moved slowly along. Many times we stopped so long we feared we might be completely stopped, but then we would move again. The villagers enjoyed watching the children brush their teeth and laughed at them. We had to use our car for toilet needs with the children's potty inside. Everything was confined to the flat car.

When we approached the deepest water, we were glad that the children went to sleep with the constant shaking of the flat car and chugging of the engine. If they had seen the water high on the railroad car they surely would have panicked. We began praying fervently for God's grace and protection. Neither of us could sleep.

About three o'clock in the morning the engine started to enter drier ground. We could see the ground near the tracks. Our hearts thanked God with our deepest gratitude.

Shortly, we pulled into the Tabora station. They kept cutting off the train cars, placing them in certain areas and then left ours stranded. We couldn't off load our vehicle.

Carlos had to jump off and run to the main station, way down the tracks. No one was there. He finally found a guard who agreed to call the station master but he was very fearful of awakening him. The station master had to get up in the middle of the night, ordered the engines to move around again and bring our car up to the off load ramp. He had missed the communication that we were to be off-loaded there.

Our ordeal was now over. How grateful to God we were. We headed down the main gravel road toward the north to the Kenya border but we still had at least another fourteen hours or more to go before arriving at the conference center.

Though we were exhausted from the stress, we felt such a wonderful assurance that we were really able to make the meeting in time. The bumps, the dust and long journey didn't even seem difficult now.

As we finally pulled into the conference center late that night, we only could thank the Lord for providing the way. We hoped we wouldn't have to experience such a trip again. We were dogged tired but we were there for our responsibilities.

As we talked to some fellow missionaries and pastors later, telling about our adventure, they were very surprised we even came. One of the pastors said, "I would call that real dedication to the task!"

God did bless that great revival campaign with many thousands coming to the Lord and experiencing salvation. All the scheduled American pastors came; all had interpreters, and the churches worked in beautiful harmony to proclaim God's salvation in many places in these two countries.

> *"May the God who gives endurance and encouragement give you a spirit of unity among yourselves as you follow Christ Jesus, so that with one heart and mouth you may glorify the God and Father of our Lord Jesus Christ.."*
> *Ro 15:5-6*

C: Without Sound of Hammers

I first baptized sixty-eight. Others followed. Soon there were more than 200 baptized members. They built a small, pole and grass church but it didn't last long. The first heavy rains found it lying on the ground. Something better was needed.

I had not been to Kibanga for quite some time. Danieli wrote that they were making ready for a new church building. When I did go, I found much activity at the church site. Both men and women were coming and going.

Danieli told me that men were in the forest up in the hills, cutting down and sizing poles with their machetes. As some men cut down trees and sized the poles others brought them down and piled them near where they would build the church. The poles were for the walls, for roof beams and for benches.

Women and girls with their machetes were stripping the bark from the poles and putting it in a drum of water where it would soak until needed. Builders would use the bark for tying things together.

As Danieli and I talked, a group of women and girls walked in with large bundles of grass on their heads -- grass for the roof. They added their bundles to the large pile of grass, which they and others had already brought. They were just about ready to begin building.

A great crowd of happy people soon gathered, having heard that I had arrived. Work stopped for a time as we worshipped outside—on the spot where their new building would go. How proud they were. I rejoiced with them.

The next time we came to Kibanga the building was finished. More than two hundred people sat on low benches made from single poles supported by forked sticks in the ground. Wonder and amazement overwhelmed us. The building was well structured and appeared to be secure. With their machetes they had dug holes in the ground and stood poles in them for the walls. A roof structure of thinner poles served to support the grass. They securely tied everything together with the strips of bark. The amazing thing was that they had neither used hammers, saws nor nails anywhere in the building. Theirs was the church built without the sound of hammers.

> *"In building the temple, only blocks dressed at the quarry were used, and no hammer, chisel or other iron tool was heard at the temple site while it was being built." IKi 6:7*

M: Marshmallows

The small Cessna airplane buzzed our house several times. We ran outside to see if it had a cross under the carriage. Sure enough, someone wanted us to meet them at the air strip. Since this was a regular occurrence, we felt that we had a special ministry to our missionaries of other faiths. Our special encounters provided new friends, and showed how we depended on each other in times of crises. Mission pilots knew we were in Kigoma and that we would be available to assist them when they needed to stop due to time or need of fuel.

Carlos happened to be home and hopped into our Land Rover to pick up whoever was coming for overnight. We had been hearing on the BBC (British Broadcasting Corp.) news report on the radio about the horrible attacks during the civil war in the Congo at that time.

Shortly, he returned with the Methodist pilot, a couple from the Berea Mission and their three children; complete strangers to us. You could see they were in shock. As soon as they arrived we greeted and hugged them assuring of our love and help. Then they began to tell of the horrible massacre all around their mission station.

Many of their church members were slaughtered and they were being pursued as they dashed out, leaving everything they had. They had managed to pick up one small bag. They were crying and rejoicing that the plane had arrived just in time to take them out.

They told of the massacre of several at the Roman Catholic Mission Stations and how the parts of the priests' bodies were on sale in the market place. Our hearts went out to them as they shared the horrors of war. We prayed with them and tried to be listening ears and consoling friends.

After our evening meal, we prepared beds for them by bringing our three girls into our bedroom, their family in their room and the pilot in the office on a cot. They stayed a few days to work out plans and schedules for their future.

During the times we had for sharing with them, in the midst of caring for our own busy schedules, the wife loved talking about their problems with food and caring for her family in the remote area of the Congo. We had a lot in common, laughing and finding how we each improvised in order to have fairly normal meals.

She shared one of her favorite secrets; how to make marshmallows. Our own children had often begged for them since I had used them as treats in the States. While they were with us, we made marshmallows together, amazed at the wonderful results. Some were coated in powdered sugar, others with browned coconut, and some with chopped peanuts.

All the children ate far too much but we just couldn't refuse their having a special treat since they didn't even have chocolate of any kind, or other candy except the hard sugar kind. Marshmallows soon became a regular extra special goodie for birthday parties and special holidays. We all enjoyed this special treat which could not be bought in Tanzania.

While on furlough, we told many church groups about our work in Africa, and we now realize that the story about making marshmallows was remembered more than many others. Most never knew that anyone could make marshmallows at home, so I was called the "missionary with the marshmallow story". We do what we have to do to make our families maintain a balanced and healthy attitude in this isolated area in the mission field.

Since our home became a place of constant visitors from all parts of the world, we made much preparation to entertain them with unusual as well as very common American food. Trying to make Fritos didn't turn out too well, but when I tried soda crackers and potato chips, they turned out well enough that I made them often.

Hospitality is a well-worked gift in the heart of Africa. To keep life and the home atmosphere fairly normal for our children's growing up we did our best to make their life memorable. With Congo missionaries fleeing, chimpanzee reserve visitors, American Ambassador touring, National Geographic personnel, hungry and lonely Peace Corp youth, plus many visits by fellow missionaries and mission executives, life definitely was very interesting and challenging. Our home was a haven to many and in turn we were equally blessed with them.

> *"Offer hospitality to one another without grumbling.*
> *Each one should use whatever gift he has received*
> *to serve others, faithfully administering God's grace*
> *in its various forms." IPe 4:9-10*

C: Hippo Hunt

The grunts of hippos on our lawn in the middle of the night amused us. Looking out windows we could see the giant creatures in the moonlight. However, a slight movement or sound would send them scurrying back to the lake only one hundred yards below our house. We put up a chain link fence before planting our garden, knowing that the hippos would otherwise eat and destroy everything. After putting up the fence, we could still hear their grunts on many nights from nearer the lake. We got the occasional report that they came into and destroyed many gardens in villages along the lake.

Quite early one morning, strangers came through our gate and down to our house. They told us that they lived in the village across the harbor from the docks and that a hippo was coming in the night and destroying their crops; corn and cassava. Having heard that I had a gun they wanted to know if I would come and kill the hippo. I knew that it would be next to impossible to shoot a hippo at night and that they could usually be seen some distance from the shore very early in the morning. I told them that I would come early the next morning.

At daybreak the next morning I and three villagers sat quietly on the shore. Soon, we could see the eyes and nose of a very large hippo just above the water, less than one hundred yards away. The men verified that this was the rogue hippo. That was not too far for my 30-06 rifle. We waited since the hippo, though spending most of the time under water must come up for air every twelve to fifteen minutes. Sometimes only eyes and nose would appear. At other times, most of the head would appear above water and we would wait for this to happen. I sat poised with my rifle.

It was not long until most of the hippo's head came out of the water. One shot behind the ear sent the hippo churning around in the water. Moments later, with no more motion, we knew that he was lying dead on the bottom of the lake. We waited knowing, that within an hour, he would float and we could be ready to tie a rope to one leg and tow him to shore. Several men joined us in canoes as we waited with the rope, over the place the hippo went down.

In just about an hour, the hippo did come to the surface. We tied one end of the rope to a hind leg and one man in each canoe took hold of the rope while the other man in each canoe paddled and pulled the hippo and us to the shore where others were waiting to assist in rolling the two-ton carcass onto the shore. The entire village celebrated our kill, since the hippo had been destroying their crops, now we knew that its meat would fill many hungry stomachs.

I told them that I only wanted some of the inch-thick skin from the hippo's back and the tusks, which would make good souvenirs. They complied.

We had not attempted to begin a church in this small village. Gungu was only four miles away so, before leaving, I invited everyone present to be with us on Sunday at Gungu. We were pleased to see several come. Not very many weeks later, the Gungu church arranged to have a baptizing at their village. Of those we were to baptize, seven were from the village. Every one of them recalled how I had helped save their crops by killing the hippo.

"He will deliver the needy who cry out." Ps 72:12a

M: Six Toes

To assist in the work of evangelism we often were invited to other stations to join in a revival or weekend Christian Growth Conference. We also invited others to join us to assist in promoting the work in the Kigoma area.

We enjoyed the opportunity to be with missionaries on the coast north of the Mombasa, where Carlos was to preach in their evangelistic services. This area had as large a population of Muslims as we had, but they also had a unique tribe in the area called the Giriyama (Geer-ree-YAH-mah). Most of them were pagan.

The men dressed in the normal wear of shirts and shorts, as other non-Muslims did, but the women held on to their old tradition of wearing very short skirts made out of multiple layers of mosquito netting that fluffed out like a tutu. Beads were the only thing worn above the waist

In each service, our family was present but we sat near the back so I could take the girls out when needed during the long services. Some of the Giriyama, who had been saved, had changed to dress more modestly, like most of the other women; with their cloth khangas wrapped around them covering them up adequately.

During one of the services a middle aged Giriyama woman, in the customary dress, sat at the end of the row where we were sitting. Our daughter, Debra, who was nearly four at that time, was closest to her and continued looking her way. I kept whispering to Debra not to stare at her since this was improper but also I wanted to keep her from staring at her bare chest. Debra kept whispering back, "But look, Mama, look."

I had to ask her again not to look at the woman but to look at Daddy in the front.

She seemed fascinated with this lady. Again she whispered back, "Mama, look! Just look! She has six toes on her foot!"

I was a bit chagrined to realize that Debra had no interest in the topless woman - only her excess of toes.

> *"Let your eyes look straight ahead,*
> *Fix your gaze directly before you." Pr 4:25*

C: Death Threat

Paul Ebomielin, a pastor and convention leader from Nigeria, came to Kigoma to assist in Tanzania's countrywide revival crusade. Each day we would go to two or three villages for services. One afternoon we went to Ujiji. We wanted to walk around and witness, if the occasion presented itself, in this town which was 99.9% Muslim.

We were in the main street when three Muslim Sheiks confronted us.

One, in a loud and angry voice said, "You are here to confuse our people with your words about Jesus. We will not allow you to do that."

As kindly as I could I said, "We will only do what the law allows. We will talk about Jesus and the people will decide what they want to do about what we say."

With increased anger another of the sheiks said, "Ujiji only worships Allah. Islam is our religion. We want to hear nothing about your Jesus."

Sensing their increased anger and noting that many other angry people were joining us in the street I did not reply.

"If you preach Jesus in Ujiji we will kill you," one of the sheiks cried out.

From the crowd I heard someone shout, "Kill them!"

The entire crowd joined in shouting, "Kill them! Kill them! Kill them!"

Looking about, I could see that many had taken stones and sticks of various sizes. I felt that at any moment one of the sheiks could say something which would incite them to fall upon us.

Leaning over to Paul I said, "Paul, pray as you have never prayed before and follow me."

Completely overcome with fear, I turned my back to the sheiks, faced the crowd, and took a step forward. As I moved forward those before me stepped to each side. Each time I took a step forward more of the crowd moved to the side. With Paul close behind me, we passed through and away from the crowd, which by this time was completely silent. The sheiks also remained silent; everyone looking at us as we moved away. I 'felt' the sticks and stones on my body but they never came.

When we were some distance away from the silent masses, I took courage and looked over my shoulder. They were still there and still silent. I could not see the sheiks. Perhaps they had gone away into the nearby mosque.

Paul and I did not talk as we walked on to the Land Rover, which we had left some way ahead. When standing beside our vehicle, however, we praised and thanked God for our safe exit from the angry mob. We both were confident that the Lord had delivered us.

*"But he walked right through the crowd
and went on his way." Lk 4:30*

C: Look Behind You

Local authorities in Kigoma gave us permission to have church services on Sunday mornings in a school in Ujiji. Having received a death threat already, we began services cautiously not knowing what the Muslim reaction would be. At first, few attended but soon there were many. Among them were spies from the mosque.

Only a few weeks passed when people began coming secretly to us in Kigoma expressing a desire to accept Jesus as their Savior. Sometimes two or three would come together. When someone accepted Jesus as Savior he/she would usually first ask how he or she could react when the Muslim community found out.

I would usually say, "Do not tell anyone for the time being. One day God will let you know when you can share what you have done."

From Sunday to Sunday, we preached in the school at Ujiji. I could tell from facial expressions that those were present who had accepted Jesus already. At the close of each service, we would offer an invitation for people to accept Jesus even though I had told those who had been saved to keep it to themselves for the time being. We waited upon the Lord.

One Sunday following preaching, I gave the invitation. Immediately, as we began singing, a man who had accepted Jesus at our house in Kigoma came forward saying, "I can not keep it inside any longer. I have to let people know that I have accepted Jesus."

He began shaking. Fear overtook him. Holding tightly to my hand with both his he erratically began, "What can I do? What can I do?"

I said, "Turn around."

On turning around, he could see that twelve others had come and were standing behind him. His coming had given them courage to follow. We rejoiced but expected the worst. By that afternoon, the persecution had begun. Some came to tell us that someone had already burned a new convert's house. Two Muslim men had severely beaten their wives. By midweek, we heard that another woman, severely beaten by her husband and fearing that he would kill her, ran away. We never heard from her again. Some said that she was back with her family in Burundi.

On the following Sunday only three of those who had come forward came back to church. Eventually we were able to baptize eight of the thirteen, openly in the lake at Ujiji, along with others who had joined them.

*"So the word of God spread. The number of disciples
in Jerusalem increased rapidly,."Ac 6:7*

Chapter Six

Joys of Success

After our second furlough, we flew in to Nairobi and then the 800 air miles on to Kigoma in a missionary plane. We found more than 300 people waiting on the red dirt airstrip to greet us. Some of those who had come to welcome us back were church members from Kasulu. Some had come by bus but many, not having money, had walked more than sixty miles just to be there for us.

We settled in and soon were back to our schedule of work with backdoor clinics, visits to and preaching in the churches, Bible study and special classes for church leaders, childcare, sewing and cooking classes for the women, assisting in putting up church buildings and going to places where there were no churches.

Again, we enjoyed our house on the shores of Lake Tanganyika. After those eighteen months behind the shop in town, the new missionary house, overlooking the lake, was delightful. It was especially nice to have supper again, on the patio at 7:00 o'clock each evening. Our being so close to the equator meant that the sun rose and set at nearly the same time each day. While eating, we could watch the sun as it slowly disappeared behind the Congo Mountains - across the Lake.

C: Pastor from the Congo

In the early 1960's, the Civil War in the Congo affected all of us in Tanzania, especially those of us who lived in Kigoma, on the shores of the lake, which separated the two countries. Refugees came with tales of carnage and horror, some with only the clothes on their backs. We often took them in and assisted in any way we could. Our church members at Kalalangabo (Kah-la-lahn-GAH-bow), most of who were from the Congo, told of family members who had been killed or tortured.

Late one morning, Heri, (HAY-ree) our pastor at Kalalangabo, came to our house with Jeremiah, a pastor from the Congo, and a relative of his. We listened in horror as Jeremiah told of what was happening in his country and what had happened to his own family.

The rebels, supported by the Communists, were killing Christians and burning their churches. Fearing for his life, Jeremiah had hid out in the mountains for nearly a month until he found someone with a boat who agreed to bring him across the lake to Kigoma. Because he was a pastor, the rebels were searching for him. They had burned his house and killed his wife and two of his children. They tortured his sister in an attempt to get her to divulge his whereabouts. They had cut off both her ears but she still did not tell. Relating this tale, he wondered if his sister were still alive. He would wait at Kalalangabo and pray for his family and his people. We had a special time of deep fervent prayer for his sister and those surviving in his congregation.

When the conflict was settled, Jeremiah went back to the Congo and to his people. We sent him back with Bibles and song books as they also spoke Swahili in that area. We promised to continue to faithfully lift him up in prayer. He came back twice to get more Bibles, literature and encouragement. We gladly provided them for him. He said that even though the rebels had killed many of his church members, those remaining were worshiping and had built a mud and pole church with a grass roof. They were depending on God to help them rebuild the church and their lives.

> *"Have mercy on us, O Lord, for we have endured much contempt." Ps 123:3b*

C: Stolen Goods

Soon after our arriving in Kigoma, thieves stole our car from the street in front of the store behind which we lived. It was found a week later in Burundi; wrecked and worthless. Daily, there were reports of break-ins and thievery. Thieves broke in and stole from houses and shops. Seldom did the owners get anything back. The Burundi border was thirty five miles to the north and the lake separated Tanzania from the Congo. Most often thieves would take stolen goods across the lake to the Congo or into Burundi. Since they were afraid of dogs, most residents kept watchdogs at their homes and in their shops. We had a chain link fence surrounding our property and kept a big, black Labrador. That seemed to help, as we never had a break-in while in Kigoma.

Early one Sunday morning, I left Kigoma in our boat, Wajumbe (Wah-JUME-bay), to visit a church to the north; on the lake. The lake was calm. It was a beautifully cool and sunny morning. Myrtice and the girls remained behind in order to attend the church at Gungu.

Backed up against the mountain were small, sandy beaches on the lake. Caves in the back of two of these beaches afforded shade and shelter in case of rain. From time to time, we went to these beaches for picnics, swimming and relaxation in order to have some privacy. The beaches near our house most often had crowds of people; some fishing, some bathing or doing laundry and some appearing just to watch us. Even when not stopping, I observed these small beaches as I made my way up the lake.

On this particular Sunday morning having a little extra time, I didn't get into a hurry and took special notice. I could see that there was a large amount of stuff in one of the caves.

Seeing no one around, I beached Wajumbe and walked back to the cave. From the items found there I suspected that thieves had stolen from a shop or shops in Kigoma and hid their loot in the cave to await opportunity for passing it on to the Congo or to Burundi. Even though I would be a little late for church, I felt it necessary to return to Kigoma and report on what I had seen.

On returning and beaching Wajumbe in front of our house, I made my way to the police station. The ones in charge told me that thieves had burglarized three shops the previous night. They and the shop owners were grateful for my reporting on what was in the cave. They immediately sent boats to collect the stolen goods.

I went back to Wajumbe and again, on the lake, I made my way to the church where the people received me with great enthusiasm. Not knowing who the thieves might be or from what village they came I felt it best not to report to the church or the village what I found and had done.

We had an exceptionally good service that day with several publicly accepting Jesus as Savior. After the service, I baptized more than thirty who had previously accepted Jesus, bade the people farewell and made my way back to Kigoma in Wajumbe. It was a great day in the Lord and for justice.

"If you do what is right will you not be accepted?" Ge 1:7a

M: Walking on Water

Lake Tanganyika (Tanga-, sails and -nyka, forest), meaning sail in the wilderness, was named by early explorers whose porters, while trekking towards the lake, could see the sails of the boats before seeing the lake. It is reported that some of them, fearing what they saw, dropped their loads and ran away.

Along the shore of the lake there was very little sand; many rocks and smooth stones. One could swim only very close to the shore, since the bottom dropped off very quickly. It had some of the most unusual and beautiful tropical fish in the world. In the clear waters you could identify and watch the schools of fish of various colors, shapes and size.

We tried to make special times, usually on Saturdays, to take the children to the lake with picnics or just riding in the boat to quiet inlets. After a few seasons, we decided to find some water skis and try our luck at this enjoyable sport since physical activities were limited. While we were in Nairobi for one of the missions' meetings, we found a basic pair of water skis and took them back to try our new sport.

When I drove the boat to help Carlos get started, he had more disasters than success. But after many attempts, he finally got the hang of it and started skiing right in the close vicinity near our house. When he started to pull me the first time, I was able to get right up and enjoy the wonderful exhilaration of skiing on the beautiful, calm water. Many children and passersby would always check us out even if we were just sitting on the shore watching the water and the children at play.

Once, looking up from swinging through the area on the skis, we saw a huge crowd on the shore - cheering.

"Look, they are walking on water! Really walking on water!" they yelled out in Swahili.

After that, we always had a tremendous crowd to view us, trying to see how we could really stay on top of the water.

> *"The earth is the Lord's, and everything in it, the world, and all who live in it; for he founded it upon the seas and established it upon the waters." Ps 24:1-2*

C: Thirty-two Men

We had been to Kenya for an annual mission meeting. This special meeting was for planning our work for the ensuing year. It also afforded wonderful times of inspiration as well as fun and fellowship with our fellow missionaries. It was exciting to be with them since Kigoma was far away from other mission stations. The girls were especially happy being with friends. They had not seen most of them since the previous year. We spent the first night on the way home with missionaries in Arusha and the second night in another mission's guesthouse. It had rained on us most of the way. We were anxious to get home.

Although we passed scattered villages, most of the way was desolate. From time to time, elephants, zebras or giraffes would cross the road in front of us. On the morning of the second day as we drove through a very barren area, a huge spitting cobra was in the road ahead of us. It was at least seven feet long. His neck spread to six or seven inches. We slowed down and as we came close, it raised its head about a foot off the ground, spread his neck and spit at us and then slithered off into the bush.

Late on the afternoon of the third day, when we were about eighty five miles from home, the roads were slippery and very muddy. Several times I put the Land Rover into four-wheel drive to get through some very difficult places. As we were driving down a long grade, I could see a great expanse of water covering the road for at least one hundred yards. We stopped to appraise the situation and decided to drive slowly, in four wheel drive, and go through.

We drove into the water. At first it was only a few inches deep but, as we proceeded, the water got deeper. Soon it was up to the floor board and then began coming into the Land Rover. The children were in the back with their feet on the seat. Myrtice was doing the same in the front seat.

When there was about six inches of water inside the cab, the engine died. The fan had thrown water onto the engine and caused it to stop. I had not learned that one could take the fan belt off and put it back on when you are out of the water. We were about halfway across the flooded part of the road. There was so much water everywhere that our hearts sank in fear. We sat there and prayed. The children were crying. So much water inside the Land Rover frightened them.

Before long, men appeared and offered their help. There were thirty two of them. They waded into the more than hip-deep water—some on each side. Slowly, they pushed us through the water and out on the other side. We thanked them profusely and gave each man a shilling; about 14 US cents and a days wage for many.

We wondered if the engine would start. It did, on the first try. The men chattered with joy from getting the money. They were happy and we were more than happy, thanking our Lord for His provision through these helpful men. Otherwise we might have had to stay until the water receded. How thankful we were to be on our way home!

"The worker deserves his wages." Lk 10:7b

M: Burned Arms

Very early one morning, before we had even gotten out of bed, we heard a call; "Hodi, Hodi, Hodi," at our kitchen door. There was a sense of urgency in the voice. Quickly, I got up, put on my robe and went to the back door. When I opened it, I saw a small, distressed woman with her 'khanga' (African cloth) covering her head and around her shoulders.

"May I help you?"

"Are you the white lady who helps the sick?" "Yes, but the clinic does not open until 8 o'clock."

Seeing her distress I quickly added, "What is your problem?"

She slowly removed the cloth 'khanga' from her arms revealing two badly burned and smelly arms.

"Oh, I'm so sorry. You do need immediate help. Let's go into the clinic room and see what I can do." I needed to examine the extent of her burns.

Still in my nightgown, I began to care for this dear suffering woman.

She said that her name was Mulagi. She shared her story; "While I was carrying some hot corn meal porridge, I stumbled and fell, spilling the thick liquid all over my arms." She moaned, "I had no water at my house and I couldn't get the hot food off my arms fast enough. I had to use dirt to clean it off."

As I examined her arms, I could tell that this must have happened several days before, because infection was already invading the burned areas. After giving her pain medication, I told her that she should have come immediately for help.

"I did! I have been walking for four days."

She told me of her village that I perceived to be some seventy five miles to the north.

My heart empathized with her. I asked, "Why didn't you go to the hospital on the way? I have heard there is one near you."

"Oh, I couldn't do that! Nearly everyone who goes there dies. They don't have good medicine."

"How did you know about me?"

"I kept asking along the way to find someone who could give me help. Several told me about your good medicine and your kindness. I knew this is where I must come."

"Your burns are very bad and you will need to stay nearby so I can give you care and medicine every day." I knew that she would have to get her antibiotics by injection and that I would need to clean and remove dead skin particles from the wounds, putting on fresh dressings regularly.

After getting her some relief, I began to gently remove the dead skin. It was a painful process, so I tried to engage her in conversation to keep her mind off the process. On seeing the 'hirizi' (fetishes) around her neck I perceived that she was a pagan. I asked her, "Do you know Jesus?"

She answered by shaking her head "no." She answered, "I do not know anyone by the name of Jesus!"

I could hardly believe it for this was the first person who actually told me they had never even heard of the name of Jesus Christ.

"May I tell you about this wonderful person?"

She nodded her "yes" answer because she was still in much pain.

I immediately began sharing with her about the One who loved her and all the people of the world. I shared how he gave His life as a sacrifice for her sins. She listened intently and began to ask questions. Time passed quickly. I bandaged her arms, gave her medicines and sent her to find a place to stay. "You must come back every day for a while," I reminded her as she left.

I enjoyed thinking of new things to tell Mulagi about the wonderful stories and life of Jesus, during our cleaning and treatment sessions. She always seemed interested but did not converse much. I knew that her distress from the pain distracted her. After regularly meeting with her for about five weeks, one day, she came for her treatment sessions. I took off the bandages and could see the arms were healing very nicely.

"Mulagi, I believe you can go home now because you do not need any more treatment here. You know how to care for the few bad places remaining, treating them as we have been doing," I advised her. As I began telling her how very pleased I was to see her healing, she stretched out her arms in front of her.

As she intensely examined them she said "I am glad I burned my arms!"

Her statement utterly shocked me. "What did you say?" I questioned, doubting that I had understood her correctly.

"Yes, I am so glad that I burned my arms. If I hadn't burned my arms I would not have heard about Jesus. I want this Jesus to be my Savior and Lord."

I flushed with joy from her response and gave her a big hug. After talking with her and helping her to understand what she was doing, she confessed that she trusted the Lord as her very own Redeemer. Before leaving, she asked us to come to her village and tell her friends and family what we had told her. We set a date with her.

Two weeks later we drove more than seventy five miles and, leaving the main road, traveled yet quite a long way into the bush to find her village. All the way we were thinking of her walking so far.

Upon arrival, we found the whole village eagerly waiting for us. Mulagi had told everyone of her wonderful care, healing for her burned arms and in finding the Lord Jesus. This day became a great day of rejoicing when we shared the basic truths of the Christian message. Many villagers joined Mulagi in committing themselves to Christ before the end of the day. We felt like Paul going over to Macedonia to preach the gospel to a people eager to hear the good news.

After many trips, with preaching and teaching in this village, we saw a new church born. God had brought this dear person to us in order that her whole village could hear the good news of our Savior. Through one person hundreds became believers. The Lord does work in mysterious ways His wonders to perform!

"Everyone who calls on the name of the Lord will be saved." Ro 10:13a

C: In Somebody Else's Hut

A young man, in his early twenties, came to our door. He said that his name was Juma (JEW-mah) and he wanted to talk.

I brought him into the office where he related his story: He had come to Kigoma from Salagala (Sah-lah-GAH-lah), a village many miles down the lake, three days before, to purchase things he and others in his village needed. Salagala was two days' journey south of Kigoma by Lake Steamer. He planned to board it in the evening and return to Salagala.

He said that his first night in Kigoma he stayed with friends who were members of our church. They told him about Jesus and encouraged him to visit us. Juma wanted to be a Christian. We shared from the Bible and prayed. He made a profession of faith and immediately began asking if we could come to Salagala and share with those in his village. We set a time for my journey and he went off to catch the lake steamer.

Three weeks later, I put things together which I would need for my journey. I would be away from home for five days. It would take that many days to get to Salagala, spend time I needed there, and catch the steamer on its way back to Kigoma. I also took Bibles, gospel tracts and other literature which we had prepared to be used in our Sunday schools.

Myrtice and the girls took me to the docks where I boarded the Liemba (Lee-AIM-bah), one of Lake Tanganyika's steamers; an old, old steamer that had been on the lake for many years. During World War I the Germans scuttled her. Later the Belgians brought her up and refurbished her. It was again the best and main steamer on the lake. It carried tons of freight as well as passengers. On this eventful day, many passengers had crowded onto the steamer. I reserved one of its small cabins for the night. I brought my own food.

On the afternoon of the second day the steamer anchored, quite a way off shore, at Salagala. Many paddled their canoes to the ship's side. The workers on the ship lowered the gangplank and passengers, with their loads, disembarked. In the distance, I saw my friend, Juma, and some others, in canoes, making their way to the ship's side. They came aboard and assisted me by taking and placing my loads into one of the canoes. I got into Juma's canoe and he paddled us to shore.

When we arrived on shore, there were many to greet me. Juma had told just about everyone that I would be coming. They were cautiously observing me since few whites had ever visited Salagala. There were fond greetings and we went, single file, into the village. I saw many banana trees, patches of cassava and many date palms, laden with large clusters of near ripe, yellow dates.

We approached a rather small hut and Juma told me that this would be my hut for the duration of my stay. I did not know who, but someone had given up his hut for my visit. Juma and friends had completely re-plastered the walls and floor with fresh cow dung; the common plaster for African huts in the area. They placed my loads near the door and told me that they would leave me to become settled in and would return shortly.

As I inspected my place of dwelling for the next two days, I took note that the cow dung was indeed fresh; still not completely dry. I took out some of my loads that I had wrapped in a small tarp. I spread that on the floor, put my loads on it, and set up my cot. I waited a while until Juma and the others returned.

During the next two days we had meeting after meeting. Many were pleased to accept Christ. We made tentative plans for a church.

There was one very old man who was openly delighted that I had come. He told me that he had never heard about Jesus but knew, in his heart, that there must be someone like him. He knew that there was a god but had little idea what he was like. He, without hesitation, said that he wanted Jesus as his Savior.

This man did not know when he was born. He said, "Our parents never told us things like that." He well remembered when the Germans were rulers there. He said that he was a grown man with a family when the British came. I figured that he was born quite some time before the turn of the century.

Because of the distance from Kigoma and not readily knowing when I could return, I felt it expedient that I baptize those who had accepted Christ. They agreed that Juma would be their leader. When the Liemba returned, I boarded and made my way back to Kigoma rejoicing in how God had opened yet another village for the gospel.

"Do not forget to entertain strangers." Heb 12:13a

M: John Glenn, the Astronaut

Being in such a remote area, over one thousand miles from the capitol city, we didn't ever dream of all the famous people who would come to our home. We had no television or newspapers; only a short wave radio to which we would listen once a day to keep up with important world news. We had heard of the famous flight into space by John Glenn, the first successful astronaut, never dreaming he would show up in Kigoma.

About noon one day, a Land Rover drove into our driveway and four men, in safari gear, got out. Our big, black Labrador - barking - jumped from his resting place high up in the mango tree in the front yard, letting us know someone had arrived. When they knocked on the door we had no idea who they were.

As they introduced themselves we were amazed that this was John Glenn, with his son David, and two men from Wolpen Productions. They were filming a documentary for TV. They told us that the purpose of their coming to Tanzania was to make a film with John Glenn enacting the journey of Henry Stanley across the country to Kigoma to meet Dr. David Livingstone in Ujiji. They were told of our being in Kigoma by the American ambassador, who had visited us previously. Since Glenn was such an adventurer, this seemed to fit for his making this film.

Warm, cordial and flowing conversation described our meeting. After finding they had been on safari, sleeping in tents and eating mostly canned goods for several weeks, we invited them to have supper with us. We knew they were starved for some regular food.

"But we have more than twenty men with us. That would be too many for whom you would have to cook," Glenn said.

"No, not at all, we'll make plans right now to give you some good American food."

"They may not all be able to come, for some have their equipment to clean from all the dust on the trip. Maybe around fifteen or less could make it."

"We welcome all that can come." We encouraged them, knowing how difficult it was to travel in this country. I had to start immediately to prepare a big meal for them. Carlos helped since he didn't have any meeting that day nor did I.

Fortunately, we had frozen many chickens that we had raised from day old chicks. Quickly, plans fell into place to have lemon-grilled chicken, potato salad, green beans, which we had grown, fresh salad, fresh rolls, cake and brownies. We grilled twelve whole fryers, cut in half to be sure we had enough. Things started really buzzing in the kitchen.

The evening was perfect with clear skies and a gorgeous sunset. Twelve men joined us for dinner on our large, front porch, overlooking the lake and viewing the Congo Mountains.

Conversation just stopped when the men started eating. They looked like hungry animals relishing their food. When they did talk, we were delighted by the hilarious stories of their journey. When the evening was over, there was no chicken or anything else except one large pan of brownies.

"Can we take these back to camp for breakfast?"

'Surely, and be sure to share some with the men who couldn't come," I admonished.

The next day, John Glenn came by to return the large, brownie pan and to thank us again for having them. His son David said, "You have restored my faith in food!"

John Glenn never spoke of his space journey without our asking, for he constantly asked about our mission work and the responses that we were having. He showed that he was truly interested in missions and supported it through his own church. This was a real turnaround to us as most visitors seemed to like to talk about themselves.

He left a memento; an artifact of the world with the space craft swirling around it, which was a marvelous reminder of his visit. He was such a humble, kind and thoughtful person. One would have never known that he was famous by just talking to him and that he loved missions. We treasured this time with him and felt his encouragement in our endeavors.

*"The mouth of the righteous man utters wisdom,
and his tongue speaks what is just. The law of his God
is in his heart; His feet do not slip." Ps 37:30-31*

C: Working for Salt

Danieli Bihali had taken us to Munyegela (Moon-yea-GAY-lah). As he had told them that we were coming, a large crowd welcomed us. We met in an open field where the people sat on the ground or on rocks, which they had collected for that purpose. There were no trees, only African huts across the landscape as far as the eye could see and lots of rocks of all sizes scattered everywhere.

Everyone present wanted us to help them have a church. Many made professions of faith that first day. We went away extremely happy and praising the Lord for his having brought us there.

On our second trip to Munyegela, more people accepted Christ and everyone was anxious about having a church. We spent quite a long time examining and teaching those who had made decisions and promised to baptize them when we returned. Zabroni (Zah-BROE-nee) Mpona (Mm-POE-nah) had taken the lead and was meeting with the church group from time to time. It was evident that God was using him to become their leader. We asked if they would not begin collecting stones for building a church building. They agreed.

We returned about six weeks later for the baptizing. On the way, we met several people on the side of the road who, upon seeing us, ran away in fright. We could not understand why, as the people in the area had been very friendly to us. When we arrived and told Zabroni about this, he told us that there were people in the area who did not like missionaries or white people and were spreading the rumor that we would kill people and drink their blood. We were not surprised, as we had heard this rumor about us in other places.

We baptized eighty-one people that day in a hole of water that, before we finished, had turned to a real mud hole. One little fellow stood on the bank ready to be baptized. I pushed him aside as he was so small and looked too young to understand. He kept coming back and I kept sending him away until Zabroni came close and told me that he was older than some of the others I had baptized. He said, "He is just little."

When I took a good look at Zabroni, I understood, for he was only about four feet and six inches tall. Most of those baptized were very small like most of the Ha people. I then motioned for the little one to come on in and I baptized him. Before we left, the people promised to be collecting stones and grass for a church building. They would let us know when they were ready.

Knowing that the people had little money, we decided to provide sand and cement and metal for the roof. We felt that we should pay some of those who would work full time on the church. The next time I saw Danieli, I asked him how much to pay a worker for a day's work.

"They don't really have much need for money. There is no salt in the area. Let us give each man a can of salt for a day's work. They will be happy with that."

What he said was hard for us to comprehend -- a can of salt (about two cups) for a full day's work. How could a man work a full day for two cups of salt? When we told them what we would do, they were very excited.

The members chose Zabroni as their pastor. He would continue to lead them well. They were very poor but were rich in what they had; a church, a good pastor and a wonderful fellowship.

When we were nearing time to go on furlough, we put together all the clothes we could which we would not take with us to the States. We took them to Munyegela, gave them to Zabroni and asked him to divide them among his church members as he saw fit. He was pleased to do that.

When we returned on our last visit before going on furlough, we recognized most of the clothes we had brought. Various members of the church were wearing them. Zabroni was likely the best dressed; wearing my pajamas, a leather thong for a belt and one of my neckties.

"Is tasteless food eaten without salt?" Job 6:6a

M: My Son is Dead

At three one morning, loud sounds came from outside. We couldn't figure out who was calling us, but we both quickly got up and went to our door, turning on the outside light. Yusufu, our beloved pastor of Gungu, with a church member, were standing there with long faces.

"My son is dead," cried Yusufu, sobbing so hard we could hardly understand him. He had a beautiful son only one year old, born after his two daughters.

"He was fine yesterday. Today, Mariamu noticed he had a fever and chills. We were going to bring him to your clinic today, but he had a seizure and was gone."

We both put our arms around Yusufu and cried with him. We knew how he loved his little Amoni (Ah-MOW-nee) and how proud he was of him. This was a huge tragedy for our young pastor, a Muslim convert.

Most likely the child had succumbed to deadly cerebral malaria. Malaria was one of the biggest killers among all the diseases of Africa. We too, and our children, had had malaria several times, but we always could discern its early symptoms and treat it immediately.

Carlos and I took Yusufu and his companion back to the village, after we had called our helper to stay nearby our sleeping children.

Many people had gathered around Yusufu's home, a mud building with thatched roof. Since he had been a strong political leader in the community before his conversion, many people knew him and had gathered around.

Mariamu, his wife, was in deep grief. We sat with her, comforting and consoling her with our presence and silence. She had also left the Muslim faith to become a Christian. We knew she was young in faith but she also knew that her little son was now with God. Though such a personal tragedy had taken place in their lives, they both remained faithful to the Lord, showing an even deeper faith and a strong witness to those around them.

Our hearts have been torn so many times with the useless deaths that seem to hit so many African children. During our years of service there nearly half of the children died before they were five years old. One of our hardest tasks was to bury a child that we knew so well and felt to be a part of our family.

One day Joha (JOE-ha) came to the clinic. Her baby was over nine months old and laden with fetishes from the witchdoctor. He didn't weigh five pounds, looking gaunt and frail. "What has happened to your child?" I asked.

"I don't know. He just keeps getting thinner and cries all the time."

"What are you feeding your baby?"

"I give him uji (OO-gee)—(thin corn meal porridge) every day."

"Don't you nurse him?"

"No, because I am pregnant and the medicine man told me I must not feed this child my milk."

I found powdered milk for the child and told her to please come back as soon as the milk was out. I suggested she go to the local hospital if the baby worsened.

She shook her head, "That hospital is just a place to die," she stated emphatically.

In two weeks she returned without the baby. I realized that the child must be dead. Her eyes filled with tears, she confirmed this. I talked to her a long time sharing with her that she needed the Lord in her life to help her through these difficult times. I emphasized that she should search out help from the hospital or clinic when a child or she is sick and not depend on the witchdoctor, who brings more harm than good.

The suggestion fell on deaf ears. I also knew the hospital was often without necessary medicines. This very week, they had been out of medicine. Yes, I knew this was a problem, since even the medical officer of the hospital had sent his wife and children to see me that week. When the main doctor in town sends his family to me for care, there is no doubt that supplies are exhausted. A poor, third-world country was simply unable to afford the needed care for its own people. This is one major reason that mission medical care has an open door with a strong witness in its outreach; caring for the hurting and sharing the love of Christ to people who may never be reached otherwise.

> *"Whatever you did for one of the least of these brothers of mine, you did for me." Mt 25:40b*

C: Call from America

In the early 1960's there were no satellites. Phone calls from the US to Europe were by the Trans Atlantic cable. Calls from Europe to Africa were by radio signal. Calls from

Africa to the US would use radio and the Trans Atlantic Cable, so were somewhat complicated.

We had a letter from a church in my home county. They wanted to call us. Two men in the church who worked for the phone company had agreed to set up a phone on the pulpit. The entire church would hear. They would make the call during prayer meeting on Wednesday evening.

Church members spread the word so many came from throughout the county. The church was full.

Seven in the evening back at home would be 5:00 o'clock a.m. in Kigoma, so we set our alarm to be sure to be awake and ready.

The phone rang on time at 5:00 a.m. I answered the phone but the pastor did not hear me. I could hear him well. Something was wrong with our phone.

The operator had called earlier explaining that our message to England was by radio and it would be necessary to keep speaking. If we stopped, she said, the signal would not be strong enough. I continued speaking, even though I knew the pastor was not hearing me.

"How are you?"

"We are all right."

The more he asked the louder I replied.

We were disappointed that we did not get to speak as we had planned.

Later that morning, I called the local telephone operator and explained what we had done. In a few minutes, a technician came and found that the battery in our phone was weak and needed to be replaced. How we wished that we had known! We would have asked the phone company to install a new one.

A little later that morning, a woman who lived across the street and down a little ways, came to inquire as to what was going on at our house so early in the morning.

"I woke my husband and told him to go over and see what was wrong. Maybe you needed some help.

"He was putting on his clothes and suddenly took them off and came back to bed.

"They keep hollering, 'we are all right.' Guess they must be."

"My soul yearns for you in the night; In the morning my spirit longs for you." Isa 26:9a, b

M: Broken Arm

Screams came from the front yard. I quickly looked out to see the children running around, except Debra, four years old, lying on the grass. The cry was surely one of pain. I went out to check on what was happening. As Debra tried to sit up I could see she was holding her arm and crying in agony. As I checked her I knew it was broken.

Having had many sad occasions with patients who had gone to the hospital, I was a bit hesitant to consider going to it for help. But I reasoned, surely they could X ray and put on a cast. After only a short wait, an Indian doctor saw her; X rayed the arm and showed me the break. Being a simple, 'green' fracture, which is a crack; he proceeded to put on the plaster to secure it. I was mostly concerned with comforting and assuring our little four-year old and was not paying too much attention to the procedure.

"Mom, look at my fingers," Debra said as she came into our bedroom early the next morning. Those little fingers were swollen and black and blue. The cast was so tight that all circulation was cut off. Checking, I realized that the gauze sleeve had been left off and the plaster was tight on her skin, not allowing any room for adequate circulation.

Only cutting off the cast and applying a new one was necessary but I surely didn't want to have another mishap with the local hospital. Since Carlos was away, I made the decision to go to the nearest mission hospital which was ninety miles to the northeast. We appreciated the work of the Catholics who maintained this ministry and we knew their doctors were well trained.

After two hours of struggling to cut off the cast and pull it off her hairy, little arm, we finally were able to relieve it. The process was painful for Dr. Mary and me. It was more so for Debra. During the doctor's lunch break we gave the arm time to rest and Debra's tears to dry. A fresh, new cast with a gauze soft sleeve added first, gave me assurance that we were now in good shape.

In two weeks the cast began to soften and crumble.

Without doubt, the plaster had been old and was not holding. Luckily, we had a planned road trip to Tukuyu, in the south, for assisting another missionary couple near our own mission hospital. In a quick stop there, the doctor decided it would be too traumatic for Debra to endure another cast. He decided to add more layers of plaster.

Now we had a child with a cast that looked as big as she! She found she could use it to her advantage for knocking around her sisters and anyone else who bothered her. Thankfully, this was the only the second broken bone during our service in Africa. God took extra good care of us.

"For surely, O lord, you bless the righteous; you surround them with your favor as with a shield." Ps 5:12

M: Death on the Mountain

Along the lake, the mountain range rises up enclosing the small villages between them and the lake edge. Most of these are fishing villages but they have small garden patches for raising food. In the Kalalangabo village, we established our first lake village church with the use of our boat, Wajumbe. The church grew rapidly, responding enthusiastically and reaching the majority in the village.

Everybody profited by church services. The men received specific training by coming into town on their fishing boats for scheduled teaching. I felt the need of the women to grow in the Lord.

At one of our Sunday services, I planned, with the women, for a special day to meet with them for Bible Study and women's work, as a special ministry in the village.

When that day came, our boat was out of commission. One of the motors had failed and we had sent it for repair. Since I did not want to disappoint the women, I asked if it were possible to cross the mountain on foot. Nanki, one of the ladies in the town who had previously lived there, agreed to go with me showing me the way. Loving hiking, I felt this would be a good day to work as well as getting my exercise.

After parking the Land Rover in the nearest position to the lower side of the mountain right outside of Kigoma, we saw the best route was to wade through the lake's edge to the area where the hill began to climb upwards. It was a beautiful and sunny, hot day, as usual. My friend and I enjoyed the hike and had some great time of sharing.

We climbed higher and higher, finally reaching a plateau. Because I began to be short of breath we stopped for a quick break, and then trudged on. I hadn't had time to think about exercise and was out of shape and also not used to the higher altitude. After going for about an hour and half we could see the edge of the village tucked down below, our being considerably above them. When we saw it, the ladies there also saw us. Cheering and singing, the women headed our way and joyfully escorted us into the village. We just felt so honored by them.

Around forty-five women sat in our meeting and all seemed eager to learn. After a long time of teaching from God's Word and sharing ideas for them to serve, I passed out cookies that I had baked. Rarely did they ever eat anything sweet. They tasted them slowly and were delighted with the special treats. I had also tucked some chewable vitamins for the small children into my bag as well as some eye ointment, knowing I most likely would see some need there.

After class was finished, I gave the vitamins to those with children present and cared for the few that I saw had eye infections. When they saw I had some medicines, someone sent word to one of the ladies who had just had a baby.

This young woman, perhaps fourteen years old, came to me holding her tiny infant all wrapped in cloths. She simply handed the child to me without a word. As I unwrapped the cloths, I could see the baby was extra small and distressed. His color was ashy and breathing labored. I knew he needed to be in a hospital with oxygen and medicines for newborns.

We had no way to hurry since all the boats were out from the village. I insisted on leaving immediately so we could try to get the baby to the hospital. Half of the women crowded around assisting the mother, we prayed and then we began our walk back. We were trying to hurry to walk these five miles but since we had to climb higher it was slow going. I was leading the way trying to walk as fast as I could and praying that we could make it in time for the child's sake.

After going for about forty-five minutes I heard a loud scream. Looking back, I could see the ladies gathering around the mother. We, who were up ahead, ran back to be with them knowing the child must have expired.

Yes, the child was gone. If only we could have known sooner and been able to help the child. All the women began to sob and groan. After having a prayer with the group, I knew I must go on since it was getting so late in the day it would be dark before we got through the pass.

The crowd stayed behind and just Nanki and I proceeded. On the trek back, all I could think about was the sadness and uselessness of the death of this infant. My heart ached for the mother and family. I began crying, feeling there is just so little I can do when so many children are dying. I felt helpless but also determined to do all that I could to care for the sick and teach the mothers health care. I prayed, "O Lord help these dear people."

*"On the mountain he will destroy the shroud
that enfolds all peoples, the sheet that covers all nations;
he will swallow up death forever. The Sovereign Lord
will wipe away the tears from all faces;" Isa 25:7-8a*

C: Bananas for Shoes

Zabroni walked through our gate looking rather bedraggled. We invited him in and showed him where he would sleep for the night. We also showed him to the shower we had in the school and clinic rooms out back and gave him soap and a towel.

From time to time, our mission planned training for church workers. Each year we met in a different place— sometimes in Kenya and sometimes in Tanzania. On this particular year, the meeting was to be at Tigoni in Kenya. That would be a three-day trip from Kigoma. Even though it was far we wanted our church leaders to attend. We made our plans.

Five pastors planned to go. Each one would pay ten shillings; about $1.40 in US money. We felt that for them to appreciate going they needed to pay something. The mission would bear the rest of the cost. Most of them lived closer to Kigoma than Zabroni, who lived more that eighty miles to the north. The others had given me their money. Zabroni handed his ten shillings to me when he arrived.

I had sent Zabroni money for a bus trip to Kigoma. When he arrived at our house, he appeared not to have come by bus and he had not! He had no money of his own so he saved his bus money in order to pay the 10 Shillings for the trip. He had walked those eighty miles, stopping on the way and sleeping with strangers who, as was their custom, took him in.

I quickly noticed that he was barefooted. It would be cold in Limuru but I knew that others would likely come barefooted, so I made no effort to provide shoes for him. We washed his clothes and gave him supper. Some of the others also arrived that evening but stayed with a pastor who lived near by.

The next morning I gave each pastor his food money. We got into the Land Rover, said bye to Myrtice and left.

At noon we stopped at a road-side market. The other men and I bought plates of rice with sauce. Zabroni bought only two small bananas. Late in the afternoon when we stopped for food, Zabroni again bought two small bananas.

Farther on we stopped at a government guest house to spend the night. When we got up we had sweet African tea with bread and continued our journey. That day we stopped two times for food and Zabroni again had his two small bananas.

We spent the second night in Arusha at our seminary and on the third day drove on to Tigoni in Kenya stopping only once for food. Zabroni again ate only bananas.

We arrived late in the afternoon and checked in. Zabroni disappeared. When he returned, he was wearing cheap, canvas shoes. Then I knew why he had only eaten bananas on the way. He used his food money to buy the shoes. To him, pastor training and having shoes to wear were worth eating only bananas those three days.

"Here am I, send me." Isa 8:8c

C: From Calm to Fury

I had been to Kagunga (Kah-GOON-gah) twice and was excited that Myrtice and the girls would be making this trip with me. As I backed the Land Rover down the grade, I could see the boat on the trailer in the rear view mirror. On the side of the boat was the name, Wajumbe (Wah-JOOM-bay) meaning Ambassadors or Messengers. We had given the boat this name because the Royal Ambassadors, a church organization for boys in Tennessee, had collected money and had bought her for us in order to reach the villages along the lake.

As the boat and trailer glided into the water, I had a sense of satisfaction. There was no breeze and the lake was glassy calm. The sun was just coming up over the hill back to the east. Surely, this was to be a delightful day for our family.

The boat was floating above the trailer. I tied her to a nearby stake and pulled the trailer from the water and onto the shore at the side. Myrtice and the girls had joined me and were standing close by. Myrtice assisted as we took our loads from the back of the Land Rover and placed them in the boat. I locked the Land Rover.

As I steadied the boat, Myrtice and the girls climbed in. The girls took their places on the middle seat and Myrtice sat on the front seat next to where I would be operating the boat. We had brought life jackets in case of bad weather. I pushed the boat away from the shore and climbed in. After pausing for prayer, I pulled the cords on the engines. Both started with the first pull.

As I maneuvered the boat onto the lake, I glanced back to see our house right there next to the lakeshore. God had provided a wonderful place for us to live.

Headed north on the lake, the harbor was to our right. Three ships were at the docks. We could see the men manually carrying loads onto two ships and others offloading the third ship. The heavy burden of the loads caused for bended backs for the men.

To our back was Elephants Foot, the large mesa at the top of a steep cliff where sometimes we would go for picnics. John Glenn and his crew had camped there on their visit to the area.

Its being a clear day, we could barely see the mountains of the Congo, forty-five miles away on the other side of the lake. Fish eagles soared above, occasionally swooping down and taking a fish from the lake.

Two miles from Kigoma, we came to Kalalangabo, the first village where we had a church. Hearing the sound of our boat, many children had gathered at the lakeside. They waved and shouted with jubilation, "Wajumbe, Wajumbe!"

The girls were excited each time we saw another fish eagle soaring above or perched in the top of a large tree. There was an occasional small animal in a cove or drinking from the lakeshore. From time to time we would see monitor lizards basking atop large rocks at lakeside.

We passed Gombe Stream but did not expect to see Jane Goodall. She would have left her camp at daybreak to return to where she had left the chimps the evening before -- where they had bedded down in the trees. Otherwise, she would likely not find them for three or four days. We did see her servant and waved to him as we passed.

Not far past Gombe Stream there was a sudden change in the weather. Clouds formed overhead and the wind began to blow. We could no longer see the mountains on the other side of the lake. At first, there were small waves and then some whitecaps. The boat moved about erratically in the rough waters. Having maneuvered the boat farther away from the shore, I felt comfortable but knew that I must soon go ashore.

The waves were choppy and began breaking over into the boat. I took the boat farther out where the swells were high but less water came over and onto us. The lake had become so rough that I feared for the safety of the boat and of my family.

In the distance, I could see the crowd gathered on the shore at Kagunga. They were anxiously awaiting our arrival. I could also see the waves lapping onto the shore and wondered what would happen to the boat and to us when we landed. The crowd standing on the shore was watching us but I could not think of anything they could do to help.

We prayed silently. Myrtice and the girls had put on their life jackets and held on.

We left the swells and moved into the high, choppy waves. The boat began to move about erratically. I felt that I had little control of her. I envisioned the waves slamming us onto the shore. I wondered if hitting the shore would damage the boat and how much injury we would receive.

The boat was about twenty feet from the shore when a crowd of men lunged into the water—a dozen or so for each side. The men took hold of the boat and manually carried it and us ashore and beyond the waves.

Everyone on the shore clapped their hands and shouted with glee. We sat amazed. It seemed as if God had reached down to us when we were in distress, taken us in his hands and brought us to safety. God had used those men to do just that.

The services were tremendous and the lake was calm for our return to Kigoma late in the afternoon.

"Take courage, It is I. Don't be afraid." Mt 14:27b

C: Shoot-out on Lake

Loud sounds of shooting woke us. It was just past midnight and the shooting was very close. When we got up and looked out the window towards the lake, we could see the flashes and hear the sounds. They were very near but we did not know what was going on.

After quite a long time and not knowing anything else to do we went back to bed and lay quietly. The safest place seemed to be the bed. It was a fearful time. Finally the sounds subsided and we went back to sleep.

Early the next morning we saw people coming from towards town and going into their houses. We talked with some of them and found that the entire street, except us, had been evacuated. They had spent the night at the railway station.

After breakfast, I drove into town to the police station. The regional police commander was our friend. I felt that he would tell us what happened and why he had required the others to leave their homes but not us.

He greeted me fondly. He shook my hand and smiled.

"Tell me about last night."

"Well, a ship sank near your house. Congo freedom fighters were coming from the Congo and others were going from here to the Congo. Neither knew whether the other was friendly or the enemy so they began shooting at each other. One ship sank the other."

"Wow, I understand that you had the people on our street move to the railway station."

"Yes!"

"And why were we not asked to go?"

"You are Americans. We do not care if you are killed."

I stood stunned for a moment, noting the hard look on his face.

Then, with a big smile he said, "Pastor, I told my men to go to you first. I wanted to be sure that you were safe."

"Well, what happened?"

"When my men got to your house, your black dog jumped from the mango tree and came to the gate. They would not open the gate and go in. They called but you did not come so I guess you did not hear them."

We shook hands. I thanked him and, with a smile said, "I guess that we were the only ones on our street who got any sleep last night."

"I am just glad that the fighting did not come ashore. Your house is right there and they would have got yours first."

How marvelous is the protection of the Lord even when we are uninformed.

"Hide me in the shadow of your wings." Ps 17:8b

C: Back from the Dead

The civil war continued in Burundi. They burned houses and churches with people inside. There was massive slaughter in the marketplaces and reports that so many bodies were in the rivers that the crocodiles could not eat them all. Since many of our Christians on our side of the border had relatives in Burundi, we had much concern. Kagunga, where we had a church, was only five miles from the border.

Members from Kagunga came to Kigoma on a Monday to tell us that their pastor, Yakobo, had gone across the border to visit relatives and to preach at their church on Sunday, the day before. They had received word that rebels surrounded the packed church and set it afire. If people tried to escape through the doors or windows, the rebels shot them. The report was that everyone in the church had died. Knowing that Yakobo was to have preached, they assumed that he had also died along with the rest. They said that the entire Kagunga village was in grief.

I went to Kagunga in our boat the following day to comfort Yakobo's family as best I could and grieved with the Kagunga village and our church. There were more reports of extensive fighting all across Burundi. I left in time to get back to Kigoma before dark.

Some days later, a messenger came from Kagunga. I could immediately see that he was excited and had good news. He told us that Yakobo, alone, had escaped from the church on Sunday and had gone into the mountains where he hid from the rebels. With neither food nor water for five days, he made his way through the mountains and across the border back into Tanzania. When no one expected it, he walked out of the mountains and into the Kagunga village.

The messenger said, "The entire village was shouting with joy and saying that Yakobo had come back from the dead. The church was full that afternoon to hear him tell of his ordeal."

He continued, "Many came forward to say that they wanted to follow the Jesus who had brought Yakobo back from the dead. We now have many for you to baptize the next time you come."

"From the Lord comes deliverance." Ps 3:8a

M: Boarding School Tears

Our children missed being with other children their age who could speak English and play the games of make-believe. They loved the times of romping with the African children and playing their games. One day the girls came in singing and dancing.

"Hey, stop for a minute. I want to hear your song." I said to them as they ran by. They all three paused and started their song and swaying.

"Matumbo, matumbo; yameona mapela," meaning "Stomachs, stomachs have rash and itching." Then the song ended with "scratch, scratch, and scratch!"

We realized more and more the children sing songs of their lives and experiences. They failed to dream of the fairy tale world in which our children seemed to enjoy playing. Our girls all loved reading and spent more time in books than anything else.

The time came when we realized that our oldest, Janice, was pulling away from everything else happening, in order to read. She loved being in her own little world. When company came, she often would retreat to her room to read. I had continued home schooling her but now realized that she needed companions and friends her age to share with and enjoy. We feared she would become a real recluse.

We began praying for wisdom on what we should do. Several of the other expatriates who lived in the community sent their children to boarding school when they were in their first grade. They all seemed adjusted and well balanced when they returned home for holidays.

After a time we felt that the boarding school where many of our mission children attended at Rift Valley in Kenya would provide a good Christian education and give her the needed contact with other children for sports and social relationship. So, our first born was taken to the academy the beginning of her fifth grade.

Though she seemed brave, inwardly, we knew she felt as scared and sad as we did. We helped to settle her in her room, putting her clothes in the cabinets and making her bed. The dorm parent was understanding and promised to tuck her in each night. As we walked out my tears started flowing and I could hardly stand to leave her behind. But we really felt this was the right thing to do in our isolated situation.

We did all we could to keep up with Janice. Telephoning was out of the question since they were not allowed to use the limited phone lines. We wrote her every week, sending cookies or other homemade goodies to cheer her on. We knew she had some difficult days of crying herself to sleep and learning to relate to others in the school. We felt deeply with her but always tried to encourage her to be strong and make the best of it.

At the end of the first semester we went to pick her up. They have semesters of three months each and spend one month at home in December, April, and August. She was so excited to finally be getting a chance to be with family again. The girls could hardly get enough of each other since they had missed their close relationship. We had a big celebration in the nearby city by eating at one of the nicest Chinese restaurants. We couldn't hear enough about her friends and school life.

On her return trip we were able to secure the Missionary Air Fellowship plane to take her back to school. We lived over a thousand miles from the school which would take three days of travel over very rough roads. She was excited, a bit scared but proud that she could actually go on the plane back to school. After leaving the airfield the weather worsened and the plane had to land on the compound of one of the other mission groups. We had never dreamed that she wouldn't be back in the dorm that night.

She was taken into a strange missionary's home to sleep. Though frightened and fearful and being alone, she braved the situation. The next day she was actually glad to arrive at school in a place where she knew the staff and students.

Missionary children have to face so many uncertain situations that they learn early to be flexible and adjust to whatever may come. Because of so many insecure events in their lives many of these children have a difficult time adjusting to adult life while their parents still serve overseas. Our daughters grew to be lovely young ladies of whom we are immensely proud. All are certain of the commitment of their parents to the calling and service that the Lord has led them to fulfill.

*"Obey everything I have commanded you.
And surely I am with you always." Mt 28:19c*

M: Lame Veronica

One Sunday morning at our Gungu church I noticed we had a visitor who was lame, using a crooked stick to help her walk. The left leg was small and very deformed, bending at the knee. I greeted her and invited her to the women's classes during the week. She seemed very shy and hesitant to speak. I sat with her asking about her home and family. She told me she had no children but she was married. She was very small and had a shy smile.

A few weeks later she made a confession of faith and was shortly thereafter baptized. She changed her given name to Veronika, a name heard in some Christian groups. Changing their names to a Christian name was a desire to show that their old selves were changed and they were new people in the Lord. She became a very happy person and most faithful to all of the services and classes.

After a few months passed, no one was seeing Veronika. I asked all our ladies about her. No one knew where she lived or anything about her. I was deeply concerned since she had been so faithful. Several of the ladies in the class agreed to join me in trying to find her home.

We followed the direction from which she came, asking all along if anyone knew where she lived. Each place we asked kept pointing ahead in the direction from which she came. Endless times we stopped and we realized we were going miles searching. At long last, a full nine miles from the church, we finally found her home.

We called outside her house in the customary greeting of 'hodi, hodi, hodi' and heard a faint answer. As we went inside the mud hut with a dirt floor we found Veronika curled up in the corner on a grass mat. She was desperately sick. We all gathered around and prayed for her. I asked if we could find her husband nearby to get permission to take her to the town hospital.

"He will not let you take me for help. He is a pagan and will only use witchcraft for healing," she said in a faint voice. "He is out with the men nearly all day every day."

I knew she could easily die if she didn't get some help. She was already severely dehydrated. As we ladies counseled together and with Veronika, we made a bold decision to take her on to the hospital for life's sake. One of the ladies went to the next hut to tell neighbors what we were doing so they could tell the husband whenever he came home. We knew he might be very angry with us but it was important to help her.

We bundled her up in the dirty cloth she had for covering and picked her up, placing her on the back seat of the Land Rover. We hoped we could get away before he returned.

For six weeks Veronika was kept in the hospital. We went often to see her. She gradually improved enough to return home. Knowing I would have to confront an angry husband, I prayed fervently for the Lord's strength and wisdom in handling the matter.

When we drove up, we saw the husband outside. He came over to us seeing Veronika looking well and stronger. He gave a big smile and grunted, "Mzuri (mm-ZOO-ree), mzuri" (good, good). He helped get her out and seemed pleased to have his wife back. I explained quickly how serious was her condition when we found her. He said nothing but seemed anxious for her to get out of the car.

We helped her inside, since she was still quite weak. Her husband stayed outside. We asked him to come in for prayer with us but he refused. We three ladies gave thanks for God's healing and help for her.

We kept checking on Veronika but it wasn't long before she was back at church with us again. She hobbled those nine miles into Gungu for all the meetings. We talked many times of the importance of praying for her husband to receive Jesus as she had. A few months later we left the area to go on furlough. I reminded her that we surely would keep her and her husband in our prayers.

Nine years later while we were serving in Moshi, Tanzania, we got a letter from Veronika. This was the first we had even heard from her. As my eyes glanced down to the heart of the letter after all her profuse greetings I saw that she wrote, "After these ten years of praying for my husband, I want you to be the first to know that our prayers were answered. He has now become a Christian and goes with me to church every Sunday. I am so thankful to our Lord for being so faithful to answer prayers. We are so happy now. The walk to church doesn't seem as far as it used to."

I had to stop and express my deep gratitude to God for answering our prayers as tears of thanksgiving flowed down my cheeks. God is so good!

> *"And I will do whatever you ask in my name, so that the Son may bring glory to the Father. You may ask me for anything in my name, and I will do it." Jn 14:13-14*

C: Rebeka's Friend

Rebeka invited her neighbor and friend, Raheli (Rah-HAY-lee) to join us for a Bible study in her and Yeremia's (Yea-ray-ME-ha) house in Mwanga. She only lived two doors down the road from the Rubasha (Roo-BAH-shah) family and showed considerable interest. At the end of the Bible study we invited her to join us at Gungu for church the following Sunday. She said that she would like to go.

On Sunday morning we stopped at Yeremia's house where Raheli was waiting with the Rubasha family. Yeremia, Rebeka, their six children and Raheli all piled into our Land Rover for the four mile drive to Gungu.

Raheli said that she had never been to church and showed delight in being with us. She listened intently to the message and when the invitation was given she came forward saying that she wanted to accept Jesus as her Savior. During the following weeks she was faithful in attendance in the new members' class.

A baptism service was announced to be held at the lake on a Sunday. About twenty new converts, including Raheli, were to be baptized. As previously announced, the church congregated at the lake at a place about three miles from the

Gungu church. Everyone showed up except Raheli and no one seemed to know anything about why she was not there. After the baptizing we walked back to the church for a worship service.

On Monday Myrtice went for Rebeka and they went to see Raheli finding her at her house and excited that they had come to see her. When asked why she had not come for the baptism, Raheli beat around the bush but never gave a logical explanation why she had not come to be baptized. She said that she wanted to go with us on Sunday for church.

Raheli continued to be faithful in attending church and continued in the new members' class but when there was another baptizing she again did not show up. This happened through three baptisms.

Distressed and disturbed over Raheli's not showing up for the baptisms and her not giving us any logical reason, I asked our house servant if he knew any reason for Raheli's not being baptized.

"I guess it is because she is a prostitute."

"Raheli is a prostitute? Why didn't you tell us?"

"We thought you knew. You go by to pick her up for church every week."

During the following weeks we were careful that only Myrtice would go for Raheli. She continued to come to church and we counseled with her the best we could. After a time she dropped out of church and we heard that she had moved back to Tabora, her home town. We never heard from her any more but only prayed that she found a better life and a place in church.

Jesus declared, "Go now and leave your life of sin." Jn 8:7

C: Bride Price Balance

A stranger was standing at the gate. I went out, greeted him, and invited him in. We went together and stood beneath the great mango tree just across the driveway at the end of the house. I could see that he was exceptionally troubled.

"What can I do for you?"

"I need some money and thought maybe you might help me."

"Why did you come to me for money?

"As I walked by this morning I saw you in the garden. You seemed to be a very nice man and I felt that you would help me."

"How much money do you need?"

"I need four hundred shillings."

"And for what do you need four hundred shillings?"

"When I married four years ago I had only 1/3 part of the bride price to pay my wife's father. I promised him that I would pay the balance later but I never got enough money to pay him. I am a poor man and have no work to get money. I just fish and plant some crops so that we get by. I never have anything left over."

"Do you have children?"

"We have four."

"What happens if you do not pay up?"

"The father came to my house yesterday and told me that if I didn't pay he would take my wife and children away. He said that because I had not paid in full they belong to him."

"Do you not have brothers who can help you?"

"I have brothers but they say that they will not help me."

We talked for a time and I encouraged him to urge his brothers to help. I told him that my money was scarce and that if his brothers continued to refuse help that he must come back and I would see what I could do.

He left and did not return. I trust that he found help, either that he found the money or that his father-in-law eased up on him.

"Let no debt remain outstanding. . ." Ro 13:8a

C: Danieli's Uncle

I very seldom went to Kibanga without Danieli's asking that I go with him to visit his uncle. He wanted so much that this uncle accepts Jesus as his Savior. He had never come to church. Although I had come to believe that there was little chance for this man to denounce witchcraft and accept Jesus, I would always go when Danieli asked me to.

We would walk up the hill, among banana trees and African huts and usually find the old man sitting on a low, carved stool in front of his hut.

He wore only a loincloth and had fetishes tied all over his body. They were around both ankles, above the knees, around the waist, around his wrists, above the elbows and around his neck. I had not seen before nor have seen since another with so many fetishes.

He always greeted us fondly and would offer us low stools on which to sit. He would listen attentively to our stories about Jesus. When we would invite him to accept Jesus, he would shake his head and say that he did not need Jesus. Directing our attention to the many fetishes tied to his body, he would say that the witchdoctor was all he needed. We visited him occasionally for more than two years.

One Sunday morning at Kibanga, when I had nearly finished my sermon, I saw the old man standing at the entrance at the back of the church. He slipped in and sat on the dirt floor just inside the door.

I was the only one who had seen him as the others had their backs to him and were paying attention to me as I preached. I extended my sermon just for him.

After a time we began singing the invitation hymn at which time Danieli stood before me and facing the congregation to be ready to accept those who would come. On seeing his uncle at the back of the church, he showed visible excitement.

We sang and a number of people came forward but Danieli's uncle did not move. We continued singing until no others came and still Danieli's uncle did not come.

I had decided that we would sing only one more verse. About half way through that verse I could see Daniel's uncle. He was tearing the fetishes from his body; first from his ankles and then from his legs above the knees. Then he pulled away those from around his waist, wrists and above his elbow and finally from around his neck—each time dropping them on the dirt floor in front of him. We continued singing.

When all the fetishes were off the old man's body he picked them up from the floor and held them in both his hands. He got to his feet with difficulty, as he was quite old. When he was on his feet he came very slowly to the front of the church and handed his fetishes to Danieli saying, "You take these. I do not need them anymore. I am accepting the missionary's Jesus." Then he asked for permission to speak.

We nodded that he may speak.

"Many times have Danieli and this missionary come to my hut. I was always glad to see them but when they asked me to accept Jesus, I always told them that I did not need Jesus and that I only needed the witchdoctor. When they would leave, I would always remember what they said, in my heart. Today, when I heard the singing at the foot of the hill, I knew what I must do. I will not go to the witchdoctor any more. I want Jesus as my Savior."

His coming caused much excitement among the people.

After the service, Danieli sent boys into the hills to collect dry wood. When they returned, some of the men kindled a fire in front of the church. We all watched and prayed as Danieli's uncle dropped his fetishes, one by one, into the fire.

"Be exalted O Lord, in your strength; we will sing
and praise your might." Ps 2 1:13

C: Bibles Replace Spears

Danieli stood before the church, holding three very old and well-used spears. As this was our last visit to the church before going on home leave, I sensed that something special was about to happen.

Speaking to the church while pointing to us, "These missionaries came to us with the message of Jesus. As we were bad people, many did not want to hear the Jesus message but soon we realized that it was what we needed and wanted. We decided to leave our bad ways for the way of Jesus.

"As all of you well know, we used these spears to kill people in other villages so that we could take their cows and goats. When people came to take our cows and goats, we used these spears to kill them or to drive them away.

"Now we go to all those villages, not with spears, but with the message of Jesus. There are churches in all those villages now. The people there are our brothers and sisters. We love them and we help them when we can. We are ashamed of what we did before.

"For some reason we kept our spears, not knowing for what. Today I know why we kept them. We want these missionaries to have them and take them to America. We want them to tell the people there how grateful we are that they sent the missionaries to us."

Danieli turned to us and said, "Our brother and our sister, please take these spears to America. Show them to the people there and tell them that we used them to kill people before, but have no more use for them. Let these spears remind the people in America that we now follow Jesus, because they sent you to us. We no longer travel with a spear but with the Bible."

Handing the spears to me he said, "These are our gifts to you. Please keep them and may they always remind you how we left the bad way and are now following Jesus."

There were many tears as we said farewell to this loving congregation. Danieli and his people will always be very special in our memory.

"We know that we have passed from death to life." IJn 3:14a

Carlos, Myrtice and Janice prior to going to Africa.

Carlos, Myrtice, Ruth, Debra and Janice beside train in Kigoma.

Myrtice leads the homeschooling of Debra, left, and Ruth at their home in Kigoma.

Carlos, Myrtice, Janice, Ruth, and Debra on holiday in Mombassa before Janice leaves for college.

Debra, Myrtice, Janice, and Ruth in Land Rover on train leaving Kigoma when all roads were flooded.

Tanzania's first Sunday School, in Dar es Salaam, with Myrtice playing the organ.

Carlos, in Rungwe District, conducting the first baptisms at Mwankenja.

Carlos baptizing in Mbeya.

African home setting near Mbeya.

Carlos launching Wajumbe, boat given by Tennessee RAs, for work along shores of Lake Tanganyika.

Women, with Myrtice, learning to read and sew in Kigoma.

Myrtice examines a malnourished child in one of her clnics.

Myrtice in medical clinic near Nyumba Ya Mungu, Moshi Region, Tanzania.

Leaving church service, with portable organ, at Mwankenja, Rungwe District.

Carlos greets John Glenn at historical meeting site where Henry Stanley found David Livingstone at Ujiji, on the shores of Lake Tanganyika.

Witchdoctors in Rungwe District, Tanzania

The church being built "without the sounds of hammers" at Kibanga, Kasulu District, Tanzania.

Women bring grass for the walls and roof of the Kibanga church.

Carlos baptizing Maasai at Kirya, Moshi Region, Tanzania.

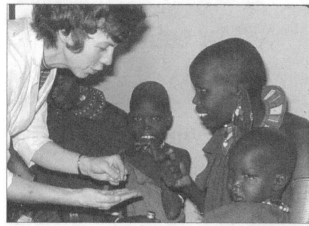

Myrtice treating Maasai women and children in clinic at Spilwe, Moshi Region, Tanzania.

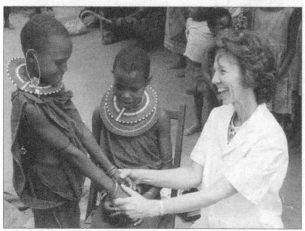

Two Maasai sisters share with Myrtice at Kirya, Moshi Region, Tanzania.

Myrtice visits with village people before a church service near Iringa.

Carlos and Myrtice supervised the building of Huruma Conference Centre at Iringa.

Water tower goes up at Huruma Conference Centre at Iringa.

Carlos confers with Jesaja, pastor at Omatando, Owambo Region, Namibia.

Carlos leads dedication service for parents and babies in Kavango Region, Namibia.

Pastor leadership training, Katima Mulilo, Caprivi Region, Namibia.

Carlos preaching in open-air meeting at Livuyu, Kavango Region, Namibia.

Kaisosi church near Rundu in the Kavango Region has its beginning under trees.

In less than eight years, the Kaisosi church has its own building and more than 800 members.

Sauyema, near Rundu, builds a larger and more permanent building to accommodate more than 400 members, next to the original grass building.

When Carlos had back surgery and could not travel, church leaders came to Tsumeb for leadership training, every second month.

While Carlos works with church leaders inside, Myrtice holds clinic outside at Kaisosi.

During time of drought, churches back home provided for distribution of food to otherwise thousands of starving people.

Carlos baptizes in portable tank where water is scarce and where there are crocodile infested rivers.

Myrtice distributes Bibles in the Lozi language in the Caprivi Region of Namibia.

Lord's Supper for church without a building.

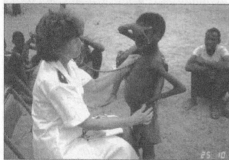

Treatment for a malnourished child.

Clinic with the Bushmen in the Caprivi Region of Namibia.

Chapter Seven

Kenya

We had been on furlough and now we would live at the Brakenhurst, near Tigoni in the Kenya Highlands.

The government's district headquarters was at Limuru, 15 miles away. We would go there to pick up our mail. We would be twenty-two miles from Nairobi and at a considerably higher elevation than Kigoma. The weather would be cool. On a clear day, we could see Mt. Kilimanjaro, 160 miles to the southeast. Coffee plantations surround the mission compound.

Our mission had purchased the Brakenhurst, a magnificent old hotel, for a very reasonable price. The owners were selling her for lack of business due to many expatriates having left Kenya after Independence and her need of repairs. The mission treasurer and his family lived there. There was also a full time agriculture missionary and his family there. Sometime after we arrived, a new couple arrived. He was an architect.

Before leaving Kigoma for furlough, the mission had asked us to move to the Brakenhurst and establish a Swahili language school. While on furlough, we purchased the equipment needed for the school.

We were also at the place where our mission had many of its meetings. This meant we did not have to travel those long, rough three days to get there. Somehow, however; it just did not seem like the Africa that we knew and enjoyed so much. Our hearts longed to be back in fulltime church planting and evangelism.

Many guests came to the area and we often had missionary friends in our home. Cooking was still a big responsibility, but fresh vegetables and imported foods were available, though at a dear cost. We enjoyed the goodies that we had missed so much in Kigoma.

M: Children with us

Our girls were delighted that we were living close enough to schools that they didn't have to go away to boarding school or be home schooled. We were delighted to have them with us.

Another plus was being on a station that had other children with whom ours could associate. We felt that our girls needed time to share with other children.

Since we were in the Conference Center compound, we frequently had visitors overnight or for several days. Special friends came from America for visits and going on safari. The girls enjoyed the fun times with visitors who made them feel special. They enjoyed sharing in the cooking and learning things that they had missed by being away in boarding school. Janice said that this was the most normal family time that she remembered in Africa.

Since many of their friends did riding, Janice and Ruth were begging for horses. Our first Christmas there, they were completely surprised to find cards with verses in a package telling of their special gifts being in a nearby barn. The screams, hugs and excitement were immeasurable!

We had found two beautiful riding horses for them. We also located someone to give the girls riding lessons. They spent hours in the beautiful coffee plantations with unlimited places to ride. They felt free and confident with this new pleasure in their lives. We were so thankful that we could provide this extra joy for them, even for the limited time we would be there.

> *"If you, then, though you are evil, Know*
> *how to give good gifts to your children,*
> *How much more will your father in heaven*
> *Give good gifts to those who ask him!" Mt 7:11*

C: Teaching Swahili

Our loads arrived from the US not too long after we did. They contained language school equipment; including materials for a language school lab. We immediately began setting up the school in rooms the Brakenhurst manager designated for our use and employed local carpenters to build tables and booths for the school and the lab. All the while, we worked on teaching plans - making ready for three new families who would soon arrive.

Our family moved into a two-room, housekeeping cottage near where the school would be. Yusufu Abdalla, with whom we worked in Kigoma, arrived with his family. He would be my assistant for teaching Swahili.

It was our plan from the beginning to set up the school and train an African administrator and teachers. When we had done that, we would return to evangelism and church development in Tanzania.

We were pleased to take two groups through language study. With Yusufu's assistance, things moved along nicely. Our plan was to make him the administrator of the school. Although that never happened, he stayed and taught at the school.

After eighteen months, we left to return to evangelism, church planting. Another missionary came to direct the school. After some months, Yusufu moved to Arusha, Tanzania, to teach in the mission's seminary.

"Every tribe and language and people and nation." Rev 5:9b

M: Chief Comes at Night

I soon had plans and equipment ready to hold clinics for the workers at the conference center and for near-by villagers. The clinic would be in the back of and under the newly completed chapel. The plan was to hold clinics three days a week.

In the first few weeks the clinic went as planned but soon so many came that I extended the time.

Late one night, someone was calling outside. We both quickly got up and went to the door to see what was happening. There stood an older man holding a small child, about two years old, in a faded tribal blanket. One of the workers from the conference center had brought him over to our house.

The man pleaded for some help for his child who had a high fever. I felt the child and knew without doubt that the fever was over 105 degrees. I asked about his going to the hospital in the town about twenty miles away. He said he had no way to go and at this time of night there was no transportation. He was a complete stranger to us, but our hearts reached out in compassion, knowing the child really did need immediate care. I would do what I could for them.

Walking with this stranger to the clinic, I learned that he was the headman of his village about five miles on the next hillside beyond the coffee fields. Position of influence was significant in our outreach, but it did not make any difference in my care.

The child's fever had risen to 105.6. After checking him, I realized that he had a severe upper respiratory infection. Without delay, I gave him an injection of antibiotics, oral Tylenol, and cool, wet cloths on his temples, neck, under the arms and on his groins to cool his fever. Every measure possible was done to keep the child from having a seizure from the fever. I stayed with them for nearly two hours until the fever had broken. Then helping to bundle him up securely on this cold night in the mountains, I sent them on their way. Then I returned to the house to get a few winks of sleep before the sun came up.

When I headed for the clinic the next morning I could see a very large number of people waiting for attention. It surprised me, for usually at this clinic only ten or more were there early. Right in front was the dear headman, with his child, showing a big grin. I had asked him to return for a follow-up and another injection but it looked as if he had brought half the village with him. I reached over to feel the skin of the child and found his fever was very low now. "I'm so happy that your child is beginning to heal," I told him.

"You have helped so much. I am so grateful for your caring for my son last night, for I was afraid that he would die. Your sharing about God's love for us has really touched me. I want you and your husband to come to our village so we can hear more."

After cordial greetings with the others, I opened the clinic door and came outside to give out numbers for calling the patients in an orderly fashion. He quickly explained to me that since his child responded so well to my care and treatment he wanted me to care for his villagers who really needed help.

Welcoming them all, I felt that God was using this late-night incident to open the way for another village to hear news of the Kingdom of God. I rejoiced deep in my heart for the opportunity the serve my Master.

Within a few weeks another young group of believers were worshipping and studying God's Word in this headman's village. Before long a new church was sharing the love of God in every direction.

> ". . .the Word of God continued to increase and
> spread." Ac 12:24

C: High in the Mountains

We came to Tigoni to set up and operate the language school for a limited time. There were several churches in the Limuru area when we arrived. We assisted in the beginning of seven more. Besides working with the language school, we had agreed to give what guidance we could to the churches and their pastors. We were happy to do that. We rotated between the churches on Sunday, offering what assistance we could.

Not too long after our arrival at the Brakenhurst, four men showed up from the Kambaa (Kah-mm-BAH) Mountains. They came seeking help for their church.

They explained that several years before a missionary set up camp in their village. He preached and baptized more than four hundred, but he never organized a church nor taught them how to run a church. In time, he left and they never heard from him again.

One of the men said, "We continued our meetings, but little by little the people dropped out. Some of them went to other churches but most are not going to church anywhere."

"What do you want from us? How do you feel that we can help you?"

"We need someone to lead us and teach us. We have Bibles but we do not know how to use them. None of us can preach."

"How many are there left in your group now?"

"We are seven all together—the four of us and three more who could not come."

"Have the seven of you been meeting?"

"Yes, we meet every Sunday. We sing and read the Bible."

After quite a long session talking about Kambaa, the people there and their needs, we made plans to visit their village. I told them that I had to be at the school from Monday to Friday but could come on Saturday or Sunday. We agreed to come to them on the following Sunday. After they had given us instructions on how to get to Kambaa, we prayed together and they left.

On Sunday, we left early and went to Kambaa. The men who had come to Brakenhurst greeted us. They, having told others that we would come, had convinced many to be there. A large crowd waited for us under some large trees.

We spent an hour talking about who they were and about what we might do to assist them. We sang and I preached. When I finished most of them stood to say that, if we would assist them, they would be a part of the church.

We left them with tracts and songbooks in their language and a promise to return in two weeks. We would come early on Saturday and spend the day teaching.

Upon our return, word had spread and there were more than two hundred eager people awaiting our teaching. It was a wonderful day. More than one hundred expressed a desire for baptism and church membership. The leaders promised to return to Brakenhurst, where we could give them instruction in how to teach the village people about Jesus and the church. They also promised to gather materials and put up a church building.

The following months proved exciting for Kambaa and the church there. It grew and we baptized many into the fellowship. The leaders came regularly for instructions and we went often there. The church continued to grow.

> ". . .*Paul had a vision of a man of Macedonia standing and begging him,* "*Come over to Macedonian and help us.*" *Ac 16:9*

M: Kikuyu Hospitality

Surrounding this area the Kikuyu tribe was dominant among the people living here. Some Luo tribesmen lived around but their main homeland was in the western provinces. Kikuyu people were very aggressive, intelligent and hard workers. Many of them developed productive farms with mainly beans, corn and arrowroot. Coffee was also planted on most of their farms. The highlands had rich soil and a cooler climate, and adequate rain for producing excellent crops. Very little hunger was seen in this area.

While the ladies were peddling their extra food products on the road sides or in market places, they usually had their hands busy making baskets to sell. Well-made baskets with beautiful colors were useful for the shoppers to carry their goods. None of the markets provided paper or plastic bags. Each shopper had to bring his or her own basket or buy one.

The Kikuyu ladies always carried their loads in these same type baskets in a unique way from all the other tribes. Most of them lived in the mountains or on steep hillsides. They carried baskets on the back with a strap pulling against their foreheads or top of their heads. This way assured them that the basket would be secure and not fall off in contrast to the way those living in flat areas carried theirs; right on top of the head, balancing it there. Many of the older ladies had permanent indentations where the heavy baskets had pulled on their heads for many years.

These ladies also loved fanciful beads in their ears as earrings, and around their necks and arms. They usually made the jewelry themselves. Most of them also shaved their heads clean. Garments were cloths wrapped around with belts holding them in place. Among the ladies, some of the earlobes had also been stretched so they had large holes in them. Being very resourceful, many planted flowers around their yards and sold them in the market in season.

When visitors came from America, we wanted them to visit one of our churches with the Kikuyu people and see their home life. We discussed with the church leaders about bringing our guests. They were delighted and planned a special service in their honor.

Sitting around one house on benches, odd chairs and stools, a large group gathered for a very spirited service with joyous singing and preaching. Even the visitors felt warmly a part of the service and fellowship.

Much to our surprise, they served food after the service. This just enriched the time with our fellow Christians. They served rice with a chicken sauce along with 'duuma' (DOU-mah) - a mixture of mashed arrowroot with cooked beans and kernels of corn throughout it. It was similar to mashed potatoes with vegetables added and mixed into it. One ate with the fingers after forming it into a small ball.

Our dear, aristocratic American visitor wasn't sure what she should do. She tried to take the duuma in her hand as they did and make it into a ball before eating it. She kept the conversation going, asking many questions to delay eating it. The more she looked at it the more she felt she just couldn't eat it. She had a lovely, expensive purse with her that she had brought on her tour. Glancing over her way I saw that she was slipping this ball of soft duuma down into her purse.

When they saw she did not have any left, they asked if she would like some more. She quickly answered, "No, I think I have had enough, thank you."

Back home we had a difficult time cleaning out her purse, for the soft mixture had stuck to and soiled the cloth interior. We laughed with her because of her aversion to the locals' food. We really enjoyed it ourselves. After that occasion we definitely tried to avoid any times of eating with our nationals while having guests.

> "As one who is in the Lord Jesus, I am
> fully convinced that no food is unclean in itself."
> But if any one regards something as unclean,
> then for him it is unclean." Ro. 14:14

M: Elephants Back in

The next outing with these American visitors was to Tree Tops, in northern Kenya, where the hotel is on large poles high in the tops of trees. This place was famous because Princess Elizabeth was there when her father, the King of England, passed away and she became Queen.

Sitting high above the animals, we could see their coming to the water hole and salt lick; any time of day or night. Elephants, lions, buffalo, zebra, giraffe, rhino and many numerous smaller, wild animals were coming and going. We stayed up late since it was so hard to leave the viewing area. Every animal was unique in its habits at the water hole. Some would hardly drink, always looking about for the dangerous animals which could catch them for food.

Right before we decided it was time for all of us to go to bed, we noticed a lone bull elephant coming to the outskirts of the area. A herd of about eight elephants had been drinking, wallowing in the mud hole and bathing for quite some time.

The new elephant slowly came nearer. Then he turned around and stood with his back to the group. Only after a period of time did he move nearer by slowly backing toward them. Each step was hesitant and very slow. He never looked around but kept backing nearer. Finally, as he was fairly near one of the elephants, this one touched him on the back with his trunk. Then he moved some again backwards and another elephant did the same thing. After standing there for quite some time, after most of the elephants had touched him, he turned around to join them.

Perhaps elephants can teach us that when we join a new group we need to go very slowly and humbly as if backing into it, to be received properly!

"Be completely humble and gentle; bearing with one another in love." Eph 4:2

C: Mission Accomplished

Eighteen months passed quickly and it was time to return to our work in Tanzania. We had set up the language school and led three new missionary groups through six months of Swahili study. We had worked with the local churches and Myrtice had had clinics for the sick; three or four days each week. Our girls had been able to stay at home and attend schools in the area.

As it had been our plan from the beginning, an African administrator and African teachers were in place. The mission wanted new work in Moshi, at the foot of Mt. Kilimanjaro. We looked in that direction.

When we moved to Moshi, Janice and Ruth returned to Rift Valley Academy as boarders. Debra went with us and entered the International School at Moshi. After a short time Ruth, having some difficulties settling in at RVA, came to Moshi and joined Debra at ISM.

"Be exalted, O God, above the heavens, and let your glory be over all the earth." Ps 108:5

Chapter Eight

Moshi I

From the top of the Livingstone Hotel, we got our first view of snowcapped Mt. Kilimanjaro. The beauty and splendor before our eyes was overwhelming. That was Christmas time, 1957 but we could not imagine then that we would see that sight many times in the months and years ahead.

Upon arriving in Moshi to live in 1979, we found that we would be living at the foot of that fantastic mountain. We would be able to gaze upon her magnificence from our dining room window on a clear morning. Breezes from the mountain would make Moshi, at 2,900 feet elevation, cool at night and in the early morning. After the sun would come up it could be very hot.

Everyone in our family would climb her before we left. I am glad I did but have said many times that it was the most miserable thing I ever did. I would not do it again.

There were 38,000 people living in the town when we came to live in Moshi. Many thousands more lived on the slopes of the mountain and in the surrounding area.

Around the slopes of the mountain were European farmers who produced high-grade coffee, wheat, dairy and beef cattle as well as beautiful vegetables and flowers, many of which would make their way to European markets. The aroma of coffee roasting pervaded the whole town and stirred our taste buds for this tasty Arabica coffee.

On the lowlands outside of Moshi were a very large sugar cane plantation, several sisal farms and one very large farm where one farmer raised beans only for the seed which would be sold in Europe where the growing season was too short to produce bean seed. Local tribal people raised cattle and goats. A tannery in the town processed their skins into fine leather.

Moshi town and the thoroughfares into and out of it had paved roads. The road in front of our house, and many others had no pavement and were very dry and dusty most of the year.

M: Beginnings at Kilimanjaro

Beginning a new work takes ingenuity, plans and many prayers. But we had one advantage in this area. Gloria and Ezikeli (Aa-zee-KAY-lee) were our feet into the door in the southeast area of Kilimanjaro region. They were a young delightful couple who truly embraced the Christian faith in their lives and home. They had become Christians in one of our churches in the Kigoma region and were strong members of the church and active in leadership.

Ezikeli had a good job with the electricity company and was transferred to the Nyumba of Mungu station where the government had built a dam to produce an electric supply. Gloria had some education and was resourceful in the church.

Nyumba ya Mungu, 'house of god' in the Swahili language, is about seventy five miles southeast of Moshi in a very hot, dry and isolated area. The Maasai in the area called the place Nyumba ya Mungu because of a very huge rock, which was formed like a Maasai hut. They surmised that God had made the rock to look like one of their houses. The formation of the lake put the rock under water and attracted many settlers for fishing as a livelihood.

Ezikeli and Gloria began a Bible study in their home, which led into a regular worship service. They wrote us to send help to them to build a church building and have training from a missionary. Since we were still in Kenya at that time we contacted a fellow evangelist in the Arusha area to see if he could go and give them some assistance.

He had a big work already going but was gracious to begin work in establishing this first church in the area though it was a very long distance from him. It was our privilege then to continue the work when we moved to plant churches in the area.

We also knew the slopes of Kilimanjaro were heavily populated because of the rich soil there. Crops of coffee, bananas and vegetables grew well on the mountain slopes.

Going around the mountain was a tremendous challenge. We did and found areas that were responsive to the Gospel.

The Chagga tribe had been reached in many areas by another church that came from Germany when that country was responsible for overseeing Tanganyika in the last century.

The further we went around the mountain we found open hearts that had been untouched, among the Kikuyu and Maasai people. It took days of camping in the area to preach and teach, strengthening the first witness.

The Kikuyu and Maasai were not friendly with one another, since they had had many battles over stealing cattle from each other.

One day while Carlos was traveling on his own, he picked up a Maasai man who was flagging him down for a ride. Carlos used the time to witness and share with this pagan man. He told him about the Kikuyu church that was beginning and asked him to visit in the service that day.

The old Maasai, who had never used water for bathing, only the urine of his cattle in the tribe's traditional custom, stared at him for a while.

Observing, one could see his much worn and dirty rust-colored cloth draped around his shoulder. He had long ear lobes which were stretched from his childhood and had heavy weights now pulling them longer; a sign of real manhood. His hair was braided fancifully in the front and back with extensions and held in place with a mixture of cow manure and red ocher.

He slowly answered Carlos, "I couldn't sit with those Kikuyu. They are dirty people!"

It must have been a case of a pot calling the kettle black. Tribalism would raise its angry head in many situations in the days ahead hindering the Christian witness.

"Do not judge, or you too will be judged.
For in the same manner you judge others,
you will be judged." Mt 7:1-2a

M: Home and Family

Though our mission had bought a house for us, the Muslim Indian owners were still living there. We were desperate for a place to live with our family. They had previously agreed to move out at a specific date, but failed to do so. When we arrived we had to do some negotiations in order to have a place to live. They finally agreed that we use the back wing of the house which had two bedrooms with an enclosed screen porch, a bathroom and a door to the outside.

Living with three children called for real ingenuity to make this place our home for these extended six months. Having our cook stove on the porch and fixing a makeshift dining area there was really a challenge, particularly since we did not have a kitchen or kitchen sink. With no place to put up the washing machine, we did laundry in the bathtub, and dishes in the bathroom sink.

We managed in the close quarters with 'shift and move' techniques. Our girls were most concerned since they were so confined and had no friends in the area. We were glad that we still had some books to keep them occupied until school started for them. They enjoyed going to the open market, trying to hunt out anything new and different. They loved checking out the little Indian shops for unusual items. They could bargain for a good price as well as I.

Fresh vegetables were more plentiful though the meat market was much the same as in the rest of the country. Janice would soon be going back to Rift Valley Academy in Kenya, for boarding, while Ruth and Debra entered the Moshi International School.

Bothering us most in this living arrangement was the 4:30 a.m. wake-up call of the nearby Muslim mosque and a repeat at five for their prayers. The owner of the house was loud in his early morning regime of bathing, which woke all of us up for this period. Because the house was open we didn't miss any of the sounds! Clearing his throat was the most dreadful one.

Since we only had one vehicle, Carlos would be out many days going around the mountain searching out places to begin churches or away on mission business. I was able to secure a bicycle to go to the market place, since carrying a loaded basket for over a mile was too heavy. The streets were always full of people walking. We had a hill to go up toward our house. When my basket was full, I had to labor to keep going up the road.

Many of the Africans would see my pushing hard on the pedals and call out "Pole sana, Mama" (So sorry, Madam). Several said, "White women aren't supposed to ride bicycles!" They were very sympathetic.

Then one day while I was pedaling with a heavy basket of food supplies I lost control and sprawled all over the road. Vegetables and fruit went one way while I slid the other. Without hesitation, several men helped pick up all my goods, and me saying repeatedly, "We are so sorry for your fall." The graciousness of the African was always shown to us!

"Words from a wise man's mouth are gracious." Ecc 10:12a

C: Rhino Church

Kifaru (Key-FAH-roo) means rhino. What an unusual name for a village and for a church! Yet there were people who recalled the time when rhino were in the area.

One man said, "We used to see them often among the sisal plants. When they were present we would not go into the fields to work. The plantation owner told us that we must go and work but we were too afraid to do that. Only when the rhino left would we go and work."

Another went on to say, "Now there are no rhino, no sisal and no work. We have permission to live in the labor camp but without work we have very little food or anything else for our families. Members of our families who got work in Moshi help us some when they get their pay."

The area was fairly dry and filled with palmettos, making gardening difficult. Some women made baskets from the palmetto fronds, to sell, making a meager income for a few.

We heard that the owners of the Kifaru Sisal Plantation had left after independence when the government took over most of the farms and plantations formerly owned and operated by expatriates. The original owners did not train the locals in management so when they left the plantation quickly ran down.

Between the overgrown brush and tall grass, you could still see sisal. We also found the factory in disarray. Having processed no sisal for quite a long time, the building was near collapsing and the machinery was unusable.

There being no church in the immediate vicinity of the plantation we talked with the people about the possibility of starting one. We told them that I would preach and that Mama Owens would come with clinics to help the sick. They were delighted.

The local authorities gave us permission to use one of the run-down buildings. Someone had stolen and taken away the doors and windows. It took a lot of doing to get the building repaired and clean enough for meetings. With the help of several of the locals, we managed and announced a clinic for Saturday and a preaching service for Sunday. Back in Moshi, I bought boards, made benches, and a simple table behind which I would preach. We took them when we went for the clinic on Saturday. It was a one room, open building with a sand floor.

The people at Kifaru responded and it was not long until we would baptize new converts and organize a church. The church grew and before long we organized work with the members to plaster the building and put in windows and doors. We whitewashed the walls inside and out so the building looked nice and everyone showed pride in what we had.

In the months and years following, many wonderful things happened at Kifaru. God takes broken things and make them fulfill a purpose to bring Him glory.

*"I showed you by this kind of hard work, we
must help the weak"* Ac 20:35a

C: Where They Keep Goats

Lydia, who lived in Boma (BOW-mah) la Mbuzi (Mm-BOO-zee) on the southern outskirts of Moshi visited friends in Kifaru on Sunday. When she met us at church there she was excited. We promised to visit her on Monday morning,

We had seen the village but knew little about it and knew no one who lived there. On visiting Lydia as promised, we found that she and Thomas, her husband, had lived at Kifaru and that he had worked for the sisal plantation. He had lost his job when the operations closed and they moved to Boma la Mbuzi. He did odd jobs and they lived scantily. He was not home when we came to visit.

Lydia and Thomas were not attending church though they had formerly been involved with a church. She had been pleased with our service on Sunday and wanted to know if we would begin services at Boma la Mbuzi. We asked her to look for a place to meet and told her where we lived.

She came the next afternoon to tell us that she had found a place—an abandoned gristmill building—and had gained permission for us to use it. Late that afternoon we went and found the building which was in a terrible mess. We agreed to come on Saturday morning and see if we could clean it up enough for Sunday morning services.

When we got to the village, Lydia had enlisted several of her friends to assist in cleaning up the building. They all agreed to meet with us the next morning. At the close of the service on Sunday morning Lydia, Thomas and six of their friends confessed Jesus publicly and said that they wanted baptism. We promised to come Tuesday afternoon for classes to teach them. Myrtice asked to meet with the women Tuesday morning at which time she started a class for Bible study and sewing.

We went to Boma la Mbuzi each Tuesday and on Sunday mornings for several weeks when we did not have to be at other places. Each time we went, we taught and preached and each time more people came. Before long, there were more than a dozen ready for baptism. We made plans to baptize them in a small stream not too far away.

The night before the baptism, it rained heavily. It was still raining when we arrived at church but stopped during the service. Knowing that it would be difficult to baptize in the overflowing stream we invited the group to our place at 3:00 that afternoon. I planned to baptize them in the fish tank behind the house. After lunch, I worked feverishly to clean out the tank. I connected a hose and began filling the tank. I put blocks next to it to assist in getting in and out. By the time the people arrived, we were ready.

It was a beautiful service with many attending—families and friends of those baptized. Remarkably, we had some new believers from the English group meeting in our home whom we baptized at the same time. It was amazing to see the comradeship and joy of the European believers gather and share in the service. What a beautiful oneness in Christianity!

Having plans to go around the mountain the following weekend we met with them on Friday afternoon for organizing their church. They chose Thomas to be their leader but since he had to work most Sundays, Lydia became the main leader of the church. The church grew and many joined regularly. Doors were opened and God was at work!

> ". . .and the Lord added to their number daily
> those who were being saved." Ac 2:37

M: Woman across Door

When we moved to Moshi, we were unusually impressed with the Maasai people, who herded their animals around Mt Kilimanjaro and to the southeast. They were extremely colorful and absolutely different from the other surrounding tribes -- the Chagga, the Kikuyu, the Luo and others. We quickly began to experience success in reaching people from these other tribes. The Maasai, however, were friendly but resistant, avoiding any significant contact with us. We could see them around the towns and herding their cattle, but we never saw any villages because they were nomadic.

Sometimes they grazed their cattle near one of the new churches. We would invite them to come join the worship services. Some would stand in the door way for a short while but would never enter. As this was one tribe untouched by the Christian message, we felt discouraged in not finding a way to reach them.

Their uniqueness was seen in their nomadic lifestyle and colorful appearance. They lived with and from their cattle which, along with wives, were considered a man's wealth. Very few cattle would be slaughtered unless they were nearly ready to die anyway or there was a very important celebration. Their main diet was blood drawn from the live cattle and mixed with soured milk. Occasionally, they bought corn meal for making mush, and picked wild greens for a vegetable.

Maasai men had fancy hairdos made red with a mixture of fresh cow dung and powdered ochre, a red-rusty colored clay dug from the surrounding hillsides. They kept their fancifully braided and extended hair in place by this mixture. After using rendered cow fat to oil their bodies, they applied the rusty ochre to the entire body, changing their skin color. A man's garment was a single, rusty colored cloth thrown over his shoulder. Ear lobes were traditionally stretched with heavy weights for length. They aimed for the ear lobe to reach the top of the shoulder.

Women had numerous adornments in the ears made from copper wire or tin. They also wore the rust-colored cloths tucked about them. They adorned their necks with many rows of multi-colored beads, some on wire frames standing out from their necks. All were unique and different. Ear-rings were also beaded and attached in the many pierced areas of the ears. Some had beautiful copper wire shaped in attractive ways for the neck and ears. Others had large copper wire wrapped around the upper arms and legs. Some stole electrical wires to make fanciful body ornaments.

As was my custom, I would return to a village with a primary health clinic every week. On one occasion, we left home at daybreak to be at the Nyumba ya Mungu church, seventy-five miles from Moshi. As there were always many sick people, I tried to begin early. This church was next to the Nyumba ya Mungu Lake. Many people lived near the lake and fished for a living. Carlos, when possible, would go with me, visiting and ministering to the people while I held the clinic.

When we arrived on this particular day there were an estimated 250 people already gathered and standing in line outside the door. Normally, Carlos would give each a card with a number while I organized my medicines. Most medicines were already prepared in appropriate containers, labeled and ready for dispensing. The people would be treated according to the number they had been given. On this day, however, things would be somewhat different.

When we moved the people aside to open a passage to the door, we found a very sick woman placed across the front of the door entrance. No one seemed to know who she was, where she was from, or who had brought her. She was not responsive and had a very high fever that I discovered by just touching her. Carlos assisted in picking her up. We brought her into the church and laid her on one of the wooden benches. She was poorly dressed, with a shaved head. She appeared to be one of the Maasai women, having some of their typical beads on her neck and ears.

Checking her over, I knew she must have had malaria, which is prevalent there and deadly. I treated her with medication by injection. Proceeding to see other patients, I took note of her every few minutes.

After quite a long time I noticed that the woman was moving a bit and had opened her eyes. I asked her who she was and from where she had come. She said that she was from Kirya, a village some way back of the church, but she did not know who had brought her to the clinic. She could only remember that she was very sick and with a high fever the evening before.

I inquired about her family. She told me that her husband and all her children had died. She was completely alone. She said that likely some of her neighbors had brought her to the clinic during the night. I gave her a drink of water and some oral medication expecting her friends to return soon to take her home.

At the end of the day when we were closing up the clinic, I saw that she was still on the bench. No one had returned for her.

Knowing she was too weak to walk, we hesitantly offered to take her home. We realized this could open a door for hundreds to ask us to do the same for them, but we knew we had no other choice for her.

After loading all the leftover supplies in the Land Rover, we helped this weak woman into the vehicle. She continued to assure us that it was just a little way behind the church along an open path.

The path was so rough that we nearly bounced out of the Land Rover from time to time. After a long, forty-five minutes, the 'little way' seemed to never end. Distances mean little to Africans.

All of sudden we came into an opening of a large Maasai village. We had looked for these villages before but since the people are nomadic, we could never locate any of them. Fortunately this was one of the permanent sites where the old and very young stay and others returned in certain seasons. Our hearts leaped as we realized that this was an answer to prayers; our finally finding a real Maasai settlement.

As we drove into the village among the many, low, conical Maasai mud huts we saw many of the colorful tribal people going about their normal tasks. Few paid much attention to us. Our patient pointed the way to her house on the far side.

When we arrived at her place all we saw was one wall standing with the roof collapsed inside. Because of natural elements and termites, this type of house would normally last only four or five years. She had prepared a small place under the edge of the fallen roof; about three feet deep, for her sleeping mat. Outside was her only cooking area with three large stones and a clay pot. This was all she had.

We gently placed her on her woven grass mat. Before we left I repeated the use of her medications and asked if I could have a prayer with her. She nodded yes.

After finishing the prayer, I told her that she must return to the clinic the next week to follow up her case.

Immediately, she responded by asking, "Could you please come to our village? I have been hearing you tell of Jesus today and we do not know about your Jesus, none of our people do. Please come tell us about your God."

Quickly, I reassured her that we would be very happy to come if she would ask the chief for permission for us to work in her village.

She gave a faint smile and responded, "I can do that."

We set up a tentative date to return to this 'open door' to the Maasai people. Again we could only thank God for preparing the way for a fruitful work.

> "And pray for us, too, that God may open
> a door for our message, so that we may
> proclaim the mystery of Christ" Col 4:3

M: Healing Shot

When our thirteen year old daughter, Janice, came home from boarding school, we tried to share as much time as possible with her. We reduced our time out in the villages and worked nearer home to be with her more.

We heard reports of an outbreak of measles in the villages and knew it was a serious situation. Many malnourished children die from measles. I knew that it was imperative that I do clinics in these villages.

"Janice, I really need to go help the people in the villages with the mobile clinic. Would you like to go and help me?"

"Yes, that would be fun if I can help you. I want to be with you."

"There are many things you can do. You can give out medicines, help the invalid, and wrap wounds. I can teach you what to do."

When we arrived at the village, hundreds were waiting since so many had illnesses. We were the only medical care in the area.

The day was dreadfully hot and flies were swarming around our faces. While we were talking to the patients, some flies flew into our mouths. We spit them out and just carried on, trying to be oblivious to these pests.

I diligently worked trying to see most of the patients. Soon I realized I was far behind on giving the injections that were needed. I asked Janice if she would be willing to help me give the shots.

"Oh, I'm afraid that I would hurt them."

"They won't mind. They feel that if it hurts it will have more effect. I really need your help!"

"I guess so, at least I will try."

After showing her how to clean and hold the skin and demonstrating to her how to put the needle in, she was willing to try.

The next patient was an older Maasai man who had spent his life out in the sun herding his cows. He was thin. His skin was toughened by the elements. I handed Janice the prepared syringe and she went with him to the side while I took care of another patient.

"How did your injection go, Janice?"

"Well, I had a hard time. I did everything you said to do, but I just couldn't get the needle to go into the skin. So I just screwed it into his arm."

I flinched at the idea of the pain the man had.

"He said it was the best shot that he ever had, so he knew that he would get well."

'I was sick and you looked after me." Mt 25:36

M: Heart Hurts

Upon returning to the village of Kirya as scheduled, we found the whole village outside and celebrating with dancing and the high jumps of the Maasai men with the women swinging hips, shuffling feet and trilling (a sharp sound made with the tongue). That day was truly a day of celebration as Carlos preached the Gospel, visited many families and I ministered to their sick bodies. We had already begun to fall in love with these dear people.

A very beautiful and colorful girl laden with many Maasai beads was there from the beginning and had offered to assist me in interpreting for those who knew only the Maasai language. She told me her name was Nsiyani (Nn-see-YAH-nee). She had been in school for a few grades and knew Swahili well since she was the chief's daughter. I used Swahili completely and she would translate into the Maasai language. She was a tremendous blessing to the work and me personally.

Late in the afternoon, after we had seen around one hundred and seventy patients we were both just exhausted. We found that seeing families together expedited seeing the long lines waiting for care. Also teaching the mother and father together how to care for the problems and understand the medicine given them, I felt more assurance that they would follow the directions correctly.

With the Maasai, I saw that they were a very touching people. I began always greeting them with a touch on their hands or shoulders and on the heads of children. They immediately began to relate to me since this action seemed to break any barriers. The children invariably would lower their heads for me to touch them before we could begin any examination. This was a custom of the child showing respect to the elders.

After the first clinics with them I found that I needed to always touch them while I was caring for them. It was a cultural thing but it really made a difference in their acceptance of me and my work.

While we were seeing the very last patients, Nsiyani came close to me and said, "I really am hurting."

"Oh, I'm sorry. You have worked so hard today. Where are you feeling pain?"

Very dramatically she motioned to her chest region. I pulled out my stethoscope and began to listen to her heart.

"No, you won't be able to hear it. It began bothering me today when you started talking about Jesus and that everyone needs Him in their heart."

A full day with this beautiful young lady made me realize that God's Spirit was working on her. I sat down right beside her. While holding her hand, I shared with her about sin and her need to repent. I told her that she could receive Jesus Christ as her own personal Savior. After a short time of discussion with her she bowed her head in prayer and put her trust and faith in our Savior.

After several weeks of returning with clinics, teaching and preaching in Kirya, a group was ready for baptism. My dear Nsiyani was growing in the Lord and just radiating her happiness. She came to me after one of the clinics to tell me that she wanted to change her name.

"I am now a new person so I think I should have a new name. I want one from the Bible."

"I think that would be fine. And what name would you like to have?"

"I like the name of Esta (Esther in English) for she was a woman faithful to the Lord and her people, and courageous in spite of problems."

We were very proud of Esta, for she truly lived up to her name and was beautiful in body and spirit. In her position as daughter of the headman, God continued to use her as a strong leader and witness for Christ in her tribe.

"And who knows but that you have come to
royal position for such a time as this?" Est 4:14b

C: Simioni's Spear

When Esther accepted Jesus, she expressed much joy. She invited her family and friends to come to church. She also invited her father, Simioni (See-me-O-nee), the headman who did come but, as he said, just to see what was going on.

Simioni appeared to be much older than he was. He had weathered many seasons by spending them with his cattle and roaming the hills and the plains in search of grass and water. He lived with, by, and from his cattle.

As it was the Maasai custom, he regularly punctured the jugular veins of cows to collect blood. Afterwards he would press and hold dry, cow manure on the puncture long enough for it to stop bleeding. He then mixed the blood with fresh milk in a long cylindrical gourd where it would remain until it had clabbered. By a leather strap fixed to the gourd, it would hang near his hut or be tied to his side and used for food. The process of taking blood was a daily ritual for the Maasai.

Along the way, Simioni had lost an eye. He no longer traveled with the cows but served as the headman of his village where the elderly stayed and where others came and went with the seasons.

While we visited with Simioni one day, he agreed to accept Christ as his Savior. He, having made the decision, became a good influence on other Maasai in his village. In one year, I baptized sixty seven from his village. Simioni offered one of his houses to be used for the church.

We were pleased when Simioni offered a plot of ground for a church building. He said that his people would help with the construction. Knowing that most Maasai have little or no money, we arranged to purchase the items they could not provide. The church members would take clay from the riverbank and make mud brick, which would dry in the sun.

They would burn them in a homemade kiln. They would bring sand from the riverbed for mortar and for a concrete floor. We would provide cement, windows and doors, roof beams and metal for the roof.

When the work began, I brought metal drums. Church members filled them at the river and we hauled them to the church site in our Land Rover. The work went well, but before the church building was finished, we left for furlough. We were away for a year.

When we returned we found the church completed and being used for services. They had made simple benches from planks we brought before we left.

Having been on furlough, a great crowd showed up for our first service with them. There were many fond greetings—much rejoicing. On coming into the building, I noticed that there was chipped cement in front of the first pew near the center isle. It didn't take me long to know why.

Simioni, as it was custom for a Maasai man, took his long spear with him wherever he went. He sat on the end of the pew where I saw the chipped cement. As I preached, he expressed his excitement and acceptance by pounding the end of his spear on the floor in front of him. I suspect that, because there was a considerable hole in the cement, Simioni had often been excited during a preaching service.

It was only a short time before I was able to baptize many more, including Simioni, the headman. A new church was born; the very first among the Maasai people. Later they were instrumental in helping to establishing three other church groups among their people in this area.

". and He sent them out to preach the kingdom
of God and to heal the sick.." Lk 9:2

M: Machine Gun

Tanzania had become very communistic politically during this time. Communes were begun. Food shortages became worse and worse. Even to find sugar, flour, oil or other basic cooking needs was impossible. We had to leave the country and go up to Kenya to buy 100-kilo bags of these basics. The people of the land were really hurting. Many were desperate.

After a long, tiring clinic at Nyumba ya Mungu one day, I was driving back late when the sun was going down. The sky was darkening and I was anxious to get home before too late. As I sped alone towards Moshi, I was suddenly surprised to see a man standing in the middle of the road with a large machine gun held across his chest. He wore a straw hat and had on regular men's clothes. I had to screech heavily on my brakes in order to stop before hitting him.

As I came to a stop he stepped around to my open window with his gun held up. Knowing that he could be very dangerous, I tried to calmly speak to him without upsetting him. "May I help you?" gently speaking his language. I was praying silently as hard as I could for protection from this man.

He looked at me, surprised that I knew his language. He remained silent as if observing to see if anyone else was with me.

"I am Mama Owensi. I have been having medical clinics at Nyumba ya Mungu today. May I ask who you are?"

Suddenly his countenance changed. He grasped his gun even more firmly and began shaking it at me. "This is who I am!" He said no more.

He walked around the Land Rover to the passenger side and got in. Then he pointed his machine gun straight at me and said, "Drive!"

My heart began pounding harder and harder. What did he want? Does he want the truck or me?

As I turned to look at him, with all control I could muster, I said, "I cannot drive as long as that gun is pointing at me! The road is very rough and we may hit a hole in the road." So I just sat there.

He then raised his gun pointing to the top of the car. I immediately sighed a feeling of relief. I was able to start moving again. The closer we got to Moshi the better I felt. We had been out over forty miles away. I was fearful that he wanted to hijack the truck and kill me. We continued to drive down the darkened road now in silence. I prayed with all my might.

As we were only about ten miles outside of Moshi town we began to see flashlights and several cars in the road. When I began to slow we could see that there were policemen present for some kind of accident.

"Stop, Stop!" he cried. I braked to a full stop. Just as quickly as he had stopped me, he now disappeared into the darkness with his machine gun.

I leaned my head over on the steering wheel in utter exhaustion and shook all over. I began praising my Lord for His protection and my release from this maniac. Tears flowed with relief.

Surely, seeing the police in the road ahead had startled him making him run away. Only God could have put those police and the accident scene to deter this man. How thankful I was to arrive safely without a scratch or any harm that night. God is so good!

> *"The hand of our God was on us, and he*
> *protected us from enemies and bandits along*
> *the way." Ezr 8:31b*

C: A Little Man

Sangaso (Sah-nn-GA-so) with his wife, Sala (SAH-lah) and their five children stood before me as the entire church looked on. Under a thorn tree with few leaves there was little shade. The sun was bright and it was very hot. We had just finished the worship service.

The Kirya village had been having services for only a short time following an invitation from a very sick woman who had been treated at the Clinic at Nyumba ya Mungu. Her not being able to walk because of her sickness, we brought her home following the clinic. It was our first time to be at her village. At her invitation we came the following week and began regular visits for preaching and clinics.

Sangaso and his wife made professions of faith at our first visit to Kirya.

On the day when I baptized Sangaso he told me that he and Sala wanted to be married. "Like Christians," he said.

Sangaso and Sala had been married as pagans—completely acceptable by everyone in the village. Now that they were Christians, they wanted their lives to exemplify the Christian life. I agreed to marry them on our next visit to his village.

For the wedding, Sangaso and his wife were as well dressed as most of those at church that day; wearing old, ragged clothing. Two of the five children, the youngest, had on no clothes. The other three had on scanty shorts. Sala held a bouquet of flowers Myrtice had brought from our garden.

As I performed the marriage in Swahili, Sangaso and his wife smiled profusely. The children squirmed as most children would have done. They were so happy. Every one present seemed to share their happiness.

Neither Sangaso nor his wife was five feet tall. Their children were small and apparently underfed. They had little worldly possessions but, upon becoming Christians, let everyone know that they were the happiest and most wealthy of those in the village. Christ to them was a magnificent possession.

> ". . listen carefully to the voice of the Lord your
> God and do what is right in his eyes" Ex 15:26

M: At the Gate

Witchdoctors really did not like us at all. We constantly won their patients over to the Christian way and they frankly lost business and their income. Knowing that they were powerful workers in the villages, we still didn't let their work bring us any fear. We just continued doing what we were there for; evangelizing and ministering to the people. We would hear that they wanted to run us out but we didn't let their threats bother us.

On our return from one long, tiring day working in clinics and holding services at Nyumba ya Mungu, we had to stop at our gate to unlock it. We had to have security for our home with the locked gate, two dogs and a house helper. Thievery was a big problem. Since I had gotten out of the Land Rover with the keys, I noticed a little pile of things by the post that someone had specifically placed there.

On picking it up I knew something was really strange. Here we had a bundle tied up. When I opened it, I saw it contained a plastic medicine spoon, feathers, piece of paper with Arabic writing and flowers. We couldn't quite figure out what this all meant.

Our house helper came out to assist us in unloading our vehicle. We showed him the little bundle. Immediately, he expressed extreme fright. He held up his hands not even wanting to touch it and began backing away from it.

"Nelson, what does this mean?"

"You have had a curse put on you by the witchdoctor! The plastic spoon is referring to Mama's clinic work, the feathers are about Baba's chickens and food here and flowers are the things they see in your yard at your home. The paper is telling about the curse on your preaching."

We assured him that we did not fear the curse of the witchdoctor because our Lord protects us from the curses of the evil one. We feel safe because we trust our Savior and His wonderful protection in our work.

Within a month, a pigeon kept coming around our home. We noticed that it had something tied to its leg. We failed to catch it but asked our helper if he could try to catch it after dark some day. He usually would do anything we asked but this time he absolutely refused.

"I know that pigeon is witchcraft. I don't want to have anything to do with it."

We didn't feel that we could insist because he was so fearful of witchcraft. We finally were able to catch the pigeon one evening while it was sitting on the back fence. When we took the little packet tied to its leg, we found nothing but writing in Arabic. When showed it to the helper, he still would not even glance at it. We again reassured him that we didn't fear this but had our trust and faith in our Savior. He was a Christian but still was obsessed with the fears he had had all his life.

When nothing seemed to happen to us from these 'curses', we realized that we were not receiving any more warnings. We felt that our witness of the power of God became stronger because of these incidents. God was able to use them for good to promote His power and witness.

> *"Love your enemies, do good to those who hate you.*
> *bless those who curse you, pray for those*
> *who mistreat you." Lk 6:27-28*

C: Postmark

We were getting ready for the first baptism at Kifaru (Kee-FAH-rue). I brought a letter which I had received, to the church and used it to illustrate about baptism. I told the people that we know by the stamp on a letter from where the letter comes. In like manner, I told them, baptism lets people know from where we come. A baptized person belongs to and is from Jesus. They seemed to understand and appreciate the illustration.

Not long after using the illustration we were ready for the baptizing. More than thirty were to be baptized. Everyone was excited.

After the preaching service we all walked together to the stream which was not very far from the church. As we were preparing for the baptizing, I noticed that a rather large crowd of strangers was approaching. The pastor told me that they were from a church several miles down the valley but he did not know why they were coming.

We proceeded with the baptizing and the strangers appeared to be favorably impressed. Each time I put someone under the water and brought them up again, the strangers, along with our church people, clapped their hands. When we had finished, the pastor spoke with some of the visitors then explained to me the real reason for their being there.

They had heard of my using the postage stamp to illustrate baptism. Not having seen my using the illustration they had misunderstood. At the time I did not know that the word meaning "postage stamp" and the one meaning "branding" were expressed in Swahili by the same word. They had come to the service to see me "brand" the new converts!

The visitors' church does not immerse for baptizing. Our immersing impressed them. They liked it and quite a few started attending our church. In the weeks and months following, a number of them, believing that what we did was right, joined us and we baptized them.

"We were therefore buried with him through baptism unto death in order that, just as Christ was raised from the dead through the glory of the Father, we too may live a new life." Ro 6:4

M: Help Me to See

The heat and humidity was tremendous under the metal roof of the Nyumba ya Mungu church. Perspiration kept running even into my eyes from my forehead. No air circulation made the room stuffy and stagnant with smells. The little church was filled with patients waiting to be seen as well as many more waiting on the outside. Flies kept clinging to my skin and trying to get into my mouth and eyes.

One of my American Lutheran friends, a nurse, who had come to Tanzania with her husband who was teaching in the International School, had joined me. She had offered to assist me on these busy days. She loved being able to do something for the people, even though she did not know Swahili. She was one of my greatest blessings, since I was always doing the full clinic on my own. While I did the examining, diagnosing, and treatment, she was able to dress the wounds, give the injections, and the immediate doses of medicines, and gather the medicines, which I had packaged at home, to give them.

About mid-day I looked up to see that my next patient was being led by a small girl holding a pole about the size of a broom stick with an old Maasai woman holding the other end. It was very evident that she was blind. The child positioned her in front of me. As the custom with all my patients and particularly the Maasai, I reached over and touched her arm and patted her lovingly.

"What can I do for you, dear grandmother?"

"Please, help me. Help me to see."

I began to examine her eyes first. They were both opaque with heavy white covering. I knew her eyes were permanently blinded. I continued to examine her to see if there were any other problems. Finding none, I responded to her by putting my hand on her boney shoulder and saying, "I'm sorry. Your eyes are finished. There is nothing that I can do to help you. I can't make your eyes to see, but I can help your heart to see. I can help you see our Heavenly Father."

She immediately grabbed my arm. "Please help me to see the Father."

Though other patients were pressing, I had to take a few moments to share with this dear woman about our Heavenly Father and our Lord Jesus Christ. Leaving, she was still holding on to the pole but with a smile on her face. I feel she had truly seen the Father.

"So we fix our eyes not on what is seen, but on what is unseen. For what is seen is temporary, but what is unseen is eternal." 2 Cor 4:18

Chapter Nine

Moshi II

Having set up the language school at Tigoni in Kenya we returned to Tanzania and spent eleven years living and working in the Moshi—Mt. Kilimanjaro area. During that time, the work developed in and around Moshi town, extended to the Nyumba ya Mungu area seventy five miles south and east of Moshi, around Mt. Kilimanjaro to Kenya on the northern slopes of the mountain and to Bukoba, far to the Western side of Tanzania.

C: Greeks Leave

The Greek community in and around Moshi had been significant. Many were well-to-do and owned businesses in the town. Others were farmers who raised dairy cattle and some had coffee and sisal plantations. We enjoyed their company, their traditions, and their knowledge of Tanzania from the 'other side'.

By the time we came, however, many had left and others were looking for ways to get out as the new government, following independence, did not look with favor on foreigners owning property.

The new regime had confiscated many of their businesses, farms and plantations. Several of those remaining became our good friends and we empathized with them in their plight of losing their life's work, property, and community, after they had been settlers for several generations here.

Just down the road from us, on a main corner, were the Greek Orthodox Church and Club. The church was the beautiful, typical white Greek Orthodox building with its dome extending upward—an impressive building, a replica of the churches in Greece.

The Greek families who remained took good care of the church property. There was little activity, however, as most of the Greeks had left. A priest would come from Nairobi for an occasional wedding or funeral. The church still had all its special items used in worship.

The Club House, across the yard from the church, was a single building: a large fellowship hall, with enough of everything to accommodate a large gathering.

Since arriving in Moshi, we had been looking for a suitable place for a town church. We were meeting in rented buildings in different "quarters" in the town. No suitable place for building a church was available. The local town planners had long since awarded the few plots designated for churches to others.

Mr. Ghikas, with whom we had become friends, came by the house one morning. He and I were members of the local Rotary Club. His wife, Rosemarie, was from Switzerland and a lovely woman. They had a farm on the lower slopes of the mountain and often brought us vegetables, milk and feta cheese, which we enjoyed. They also occasionally attended English services which we held in our home.

"Our community is now small in Moshi. We have decided to do something with our club and church and we wondered if you would have interest in buying the property."

With little thought and realizing that the corner where the Greek Church and club were located was one of the choicest sites in the town, "Mr. Ghikas, our mission doesn't have money to pay what that property is worth."

"Could you pay $25,000?"

Shocked, as I knew that the property was worth so much more, "Let me speak with others of our mission and get back with you."

Mr. Ghikas left. Myrtice and I were so elated that we immediately called several of the mission officers and decided that we should request funds for the purchase of the property. I called Mr. Ghikas and told him. This seemed to us to be an answer from God for us to have a church in

Moshi and one on the most desirable sites in the town. Only God could do that!

In the negotiations for the property, we agreed to keep the Greek Orthodox items of worship in the church so that the Greek community could use them for weddings and funerals if there were a need. The front of the church had several large painted icons representing apostles, and the dome had a beautifully painted likeness of Christ right in the top, so looking up, you could see Christ as if He were rising on the day of the resurrection. There were the font for baptizing babies in which they immerse three times, and containers for the incense used by the priests during the worship services.

We knew how important these items were to them. Another Greek man had attended our services on occasions. One day he said to me, "Your god seems so far away. If I were in need to approach my god all I would have to do is go to the church, take one of the icons and hold it close to my bosom."

I was pleased to tell him that our God is omnipresent, that He is approachable at any place at any time and always ready when we call on him.

> *"God is Spirit and his worshipers must worship in Spirit and in truth." Jn 4:24*

M: Gladness and Goodness

Soon our church began meeting at our beautiful, new Greek Orthodox Church building right in the middle of town. We wanted to reach the people who lived in this immediate area and I felt that this would be a great opportunity to begin visiting the residents of the large public housing near by.

Getting on my bicycle, I rode through the area and started methodically stopping at each house. Many were not at home or did not answer the door. Finally, a dear tribal lady, very, very pregnant, came to the door. She had been crying and looked miserable. After she invited me in we were able to have a heart to heart talk. Her name was Anna.

"My husband has been abusing me, and I have no family in the area. We have only recently moved to Moshi."

My heart felt deeply for her. "Is there anything I can do to help you?" I asked. She seemed like a poor beaten-up soul with no place to turn. Her home was bare of furniture, only a bed, table and two chairs. A small hot plate and a few pans were on the board by the sink.

She prepared some tea for me while we continued to talk. Our hearts seemed to bond immediately. She spilled out her heart and problems. She had been in a church several years before in her old home area and was very excited that there would be a church nearby. After a long conversation, we both prayed in earnest that God's Spirit would intercede to give guidance and comfort.

Anna did respond and bring her two older children to church. She seemed to take a new interest in life and living for the Lord. We had many visits and times of counsel and sharing.

At the end of that month, I knew I needed to visit again and check on her as I had missed seeing her. We had been leading another church on the past Sundays. When I knocked on the door, a very happy Anna peeked out and welcomed me warmly. She had two little bundles all snuggly wrapped and placed in a large flat basket used for selling oranges or other fruit.

"I am very happy; you have your twins!" I exclaimed, rejoicing. "Remember I told you that I thought you were going to have twins!"

She was all smiles with that proud new-mother look. "Yes, they arrived on the weekend. Everything went so well. Even my husband seemed pleased. He said he would try to go to church with me too."

"I am so happy for you. You see, God is good and He is with you during these difficult times. What did you names your babies?"

"I named them for the blessing that God has given me. We call our two girls, Gladness and Goodness, for the feelings that God has given me."

We know the Lord was pleased with Anna and did continue to bless this family as they became active in church and faithful to the Lord.

'I am still confident of this; I will see the goodness of the Lord in the land of the living. Wait for the Lord; be strong and take heart and wait for the Lord." Ps 27:13-14

M: Faith Rekindled

The town of Moshi was near the area of much agriculture and commerce. Majestic Mt. Kilimanjaro brought many tourists and visitors to the area. It always seemed to have a bustling atmosphere. We constantly saw new faces in town. However, one face seemed to keep appearing in the same places that we frequented as the Post Office, Bank and shops.

This little old European woman with white hair and a back bent over arrived at these places in a chauffeur driven Mercedes-Benz. She kept to herself, never looking our way. When standing near her in line somewhere we would smile and express a greeting but she never responded

Carlos had met one friendly European at the Post Office one day. The old lady had just gone out. He asked who this old lady was.

The man said "That's my grandmother! She's a sour and unpleasant woman. You just need to stay out of her way!"

This stirred Carlos to want to help her. "Maybe I could visit her and give her some encouragement. She seems to be so dejected."

"Sorry, but I don't think she would even open her door to you. She is very unhappy and keeps to herself. I live with her so I know her well."

When Carlos shared with me about Mrs. Anna Berkley, we both felt that she needed some spiritual help. With all the African churches we also had an English-speaking church going well in the town and felt that the fellowship would be a real strength of caring. Most of the members were from countries all over the world; Japan, Australia, Canada, Greece, Germany and Great Britain.

Later, as Carlos was passing near her house he decided to stop for a visit. He knocked on her door and waited a long time before she appeared. He greeted her and explained that he was leading the new church in town and wanted to invite her to come. She slammed the door in his face.

After a few weeks he decided to see if he could visit her again. Bravely, he knocked on her door again. This time she allowed him to come in. She wasn't very friendly but was kind enough to listen to him. He just wanted to help her in any way that he could. She seemed to soften and shared some about her background.

"I moved from Switzerland to Tanganyika when I was only a child, with my parents. They developed a huge sisal plantation and had several other businesses. I later married someone from my country. We developed a coffee and tea plantation in the Lushoto region in the mountains of Tanganyika. They produced well and we became very wealthy.

We had only one daughter who studied in Switzerland, later married and moved to South Africa and is now an invalid. I am very upset with God. My husband died in mid-life and I've had to manage the business alone for many years. My daughter was the only one I had and now she is ill all the time and I can't even visit her because of the country restrictions." As she recounted her life story she neared tears.

Her resentment came from having to work all those years on her own and then having her only daughter away with a debilitating disease. From her childhood she had been a Lutheran but she felt that God had failed her.

Carlos counseled and talked with her a long time trying to encourage her to see the good things God had done for her. Before he left he asked if he could pray for her.

Again, her deep anger surfaced. "It won't do any good," she said.

In his gentle way, he was able to persuade her to let him have a short prayer for her.

Gradually we were both able to visit with her, building a relationship of friendship. Often I would carry food and flowers from our garden to her. Her grandson had now moved out of the country and her loneliness seemed greater. I began to notice her weakening and not moving around very well. After my encouragement she did go to the doctor. He found cancer in this eighty nine year old woman. As we were ready for furlough, we asked our English-speaking church to minister to her. Before we left we knew she would be having chemo therapy making the days difficult for her.

After arriving in the states, I found a lovely white wig that I sent to help her in the days of losing her hair. The church was faithful to her. They kept us informed about her condition and response. They told us that the wig brought her joy unimaginable and she appreciated their attention.

When we returned, we found her whole attitude had taken a complete turn-around. She was responding to prayer and discussions about the Lord and the Bible. One day while we were visiting she recommitted herself to the Lord. She always wore her wig proudly, expressing her gratitude repeatedly. There were none available in this country.

When the church began meeting in the Greek Orthodox building, her driver would pull up close to the open back door where she could hear the service. Though she was weak she wanted to worship. Her anger had turned to joy, her rudeness to kindness, her conversation to gentleness, and her faith to strength in the Lord again.

After several months when I was visiting with her I saw she needed to be hospitalized. She was becoming weaker. I took her to one of the good mission hospitals outside of town on the mountain. Within two days she passed away. The church had a beautiful funeral in remembrance of this dear lady who had been estranged from the Father but was now safe in His bosom.

"Restore to me the joy of your salvation
and grant me a willing spirit, to sustain me." Ps 51:12

C: Boy Loses Leg

We knew that there were crocodiles in the lake at Nyumba ya Mungu but had heard of no problems with them. Then we heard that a boy had lost his leg to one. When we visited the boy and his family in the hospital, they pled that I find and kill the croc. I agreed to try.

The next Tuesday I went with Myrtice to the area when she was planning to hold a clinic. I took my rifle. After assisting in getting things set up for clinic, I went to the edge of the lake where the croc had attacked the boy. Knowing that crocs are very skittish, I found a place in some bushes near the water's edge where I believed it would neither see nor hear me. I waited.

After more than an hour, I could see movement in the water some distance away. A croc was coming out of the water. I watched as he moved to a sunny place on the sand. Even though I was quite a long distance away I hesitated to move or make a sound in fear of his hearing me. Although he was too far away for a good shot I decided to try. Taking aim, I shot. I could see that I hit the sand just in front of him. He slithered into the water. I waited again for quite a long time but did not see him again. It was getting close to the noon, so I went back to the church where Myrtice and I had our sack lunch.

After lunch, I went back to the lake and found a shaded place nearer where I had seen the croc that morning, and waited. After another hour, I again saw movement in the water and the croc appeared. This time he came only about half way out of the water. I could see by his uneasy movements that he was leery of my being nearby. I moved just a bit in order to take aim. He heard me or sensed my movements and quickly went back into the water. I did not get a shot. By late afternoon he did not appear again. I went back to the church and assisted Myrtice's getting things packed up and put into the Land Rover. We went home disappointed and hoped and prayed that the croc would not attack anyone else.

The people told us later that they were taking extreme caution when going into or near the lake. Even though the croc did not attack again we occasionally warned the people of the danger. Soon after that we went on furlough and when returning after a year we were told that no one else had been attacked. As he had not been seen again we believed that the croc had moved to another area.

"Protect them by the power of your name" Jn 17:11b

M: Visitors

Most days were full with clinics three times a week, women's classes, and many, many visitors passing through this area as we were half way from the coast to Nairobi, the capitol of Kenya. Hospitality was a necessity and we enjoyed our many visitors from fellow missionaries to stateside guests, or visitors from Kew Gardens in England. Carlos had begun to collect wild orchids from the trees and grassland in all the areas where our churches were located. The scientists were encouraging and helpful in identifying many species.

The yard behind our house became filled with wild exotic tropical plants which we collected and enjoyed immensely. The old cement fish tank that was there when we moved had been used to baptize many of our town church members from the group at Boma la Mbuzi (Goat Corral) as well as our English fellowship.

Christmas and Easter were special times to invite 'lonely' town folks from many different countries. Our daughter, Debra, had friends from many countries around the world, since she was in the International School. One day she brought home a friend named "Mena Hemingway." Of course our thoughts went to the famous writer Ernest Hemingway.

When we asked her about him she casually responded, "Oh, he was my grandfather." Mena told us about her situation up on the slopes of the mountain. Her father, Pat Hemingway, was in charge of the wildlife management in all the country. Her mother had died when she was just a small child. She had been adopted. Her father continued to take care of her.

Several holidays we included them in our family celebrations. They loved the family atmosphere, decorations and holiday food that filled the table with extras to take home.

"This is some of the happiest times with you folks on holidays. It's so good to be with friends and have so much fun," they told us.

We were as pleased as they were to have them join the festivities with other lonely people in town. Our house was usually packed for the Christmas meal. We usually went all out for making it like a traditional meal we would have at home, even with turkey which Carlos raised, coconut cake, boiled custard and divinity, all homemade. Everyone ate to their fill and over!

Pat, Mena's father, was deeply dedicated to preserving the wildlife and expressed his faith in the Lord. They were very interesting people that added a new dimension to our lives.

Some of our most unusual visitors were from communist Hungary. They were promoting agricultural incentives to the local farmers. We had met them and realized that they were never associating with anyone in town. On one Christmas we invited this family with their two small children to share this special day with us. We always have a Christmas crèche on display on our main coffee table. This opened up the opportunity to share about the real meaning of Christmas.

They had many questions and talked freely about the occasion. After some time the husband shared that this opened his memories of his grandparents who were Christians.

"I have not thought about my grandparents who passed away a long time ago. But now I do remember that they attended church but had to do it in secret. I thought they were idiots because the state imprisoned those claiming Christianity."

With nostalgia, he began to refer to these times with tears. He had previously blocked these memories in the years of his atheism. God used this incident for us to share fully again their need for the Lord in their lives.

> "Seek the Lord while he may be found; call
> on him while he is near. Let him turn to the Lord,
> and he will have mercy on him, and to our God,
> for he will freely pardon." Isa 55:6,7b

C: Preach Again

Soon after arriving in Moshi, a fellow missionary told us about Muturi (Moo-TOO-ree), a Kikuyu who with his family was farming at Endoneti (Aa-n-doe-NAY-tee), high on the northern slopes of Mt. Kilimanjaro—opposite to where we lived in Moshi. As the Tanganyika / Kenya border stretched across these northern slopes, much of the northern side of the mountain was in Kenya. The Kenya government had designated land to Kenya families for farming. We made contact with Muturi and soon began services at his house.

Muturi's neighbors were scattered. Each family had settled on the plot of land assigned to them by the government. There were no close-knit villages as had been the case in most of Tanzania where we had lived.

At Muturi's invitation, I drove up and around the mountain, passed the district headquarters at Loitokitok (Loy-TALK-key-talk) and on to his place where I set up my tent next to his house. We first had services in his house and when the attendance grew we met outside. After only a few trips, many people were attending, coming from quite a far distance.

Maasai who lived in the area often came by. They would stand at the door with one foot resting on the middle of the other leg; spear in hand, but would not come in.

On one occasion, leaving Moshi at daybreak, I arrived in mid-afternoon, set up my tent and visited with Muturi from settlement to settlement until dark. Most of the people were digging the land preparing for planting but they promised to be at Muturi's by sundown. When we got back to his house there were many already gathered for the service.

As soon as we arrived, we had sweet tea and stewed white potatoes, which Muturi's wife had prepared for us. Immediately afterwards we began the service.

We sang, with everyone participating enthusiastically. I preached in Swahili with Muturi's interpreting into Kikuyu. The people listened, continually nodding in approval.

Following my preaching, while the people milled around outside, Muturi's wife served more food, the Kikuyu favorite -- dried beans, dried corn and arrowroot cooked together. The corn and beans had been soaked separately in water all day before cooking them with the arrowroot.

At the insistence of those present, I preached the second time.

When I had finished someone said, "Brother Missionary, we are hungry for the Word. Please preach again."

I preached the third time.

Again, someone said, "We like your preaching. Won't you preach again?"

I preached the fourth time and again someone asked that I preach once again. By this time it was 1:00 a.m. I said that we must close and invited the people to come again the following afternoon after they finished their working the fields.

The people went out and disappeared into the dark. I went to my tent and slept with a great deal of satisfaction. At the close of each preaching there had been people who publicly accepted Jesus as Savior.

The second and third days and nights were very much like the first, after which I packed up and drove back around the mountain and down to Moshi. I felt the Lord's blessings on these past few days. My spirit was so elated that I just wanted to shout and praise the Lord!

We came to Endonet many times. After meeting in and near the Muturi house, we gained permission from the Kenya government offices at Loitokitok to build a church house next to Muturi's. The church continued to grow under his leadership. God's hand was surely in this place.

"Preach the Word; be prepared in season and out of season; correct, rebuke and encourage with great patience and careful instruction." 2 Ti. 4:2

M: Kilimanjaro Calls

Wherever you drive in the Moshi region, the beautiful snows of Mt. Kilimanjaro draw your attention. Some days heavy clouds cover it, but on the clear day, it is a magnificent sight. Visitors from all over the world climb the giant of over 19,000 feet and to see its large glacier on top. We could look from our dining room window at the gorgeous view.

We kept thinking this would be a wonderful opportunity to view the area from the top of the mountain. We understood that high altitude could affect the brains of anyone under fifteen so the girls waited to make the climb. Carlos decided to join two fellow missionary evangelists for the five-day adventure, three days up and two days down.

Upon their return, we heard about the agonizing climb, cold temperatures, breathless times and extreme fatigue that comes in the high altitudes. Even with hats and sunscreen, the sun was so intense it still caused problems. Their faces were sunburned and mouths covered with fever blisters.

They all said it was the hardest physical fete that they had ever tried and one of the most beautiful sights; they all decided that one time was enough.

After our two older daughters became over fifteen, we decided that it was time for us girls to try the climb. Several journeymen girls (college graduates who serve for two years) and friends decided to join us making a party of seventeen in all. We were all excited, prepared our heavy clothing, strong boots, and extra snack food for energy. We had several guides who led the way.

Our first stop was at a beautiful mountain stream surrounded by the most unusual moss and plants, some we had never seen before. We enjoyed drinking its fresh cold water. The first night we stayed in the rough housing on the trail, which had only board bunk beds with all sexes sleeping in one large room.

Kerosene lanterns dimly lighted the room. We were all too tired to think of anything else but sleep. Our sleeping bags were warm and cozy on the hard wooden planks called beds. After a tasteless simple meal cooked by the guides, we all fell fast asleep. Toilets were hard, wood, outside latrines. The wind was so cold no one delayed in the toilets.

The next morning we were awakened before sunrise by our guides who had coffee and some porridge for us. We had only limited water to wash our faces. After packing up our sleeping bags, our climb began again.

The terrain continued to change from vegetation to areas with only a few low rough shrubs and colorful wild straw flowers. After passing this area, called the saddleback, (between the lesser and larger peaks) we entered higher altitude that had no vegetation, only rocks and sand with strong winds blowing hard in our faces. To stay upright, it was necessary to bend forward into the wind.

On the second night we were 14,000 ft high and breathing became difficult for some. The same type of housing was available. The winds being stronger and colder, most of us stayed inside for our soup and bread. It took a much longer time to heat the food since the altitude affected the fire, making the boiling point much lower. Immediately after supper, everyone fell exhausted onto her hard bed. It was good to snuggle up in our sleeping bags.

Winds blew hard again with sand and dirt hitting our faces. It was nothing but desolation in every way that we looked; only sand, rocks and desert-like land. Breathing again became more difficult, but we continued in line, following the guides. Our rest stops became more frequent and longer. How wonderful to see the cabins ahead that late afternoon. All fell into the bunks even before opening their packs with the sleeping bag. I don't believe we had ever been more tired than this time at 17,000 ft. elevation. The night was short but sleep was deep.

Before midnight, the guides awakened us to climb the scree surface. Several of the girls became altitude-sick and had to remain, others turned back after a short distance. The darkness kept us from seeing the dangerous areas through which we were passing. We all stayed close in follow-the-leader line helping each other over the difficult rocks and slippery areas.

As the first light of dawn appeared we could see that we were near the top. Waves of nausea kept hitting us, but chewing on tart dried apricots seemed to help. As the sun rose, we were right on the top rim of Mt. Kilimanjaro, seeing the magnificence of God's creation. It looked as if we could see the whole world around us in every direction for hundreds and hundreds of miles.

The snow and glacier reflected the beautiful sun rays in the depth of the crater of the old volcano. Even some puffs of smoke rose from one deep area, indicating still some type of activity there. We all had to enjoy the fullness of the beautiful sunrise and drink in the majesty of the mountain. It was a significant moment of personal worship that we were all feeling.

After filling our senses with all this beauty, we signed the book to register our climb. We were eager to return to warmer climates and easier breathing. We slowly began the descent down the mountain on the loose scree, sliding and slipping all the way, sometimes ten feet at a time.

As we returned to the sleeping quarters, we realized that out of the seventeen who went with us only my girls and I made it to the top. The others had become altitude sick. Other parties joining us along the way made a large group. We kept going, past the second building, stopping at the first one. We really 'died' with sleep that night.

The following day we made it to the foot of the mountain with funny tales of incidents on this adventure. The guides made beautiful crowns of the wild, straw flowers picked from the second level of the trip and gave them to us who had made it to the top. Our family was proud that each had received one.

The days ahead proved the trauma of the climb on our faces and feet. We lost most of our toenails from the straight decent down the mountain. Our chapped faces felt pain from sun and windburn. Huge fever blisters covered our lips in spite of all the protection we had used. We will always cherish the glorious experience, the magnificence of the mountain and the closeness we felt to God.

> *"In his hand are the depths of the earth, and the mountain peaks belong to him." Ps 95:4*

C: Koyan (KOE-yon) and the Pancakes

I sat alone on the carved wooden stool near my Land Rover, ate the two large fatty pancakes, and drank the large tin cup of sweet tea, which Koyan had instructed one of his wives to prepare for me. I knew that she had boiled the tea for quite a long time with much milk and much sugar—the customary African way. I felt that the tea was safe to drink, her having boiled it so long. I also knew that Koyan and his family were inside and drinking the clabber milk mixed with cow's blood; their normal evening meal.

Koyan Ole (O-lay) Mashunka (Mah-SHOO-n-kah), a well-to-do Maasai chief, had invited me to stay at his place. He and his family had attended services at Endonet, several miles away. At first, they, with other Maasai, would only stand at the door to look and listen. Eventually they came inside where some accepted Jesus.

Koyan wanted a church near where he and his family lived. I was there for four days visiting and preaching. I slept in my Land Rover and had those two large, fatty pancakes and that large metal cup of sweet African tea in the morning, in the mid afternoon and again late in the evening.

Koyan, not like some Maasai, had settled down. As he grew older, he had left following his cattle and had built a number of houses of varying sizes with metal roofs. He still lived with and from his cattle, however. His cows, when not taken by his boys in search of grass and water, would be in a corral adjoining his house. At times, his boys would be gone days and sometimes weeks, searching for water and grazing for his cattle.

Koyan had taken a keen interest in what we were doing. Most of the local Maasai had great respect for him. He used his own money to buy materials for building the Kikelelwa church next to his house, even though he never attended services. Although he sent his children and his wives, he did not come. I was not able to determine why. Each time I returned to his place during the day or in the evening, he was there to welcome and visit with me. He appeared to understand what being a Christian meant, but he never professed being one. While I was there several Maasai accepted Jesus as Savior.

I spent three days at Kikelelwa; preaching and visiting neighboring Maasai. Early on the morning of the fourth day I was making ready for my descent of the mountain and return to Moshi.

Koyan approached and said, "I want to go to Moshi with you."

"I will be pleased to have you go with me."

He went away to prepare for the trip and I began thinking of what to expect. I doubted that I would be very pleased to have him with me because Maasai normally avoid bathing. They are proud to tell you that they have never used soap on their bodies.

"Cows don't like soap. They will be angry if we put soap on our bodies." I had heard that many times.

I had also heard that when the cows get up from the ground early in the morning, children stood ready with their pots to collect the cows' urine. It is used to clean household vessels and for bathing. You can see why I did not expect to be happy to have Koyan in the Land Rover with me. High on the slopes of the mountain it was quite cold. I would normally close all windows and the vent above the dashboard. On this trip, I realized that I would have to leave the windows and vent above the dashboard open.

After having my pancakes and sweet tea on the fourth day, Koyan and I put our things into the Land Rover and set out around and down the mountain to Moshi.

Soon we were winding down the side of the mountain. The roads were dry and dusty but not slippery as they had been on so many trips when it was raining. I used 4-wheel drive only a few times. I was cold but I closed neither the windows nor the vent over the dashboard.

On the road, Koyan and I had some good discussions. I tried to find out why he had not publicly confessed Christ, but did not.

Once, after quite long time of silence, Koyan said, 'I don't like to be with the Luo people. They are dirty. They smell bad.'

I knew many Luo. They were from the Kisumu area of Kenya and many lived in and near Nairobi. A few lived on the mountain slopes not too far from Koyan. They bathe and use soap. In my opinion they are quite clean people.

I asked, 'Why do you say that?'

His quick and straightforward answer was, "They do not circumcise."

I had nothing else to say but thought, "Guess one's own smell is not offensive but another man's is. Their not practicing the right customs makes them 'dirty.'"

Koyan always traveled with his chief's stick. He held onto it as we drove down the mountainside. Approximately 15 inches long, it was smooth, beautifully carved, and thin with a round and pointed knob at one end. The other end had the same shape but was smaller.

On the way down the mountain, I commented on how his stick impressed me. He made no response, but when we arrived at the place where he had told me he wanted to go, without comment he handed the stick to me, saying that he wanted me to have it.

"I don't want to take your stick. It is too important to you. You will need it when you sit in judgment back in your village."

"Please take it. I want you to have it. I can have another one carved before I need it again."

I gladly received Koyan's stick and laid it on the Land Rover seat next to me. I waved farewell to him and told him that I would look forward to seeing him again in Kikelelwa.

When I see Koyan's stick, I recall the four days spent at his place, the pancakes and the tea. I recall other trips I made to Kikelelwa and wonder if Koyan ever professed Jesus as his Savior.

"Whoever believes in the Son has eternal life, but whoever rejects the Son will not see life, for God's wrath remains on him." Jn 3:36

M: Standing in the Rain

The rain was pouring heavily and had been for several hours. I was thinking how happy that I was not out in a village for clinics. It would be mud, mud, mud, and sliding around on the roads.

I heard someone calling loudly outside. Out by our gate was a small girl standing in the downpour. I could not imagine anyone being out in such weather, with frequent bursts of lightning and thunder. Usually the Africans stay close in during bad weather.

I grabbed an umbrella to go out to meet her, knowing she was scared of our dogs, which we need to protect our property. As I approached her I recognized her as being from a village ten miles out. She looked about nine years old. There was no doubt why she was there. Both cheeks were so swollen that she looked like a chipmunk with two walnuts in its mouth. I drew her close to me and we hurried back to the house.

"Rosa, what are you doing in this heavy rain? You shouldn't be out with mumps!"

"I was hurting so badly. I knew you could help me. You are the only one who helps me."

Poor Rosa had a high fever and looked miserable. I quickly wrapped a large, old towel around her to help dry her and warm her. The air was warm but I was afraid she would go into a terrible chill. I fixed some hot tea, African style, which was more milk and sugar than tea. I found some medicines for her to help her pain and recovery.

"Please stay inside until your fever is over. I am afraid you may get pneumonia. You need a lot of rest, so please just stay in bed for several days until the swelling has improved."

As soon as Carlos returned from his meeting, I took Rosa to her home. It was a slippery drive out to her village. We went into her hut but both parents were away. I tucked her into her bedding on a grass mat inside the bare room and had a prayer for her.

"Mama Owensi, thank you from my heart. You are my best friend."

"You are my dear friend too. I must go. Remember, take care of yourself and I will keep praying for your fast recovery."

Eventually she became a beautiful person who was always eager and ready to serve the Lord in her church. I had prayed that I would be a good mentor to her.

"And in the church God has appointed. . .those having the gift of healing, those able to help others," 2Cor 12:28

C: With Rats and Fleas

"Trucks stand idle along every street because there are no drivers. You see only old people and the very young," someone who had recently been to Bukoba (Boo-KOE-bah) told us. "AIDS has devastated the entire area."

It was hard for us to comprehend, as we had assisted in the development of churches there years before, prior to AIDS having invaded the territory. The plague from AIDS had come to Tanzania after we left and had transferred to Namibia.

We recall fondly our visits to Bukoba. We had not lived there but made many trips to Bukoba to assist the churches while living in Moshi and in Iringa.

The people were exceptionally friendly and had welcomed us with open arms and open hearts. The church leaders and members had requested assistance in getting their churches on track. We were happy to help.

The Convention had chosen Mahimbo (Mah-HEEM-bow) and me to serve as directors of the Department of Stewardship and Evangelism. He and I made many trips together. Sometimes I went only with my family.

We were fascinated with the things, which were distinctively different at Bukoba. The people raised coffee as a cash crop, which provided money needed for daily living. We did not see people drinking coffee, but were amazed at their chewing roasted coffee beans. Venders in the markets sold triangular banana bark packets filled with the roasted coffee beans.

Water was scarce and we did not see soap for washing of hands prior to eating. When food was ready and everyone had sat down in a circle someone walked by and swished a small bushy limb across upturned hands—a ceremonial washing. Most often this was outside under a shed or under a tree. Women and girls brought out clay pots or large tin pans with cooked bananas or arrowroot and spooned it out onto banana leaves spread out on the ground. After praying, we took from the food with our fingers and ate. Sometimes there would be sweet African tea.

One afternoon as we drove out to one of the churches, we saw people coming down a hillside with various kinds of containers on their heads. The pastor explained that they were bringing down salt, which they had dug from the hillside. We stopped and visited with a number of people.

Looking at the salt I said, "It's gray. Is it real salt?"

"Yes. We call it ashes salt because it looks like ashes."

Taking a bit between my thumb and index finger and touching a piece to my tongue I said, "Yep, it is salt all right."

It was quite strong salt. The pastor told us that most people had no money for buying salt in the stores and that the salt taken from the hillside was called 'chumvi (choo-M-vee) majivu' (ma-GEE-voo) or ashes salt. We readily understood why.

On the first night with the family with whom we stayed, Myrtice and I were given a hut to ourselves for sleeping. Someone had moved out to give us a private place. They had spread fresh grass from the fields on the floor. We had folding, canvas cots on which we would sleep. The grass smelled fresh and looked new but unfortunately, the fleas in the straw were still plentiful. When I awoke during the night after hearing a sound, I turned on my flashlight to see a large rat running on one of the poles which supported the grass roof.

Everywhere we went the people welcomed us warmly and whenever I preached, people made public professions of faith. Each place we went, there were people to baptize.

Sometimes we walked long distances to find enough water. Later, when we were told that so many had died from AIDS we were really saddened. The Lord had begun a good work but now the devil was busy destroying it. Many churches remained faithful in caring for the victims of this plague.

"After this I looked and there we was a great multitude that no one could count, From every nation, tribe people and language, .standing before the throne and in front of the Lamb" Rev 7:9

M: Nothing Left

The day had been long. The flies were swarming around us, making it difficult to speak since they often go into the mouth. We just spit them out and carried on. In the hot, humid days before the rainy monsoon season the flies, mites and bugs of all kinds seem to hunt us out. As I was winding down the clinic, Agata, one of the faithful members, came running through the open door at the Kifaru (Rhinoceros) Church.

"Could you please see one more patient?" She asked with a begging tone.

"Yes, if you have someone who is really in need."

"My friend, Nosidai, has just given up living. I found her curled up in a corner waiting to die."

"Please bring her in."

Agata, with a friend, tenderly held this frail, skinny woman. She was struggling to breathe. She did not look like she weighed seventy-five lbs. I quickly stood up to help put her on one of the benches. Her wheezing and difficulty breathing was severe. I immediately checked her chest with a stethoscope to hear the problem. She wanted to speak but kept struggling to speak and breathe.

Finally she said "I can't pay you. All I had has been paid to the witchdoctor."

"You don't have to pay here. Christians in America have helped to buy the medicines for you. We want to take care of you in God's love and mercy."

"I have been sick for several months. I went to my witchdoctor for help. He first charged me the only goat I had to buy his medicine and help. Then he wanted my chickens. When I didn't have anything else to give him, he took my clothes and sleeping mat. I have nothing else for I am a widow and have nothing more. I was still so sick. All that I could do was just die. I knew I couldn't pay for any more help." She explained with struggling breaths.

Without delay, I was able to give her an injection for her severe asthma. After examining her and finding other problems, I had medicines to help her.

"Nosidai, we are giving you these medicines, but we know that our help comes from the Lord. We want you to trust and believe that the Lord Jesus loves you and even gave his life for your sins. He has promised everlasting life if you trust him and put your faith fully in him."

"I want to believe. I want God's help. Help me to understand better."

After a short time of helping her to understand the basics of faith in Christ, she prayed a prayer of repentance. From that moment on, her life was utterly changed. We took her to her hut since she was still very weak. I slipped her a few shillings to buy some food. Agata promised to buy food for her and prepare it for that evening. Her breathing was easy now and she had an inhaler to assist her breathing, along with other medicines, which I gave her. She now was all smiles and had a real hope in living.

The next Sunday, Nosidai came forward to make her profession of faith in Christ. She glowed with joy. She was faithful to all the classes for new members to grow in her faith. After several weeks a baptism was planned for all the new Christians at Kifaru. Nosidai passed the examination that questioned her understanding of what she was doing and was sincere.

The whole church walked, or rather swayed in their walk with singing, to the nearby creek where we were to baptize. The creek was so low and the banks were quite steep. One of the men assisted the candidates to get into the stream, where Carlos baptized them. They then helped get them up the steep bank. At the top Agata stood with a drying cloth to wipe the water off their faces.

As Nosidai went down and into the water she seemed so happy and committed to following Christ faithfully. As she was helped to the top of the bank, Agata reached over to wipe her face. She threw her arms up in front of her face to keep the towel away.

"I don't want to ever wipe this water off my face! It helps me to remember what Christ did for me, how he was buried and rose again. I am really a new person. I always want to live for him."

Yes, Nosidai did have a new life and new hope. She was no longer in despair of having nothing left, but is living in the fullness of life with Christ.

> "We were therefore buried with him through baptism into death in order that, just as Christ was raised from the dead through the glory of the Father, we too may live a new life." Ro 6:4

Chapter Ten

Iringa

Iringa (Ee-REEN-gah) is a Regional Headquarters in the high ridge of mountains above the Ruaha (Roo-AH-ha) Valley. It has the only diamond-cutting factory in the land. The Hehe (HAY-hay) people who live in and around Iringa are very responsive to the gospel.

The weather is cool and, during the raining season, the landscape is beautiful. When the rains stop in May or June there will be no more rain until October or November. During this time, it is very dry, windy and dusty but still quite cool.

Coming from the Coast, you ascend a long escarpment climbing from less than 2,000 feet elevation to 3,500 feet by the time you reach Iringa. In the valley below, there are many baobabs, acacia and many others unusual trees amid an array of most beautiful wild flowers and cacti. Before reaching the top of the escarpment there is, on the left, a very large vanilla orchid vine winding profusely in several trees. When in bloom the plant is extremely beautiful.

M: Convention Calls

This new adventure in Iringa began when the Tanzania Convention requested that we direct the building of a conference center. It would provide a much-needed place for meetings.

They had tried various options for annual meetings and conferences but many had failed. They asked the government for the use of the boarding schools while schools were out of session. Sometimes, after the government had granted permission, they recanted.

On one occasion, pastors and other church leaders were traveling to the place of meeting and got word that the government had withdrawn permission for the use of the meeting place.

Many arrived, found out that the meeting place was canceled and had to return home. Not only failing to have an annual Tanzania Convention but the wasting of time and funds was overwhelming.

In a later gathering, Convention leaders decided to request of the mission to assist in the building of their own facility. Research clearly showed the need of a facility large enough to house up to 250 delegates, a meeting hall, kitchen and dining hall storage, lounge and library. It would provide for conferences as well as the training of leaders.

The mission responded favorably and requested the Foreign Mission Board to seek out volunteers to help. Funds were granted by the board and word went out about the need.

Shortly, one large church in North Augusta, South Carolina, was willing to take on the challenge. These were amazing people. They assisted in architecture, basis plans; materials needed and volunteers to come. A team from the church came out to survey the area and began planning for the buildings.

For the next two and one half years, wave after wave of volunteers came, twelve to twenty, in groups staying and working for two weeks at a time. Some from other churches came along with these or on their own. Every group brought materials, some food and other supplies which were not available locally.

Our task was that of finding land, organizing all activities concerning the construction of the buildings, temporary housing and caring for the workers. We would make arrangements for all materials needed on the project.

We met each group in Dar es Salaam and brought them to Iringa. We took them back to Dar at the end of their work period and often brought another group back to Iringa on the same trip, keeping the construction going continually.

Providing housing and meals was challenging. Keeping the volunteers involved and happy, especially when homesickness occurred, was a daily venture on our part. Working together to complete this marvelous facility for the African churches was a wonderful experience.

Searching out housing for the volunteers and ourselves was the first big task.

> *"If anyone serves, he should do it with the strength God provides, So that in all things God may be praised through Jesus Christ." IPe 4:llb*

C: Housing Woes

The town literally appeared to have no available housing. None! Time was passing quickly and we knew for the project to take off, we must find some kind of housing. After talking to everyone in the government offices and local businesses we were still stymied.

Only when we began driving around the community did we come upon what appeared to be a last resort; a small, unfinished house which, with some work, could be made ready for volunteers. Another, with part of the roof caved in, could be our living quarters.

It took some work for us to settle in. The house where we would live had no water in the small kitchen. We would wash dishes outside at the back on a raised concrete slab next to which was a water tap. We would take water from there for kitchen use. With no hot water for bathing in the old, stained bathtub, we would heat pans of water on the stove; enough to cut off the chill.

We had room for only a little furniture in the part with a roof. The rest would go into storage. We sort of camped, knowing this was the only living place available. We could manage; our knowing that our family now had dispersed.

Janice was in college in the US. Ruth was married and also in college. Debra was a senior in boarding school in Kenya.

The house we got for volunteers was an unfinished, four-room concrete block house with a corrugated metal roof. Vandals had broken much of the window glass. There were no inside doors, electricity nor water. We must find beds and bedding, cooking utensils, and other bare necessities.

We would have to find a contractor to put new doors in and replace the broken windowpanes; all of this before the volunteers arrived.

Volunteers had to use bunk beds and live in very close quarters with only one bathroom. At first, the volunteers, after finishing a day's work, bathed in a small stream near the building site. Later, we set up a temporary shower outside, behind one of the buildings.

Myrtice would cook and supervise the activities at the volunteer house. We would eat most of our meals with the volunteers there. We had our work cut out for us.

With God's help we put it all together, so that when we brought the first group of volunteers from Dar es Salaam they settled in very well. Most said that they had not lived under such conditions before but were gracious and did not complain.

"For I have learned to be content whatever
the circumstances." Php 4:11b

M: Hungry Crowd

"I'm so hungry I could eat a cardboard box," called out one of the volunteers as he came in from a full day of hard work.

I soon found out that they literally could eat huge quantities. These men were hard working and very hungry. Feeding and keeping them satisfied and happy was my biggest task.

Food supplies in Iringa were about the same as in other parts of Tanzania. There were only a few basics. Fresh food from the open market varied from season to season. Sometimes it was sparse. Since my resources were limited, the volunteers started bringing 'goodies' in their suitcases that I could use. They brought seasonings, various mixes, dessert fixings, cheese and canned goods.

Before coming to Iringa, I had prepared meals for many visitors. Doing it daily for two and one half years was a much bigger task. Organizing of menus from whatever food we had on hand was a challenging task. I had my old "Betty Crocker Cook Book" from which to plan menus.

I planned, multiplied recipe quantities and took on the job joyfully. I loved cooking and knowing that it made the volunteers happy added to my pleasure. I found two African helpers willing to learn to assist me. We also had to care for piles of laundry.

Women volunteers contributed a significant role in the project even though they were not numerous.

Several stayed for extra weeks to assist in various projects; canning vegetables, preparation of food, making sheets and curtains - a vital part of their ministry. A few even went out to assist the men in construction.

They were such a blessing to me, easing up the heavy load of caring for the workers as well as helping perform projects for the future use of the Center.

"I just won't ride in that car!" cried out my volunteer college student, as she looked in, and saw the full carcass of the pig that I had just purchased in the open market. "It's gross!"

This college student had been such a sweet and dear helper but this was the straw that was more than she could take. She had gone with me to the market and to the shops to pick up necessary supplies for that day.

Preparing for twenty hard workers took a tremendous vigilance searching in the market and in the shops. In the market, she searched out the limited fresh vegetables and fruit, while I looked for meat in the area where freshly slaughtered carcasses of animals—beef, pork and goats were hanging by large hooks.

We, personally, had a little bug Volkswagen to use for errands. In the back seat, I had placed the carcass of the pig, which I had ordered the day before and had just picked up.

The head was still in place and the skin showed and smelled of singeing. Basically he was gutted.

When she saw this pig lying on the plastic sheeting with his legs straight up in the air she panicked, never having seen a carcass of a whole animal. She was utterly in shock.

I did all that I could to plead her to go with me. I suggested that she cover her eyes while we drove home. She absolutely refused to get in. Even though we had only about two miles to go to our kitchen, she would not agree to climb into the car. She left her basket of vegetables on the ground by the car and took off walking back to our place. After that, I had to leave her at home every time I needed to pick up fresh meat!

On one occasion, a European farmer not many miles out notified me that he would be slaughtering lambs and wanted to know if I would like to have some. I ordered a hindquarter, which he brought to the conference center the next morning. We loved lamb and thought this would be something different for the volunteers. I hung it in the cooler overnight with plans to prepare and serve it at noon he following day.

The next morning my African helper assisted as I prepared roast lamb with spices and vegetables, which I had planned to use with it. From mint in the garden I prepared fresh mint sauce, which we loved to serve with lamb. I was really quite delighted to be able to have something special for the men.

The men came in at noon, washed up and sat down at the table. My helper and I placed the food on the table, we prayed and the men began eating.

Everyone took lamb and most had already eaten some when one said, "The meat is good. What is it?"

I said with a big smile of satisfaction, "It's lamb. I was able to get a leg from a farmer yesterday. It's considered the favorite meat of all the expatriates here."

A silence fell on the men. As Carlos and I watched in astonishment, each man pushed the meat to the side of his plate.

One man said, "We do not eat lamb in South Carolina."

It took me a while to get my composure but when I did, I removed the platter of meat from the table as each man silently watched. The men ate the vegetables and after a rest time returned to their work. Later, several came back to apologize.

I never again served lamb to volunteers from South Carolina. Thankfully, this was the only meal I prepared for workers that they really did not enjoy. Having three home cooked meals a day was more than most of them normally experienced.

When each group was ready to leave, they expressed the highest appreciation for the meals. That pleased me because I felt that in serving them, I was serving the Lord.

> "Serve wholeheartedly, as if you were serving
> the Lord. . ." Eph. 6:7a

C: Adjusting

He was one of the nicest men who had come, an atomic energy scientist with a Ph. D. On the day he arrived, he called me aside and said, "I have never used a hammer. I wanted to come, so, please tell me what to do and I will do it."

"That is ok. We will find plenty for you to do."

He settled in well and by late morning of the second day he was on a scaffold working with two other men nailing on fascia boards.

As I walked by he looked down, smiled profusely and called down to me, "I am doing fine. This is the best experience of my life."

With satisfaction, I nodded, smiling. As I walked away, I thought of our trip up from Dar the day he arrived.

He and the others in his group learned a custom strange to America; motorist driving on the left side of the road. It is the custom in much of Europe, and other lands. Getting used to it was just one of the many adjustments the volunteers would need to make. For some it was not easy.

The plane's having been late, we left Dar at sunset. Since they had missed hours of sleep on the flight, most of the men fell asleep on the middle and back seats of the mini bus. Our PhD was asleep with his head leaning against the window on the outside of the front passenger seat. The man between him and me remained awake. Darkness came and we moved on our journey.

Suddenly our PhD awoke, and seeing that we were on the left side of the road and a car coming towards us, he suspected that I had also dozed off. He screamed, "Carlos, Carlos, you're on the wrong side of the road." The rest of the men who had been dozing awoke. We all had a good laugh as the other car passed without incident on the side.

"The Lord watches over all who love him." Ps 145:20

C: Cement

One of my responsibilities was to procure materials for the volunteers in their work. Often this was a very difficult and frustrating task.

The next group of volunteers coming expected to pour footings and to lay brick. There was no cement—none in Iringa, none in Dar es Salaam, none in Tanzania and the volunteers could do little without cement.

By international phone calls, I made inquiry from fellow missionaries in Zambia, our neighboring country to the South. They told me that there was cement in Lusaka and promised to work through our mission there to get some. The missionary contacted a shipping company and arranged for them to bring two large truckloads of cement across the border and to Iringa.

With telephone calls to Dar es Salaam, I acquired the necessary permits to bring the cement into Tanzania and with these permits in hand left Iringa in the wee hours, had breakfast in Mbeya and was at the border by the time the trucks arrived. Going ahead of the trucks, I drove back to Iringa and on to Dar es Salaam to meet the volunteers early the next morning.

We arrived in Iringa with the volunteers to see the trucks waiting to be off loaded. We were again convinced that God is still in charge and that miracles still happen.

"He who seeks finds; and to him who knocks the door will be opened." Mt 7:8b

M: Family Triumph and Tragedy

With two of our children on the other side of the world, we often felt we were missing much of their lives. As parents, we were not able to see them for special holidays or even keep up with their problems and needs. This is one of the hardest parts of being missionaries.

During this busy time of volunteers and building with heavy daily responsibilities we tried to write weekly letters since phone calls were still so very expensive. We took a joyful short break to go to Kenya for our youngest, Debra's graduation from high school at Rift Valley Academy. Our oldest, Janice, came out to go with her back to the States. This brief time with the girls was such a blessed treat to us. Janice had now completed her college degree in nursing and was working in Vanderbilt Hospital in Nashville.

Janice sent us word of her upcoming marriage but we were unable to leave our work to go. We felt so left out, not being able to assist her in this special time of her life.

When she told of her pregnancy, we would love to have been with her, but again our construction was at such a crucial time that we needed to stay to meet the deadline for completion.

So our daughter and her husband had beautiful twins, a boy and girl, born very prematurely, weighing only one pound 12 oz. and two pounds. She stayed with them in the intensive care for over six weeks with many life-threatening problems, a time that she really needed our support. She even took them home early at three lbs each, since she was working in the premature ICU unit and knew all the special care they needed. It was a joyous time of triumph for us to become grandparents but sad that we failed to be there for them.

Our daughter Ruth was married, having completed her nurses' training, and had her first son six months after the twins were born. Her son was healthy. It was wonderful to have three grandchildren in one year. Yet we had not seen any of them.

A disturbing phone call from America told us about Ruth's three-month-old son. He was in intensive care, having turned blue and stopped breathing while he was with a baby sitter, and was on life support. Ruth was in special nursing classes at the time. Though we did not know how we could manage, we felt that one of us had to go home.

Since Carlos felt he had to oversee the project, I quickly made plans to leave for the states. The flight was a blur. I was feeling the pain of knowing that this baby possibly would not make it.

Immediately after I arrived, and after he had been one week on the ventilator, the doctor stated he was brain dead, possibly from an aneurysm. They removed the support system and the baby passed away. Nothing prepares one for the experience of death of a little grandbaby. Our children were shattered. Their church and friends were a strong support. How thankful I was to be able to be with them to seek to bring comfort and encouragement at this time.

I remember standing in the hospital hall when the doctor announced that Matthew had died. No one was with me. I literally cried to the walls. It was such a lonely, sad experience. The children were with the baby, holding him for a few brief minutes to say goodbye.

This brief time at home helped to bring our family close again, to know our new sons-in-law, our new tiny twin grandchildren, and the life situations of our girls. Going back to Africa was draining, but I felt that my place was there beside my husband, doing the work that the Lord had called us to do. Of the sacrifices of missionaries, perhaps being so far away from their own children is the greatest. The children's families have the most difficult times being without 'available' parents for assistance, but assuredly accepting that their parents had strong callings and a firm commitment to the task.

"I am the Lord your God, who teaches you what is best for you, who directs you in the way you should go." Isa 48:17b

C: Buddy's Story

Soon after Buddy's group arrived, he called me aside. I knew that he had been there before. He was with the survey group from his church, which came before they made the final decision to participate in the project.

"Carlos," he said, "I am not a Christian and I am not a member of the church. I also have some other problems. I wanted so much to come. They agreed that I could."

"Welcome, Buddy. We are glad you are here. What do you mean by 'other problems'????"

"I have a bad habit. I curse, but I promised that I would not while in Iringa if they would allow me to come. I wanted you to know so if one of those words slipped out you would understand."

Afterwards, I asked one of the other men about Buddy. He told me that Buddy was a very nice man; a hard worker and those who knew him liked him. He often attended church but had not joined. He said that Buddy's wife was a lovely person and very active in church. She had been a church leader most of her life. Like her mother, she had contributed considerably to the church.

We enjoyed having Buddy around. He worked hard and had much to contribute to the project. His ingenuity was amazing.

When I told Buddy that we would be cooking with wood at the conference center, we together designed a wood-burning cook stove. There would be two large ovens and a large cooking surface. We planned to build the stove of the same fire-burned, sun-dried, mud brick we were using for the rest of the building. We would build it as part of an outside wall, so that we could put the wood in from the outside.

When Buddy went back to the US, he took the plans for the cooking surface and oven doors, promising to build them in his metal shop. He sent his finished product back in one of the containers put together by the work groups at his church.

The second volunteer group with which Buddy came stayed two weeks, as did most of the groups. When they returned to the US, he remained, planning to return home with the next group. He would give a full month to the project this time.

Buddy, being practical, sometimes disagreed with one of the first volunteers, a single man who had recently graduated in architecture. He came planning to stay two months and was to supervise the project. He was a very precise architect.

One day, in mid morning, Buddy came back to the house where Myrtice and I were working. His face flushed and angry, I could tell that something was wrong. I followed him to the back room where we both sat down. To this point he had not spoken.

Buddy looked right at me and began blurting out his contempt for the other worker. I had not heard such language since working years before with my father, whose many construction workers were accustomed to speaking like that. I sat and listened, trying not to show any emotion. Buddy carried on.

After a while, he stopped and with shame and remorse apparent on his face apologized. He said that he and his fellow worker had disagreed on how to do something and that they had an argument. He said that he felt like hitting him but, rather than doing that, he had walked away and come back to the house.

"Buddy, you did the right thing by walking away and coming here. I am glad you did that."

"I am sorry. I should not have said all those things in front of you. I was so angry that I couldn't help it."

"Getting it off your chest made you feel better, didn't it?"

"Yes."

"I am sorry. If you and Myrtice will forgive me I will try hard not to let it happen again."

Buddy agreed that we pray together. After a while when he had settled down and was calm again, he went back to the job site. The two of them came for lunch later and, though they were not saying much, all appeared to be much better.

After about a week, Buddy began having problems with his heart. We called first and took him to Mbeya, two hundred miles away, to our mission hospital. Our doctor found his problem was not yet too serious. He gave him medications and we returned to Iringa. He finished his time there without problems.

Buddy worked hard daily and never complained. He did many things I neither could do nor knew how to do. He and I worked many hours side by side and had many opportunities to discuss the matter of his not being a Christian. He seemed to appreciate our discussions.

When Buddy came again, his pastor also came. On Sunday, we went to a village church where his pastor preached and I interpreted for him. At the end of the service, Buddy raised his hand indicating that he was accepting Jesus. What a joy! We all rejoiced.

Buddy with his wife, Helen, came for the dedication of the conference center. This was his fourth trip to Iringa. They wrote ahead that he wanted his pastor to baptize him in the stream at the foot of the hill below the conference center. This was where the volunteers bathed at the end of many days' work.

Seeing that there was little water in the stream at the time, we made a dam and dug out behind it so there would be enough water for the baptism. We also cleared away grass and bush to make a suitable place for people to stand on the bank next to the stream.

Buddy's baptism was a highlight and an integral part of the planned program on that very special day. Standing with a great crowd and witnessing what was taking place was spiritually uplifting. Over a two and one half-year period, we had witnessed this man's spiritual journey. He had moved from a way of life without Christ to becoming a completely changed person dedicated to a new way of life in Jesus. Some years later, back in South Carolina, when he died it was of heart problems.

"Therefore, if anyone is in Christ, he is a new creation;
The old has gone, the new has come!" 2Cor 5:17

M: Supper with Pastor

When Pastor Anosisye, the Convention's home missionary in Iringa, came by one day he invited all the volunteers present to have supper with him and his family. The men later expressed their concern for eating with the nationals. They were afraid of the uncleanness and strangeness of the food. We assured them that this would be a good experience to see how our brethren here show their hospitality. We knew that all of Anosisye's family were very clean and even his daughter helped in the kitchen at the center.

All of us climbed into the vehicles and arrived at the pastor's house. His home was simple. We all appreciated the warm welcome. Anosisye thanked all the workers for coming all the way to Africa to assist in the construction.

Knowing that he had such a limited income, we were astonished when he and his family passed around warm cokes, an expensive item to them, far more than they could afford. The sons and daughter began passing out plates and bowls of chicken with rice. Most everyone found a spot on the floor. A few sat on the available chairs. Some sat on rocks or small benches in the courtyard behind the house where the food was cooking. Some were still a little doubtful about eating the food and began slowly with their spoons or forks. Most ate heartily and showed their real enjoyment of the food.

After all had eaten their supper Anosisye started leading the group in some of the favorite Swahili hymns. The men joined in singing in English. It was very enjoyable and a time of bonding with sweet fellowship. At the close, Pastor Anosisye led in a very meaningful devotional with Carlos' translating.

When we left, everyone felt such an uplift and satisfaction in knowing the kind of Christian leaders that were in Tanzania.

"What a unique experience! - and the food really was good." commented one of the men.

"It was such a blessing to me to know they sacrificed for us," commented another.

"This gives us a new appreciation and love for our African brethren," another said.

"We really feel all our work here is worth while and appreciated. Certainly it is the work for the Kingdom of God."

"Above all love each other deeply." IPe 4:8a

C: Cameras and Candy

Almost everyone who comes to Africa brings a camera. Picture taking is exciting and gives everyone something to show back at home. People, animals, scenery, and buildings - - in most places there are no restrictions. In Tanzania, however, there were restrictions on photographing of certain things such as government buildings. The foreigner sometimes does not know the local regulations and sometimes knowing, does not make a difference.

One Saturday afternoon when the volunteers were taking a break from work I took them around to show them where and how the local people live. Most took their cameras along.

"Ask before you snap," I admonished. "There are places where pictures are not allowed." With that, I paid little attention to picture taking.

We had been out about an hour when suddenly two men stood before us in the middle of the road, waving for us to stop the car. They obviously were angry.

"You took pictures of the Tanu (TAH-new) building," one said.

"I don't think so" I said.

Pointing to one of the men in the back seat he said, angrily raising his voice, "That man did. I saw him."

I looked to the back seat and saw the one to whom he had pointed. He was holding his camera in both hands and had a sheepish look on his face.

The angry man reached through the back window and pointing to the camera said, "Give it to me. Do you Americans think you can break our laws? You know that you are not allowed to take pictures of our buildings."

I knew, but some of our visitors obviously didn't completely understand or thought that they could get by with slipping a few pictures here and there. The man held tightly onto his camera.

I said, "Give it to him," knowing that refusing would likely mean that we all would be taken to the local jail.

The angry man said, "Get out of the car and come with me." His anger appeared to be rising. At least it did not seem to be getting better.

We got out of the car and followed the man into the nearby building. As we walked along, I said to the men, "Please leave the talking to me." I knew that we were in serious trouble. They would likely not only keep the camera the man had in his hand but also take all the others we had with us, and that we all might end up in jail.

Inside the building, we faced four people. They sat behind a long table and we sat in front of it. The man who had accosted us appeared to be very much in control.

I started by saying in Swahili, "I want to ask you to please forgive us. I live here and know that we are not are not to take pictures of Tanu buildings. These men are all my visitors. They are helping us to build the conference center."

"Then it is your responsibility to tell your visitors that they are not permitted to take pictures."

"They have been here only one week. I have attempted to explain your rules to them but I overlooked some. I am the one who made a mistake. I promise that they will not take any more pictures of Tanu buildings."

We sat there for nearly two hours. The sun went down and it was getting dark. I knew that Myrtice and the volunteers who had not come with us were concerned about what had happened to us. I had no idea how long they would keep us or what their intentions were for us.

The four men spent most of the time talking angrily among themselves. All of this being in Swahili, our volunteers were in the dark about what they were saying. I understood but had no opportunity to explain to the other men. They were openly frightened. I did notice however that as time passed the men on the other side of the table became less angry. I began to feel better about the situation.

Finally the leader of the group said, "You know that you made a very bad mistake. You have apologized and we accept your apology."

I responded, "Yes, we made a mistake and we are very sorry. Thank you for accepting our apology."

The camera was still on the table and I began to wonder if they would keep it. I was relieved when the man now showing no anger at all took the camera and handed it over saying, "You can go now."

Getting back into our car, everyone expressed relief. We all felt that God had his hand on us, delivering us from what could have been a very difficult and painful outcome. Every one of us had learned a big lesson, Obey the Rules.

Most volunteers brought chewing gum and hard candy for snacks. Knowing how many African children loved it, they brought it in quantity to give out.

Driving down a road, they would throw it out the car window. Whenever we stopped, they would hand it out to children who thronged when they learned that there was candy.

Soon it became a problem. Everywhere we went children ganged on us. They came out of their houses and stood in great numbers by the roadside as we drove along. They appeared at the project site, calling out for candy. The volunteers would go the fence and pass candy over to them. Was it a problem? Yes, but the joy, which came to the volunteers and the children, overrode the problem

> *"Whatever you did for one of the least of these brothers of mine You did for me." Mt. 25:40b*

M: A Real Home

We were thrilled! We would now have a real house with hot water and a kitchen inside! I was so excited about again having a normal house. The volunteers had shared that it was complete and ready for us to move in.

The missionary residence was finished first, while the conference center was still far from completion. Moving day was not difficult. We had been in such poor quarters; no inside water, no hot water. We had actually felt as if we were camping the first eight months of the construction.

Volunteers helped us unpack and we were completely set up for normal living for a change. It was a joy to unpack the crates. We could again have the extras that make a house and home. They had been stored for so long.

Some caring volunteer had brought and donated a dishwasher to the new home. We could not believe we would ever have such a modern appliance. I decided to try it out in that first week to wash our dishes from the crates. It really worked, we thought. I left it running while I prepared supper for the group in the main kitchen.

After supper, we all stayed around to unwind and play Uno and other games. We left about 9:30 p.m. to return to our new home. As we walked into the back door a flood of water came pouring out. Water was ankle deep all over the house. We called for a few who were still up to help us find its source and bring brooms to help sweep out the water.

A pipe had burst behind the dishwasher. We spent most of the night sweeping out as much as we could and trying to dry out furniture, carpets, and other items on the floor. I never used the dishwasher again. Someone else could try it. I would return to the old way of hand washing!

"For every house is built by someone, but God is the builder of everything." Heb 3:4

M: Across the Road

Drums beating in the night were intense in the village just across the street. We left the windows open at night when it was cool and very pleasant. We were aware of all the activity happening across the road.

One of the first weeks we were in the new home, I decided to walk across the street to meet some of our neighbors. There was a big crowd gathered around one home.

Most were men standing around talking. I introduced myself and asked what was happening in the home. Then I heard the wailing and trilling inside.

They told me the woman of the home had passed away. She was rather old and they had expected her death. I felt it was my opportunity to go inside and express my sympathy and sit on the dirt floor with the other ladies. I stayed for quite a long time in the simple mud hut with its thatched roof. The women seemed oblivious to my being white, since we all talked in Swahili. They needed some perfumed oil to rub on the body. One lady whispered to me, "Could you help us find some oil for the body?"

"I will be happy to try to find some for you. Is there anything else that you need?" I responded.

"No. We would be grateful for just the oil."

I returned home to get my Volkswagen bug and went to one of the shops in town to find some perfumed oil. The custom was to wash the body, rub the highly perfumed oil on it to hide the smell, even though they bury within twenty-four hours of the death. They had a new blanket in which to wrap the body. I returned right away and gave them the oil.

Their simple gratitude was the beginning of friendship with many people in the village. It opened the way for us to witness and invite them to our new church, meeting in a nearby school building. We would later build a church on the Center's grounds. A little oil made a big difference.

"To comfort all who mourn, and provide
for those who grieve. ." Isa 61:2b-3a

M: Child Falls from Tree

Occasionally, I left the town church where I was teaching Sunday school and went out with the volunteers. Though I had all I could do caring for them, as soon as I saw the condition of the children in the outlying villages, I knew that I must do something to help them.

They were poor, malnourished and diseased. It was not long until I managed to go out for short days twice a week to have clinics in this poor area. Organizing the meals early, I could turn over the preparation to my helpers.

Finding so many children in poor physical condition and some with terrible burns, caused by playing near the fire where their moms cooked, kept me very busy trying to treat them all. Many also had parasites and infections of all types. This ministry time in the villages energized me to be able to help these most needy. Crowds continued to grow until it was a problem to help them all, but somehow I managed.

From this extra contact and ministry, we also saw how the preaching points began growing in numbers and more were coming to the Lord. Sometimes stretching ourselves further than we think we can manage, gives proof of God's strength and wisdom to provide what we need. God's Kingdom grows as we give ourselves fully, fulfilling His purposes. Proverbs 19:21 states, *"Many are the plans in a man's heart, but it is the Lord's purpose that prevails."*

From the time I began to have clinics, people often dropped by with small emergencies from the nearby village. One little child was brought over when he fell into a pan of boiling water. I left everything in the kitchen and took him immediately to the government hospital.

One day a young boy came running to the center calling out for help. As I went out he pointed to the road where I saw four men carrying a young boy about nine years old in a blanket tied at the ends to long poles serving as a swinging stretcher.

I quickly ran to see what the problem was. I could see his leg was bleeding heavily and had a compound fracture where the bone was actually sticking out. They said that he was high up in a tree trying to cut some firewood and fell. They told me that they had been carrying him for about nine miles and were exhausted. All I had to transport him was the little VW bug.

We carefully placed him in the back seat while his father sat with me in the front. He was in such terrible pain that I sped as fast as I could. We reached the emergency room of the little government hospital.

After finally locating someone to help him, I asked that he receive extra attention since it had been a long time since his fall. I had to leave him in their hands knowing there was nothing else that I could do. Surgery would be necessary. I told his father that I would be praying for him and would try to check on him.

After seeing him several times, we had developed a great friendship. No one was staying with him or even checking on him, since his village was far out. Visiting as often as I could, I shared about Christ with him. Time was limited for more visits with my jobs at the Center but I really wanted more time to help him understand more clearly.

One morning before going to the market, I stopped by for a quick visit to see him. As I approached the nurses' station, I could see down the long ward that his bed was empty. Concerned, I found a nurse in another part of the hospital and inquired about him.

"Sorry, but he died suddenly two days ago when we were getting him up to try some crutches."

I felt so badly for his family. Such a young boy lost his life so suddenly. He must have had a blood clot. I also knew that the care in the hospital was lacking from far too few trained attendants and shortages of medicine. How I grieved that I could not have done more for him.

We experienced many sad times such as this one, knowing we had done all we could do in the situation.

> *"Rejoice with those who rejoice; Mourn with those who mourn." Ro 12:15*

C: New Churches

When we came to Iringa our primary responsibility was to direct the building of the Conference Center. On the weekends, we visited and worked with the local churches under Anosisye's leadership. He was one of the first converts in the Rungwe District when we were there in the late 1950's. I had baptized him and most of his family.

After being a pastor in Rungwe and leading in the beginning of many new churches there, he had become one of the Convention's missionaries and lived with his family in Iringa. During the two and one half years we were in Iringa and working with Anosisye, we led in beginning of seven new churches. Anosisye was our dear friend and he had a strong and effective ministry. We rejoiced when we found that he would be in Iringa at the same time with us. He was a true man of God.

Every Sunday the volunteers visited the villages for preaching services where Anosisye had led in organizing churches. Volunteers enjoyed visiting the churches with us. Often one of them would preach with my interpreting or I would preach. Many volunteers gave their testimony.

Anosisye took us to villages where we had no church but where Christians from our churches lived. These visits became the seed for new churches. God was moving out into the villages around the center.

> *"And the Lord added to their number daily those*
> *who were being saved." Ac 2:47b*

M: Security

Before getting up at my usual 5:00 a.m., I heard considerable commotion outside. Loud calling from our night guard made me know something was terribly wrong. He screamed out, "Please call the police."

Going quickly to the door, I was told that there had been a thief on the property.

"I grabbed the first thing I could find to hit him. I didn't know it would kill him," the guard stated in panic.

A thief had slipped onto the property and was removing tools when the guard found him. During a struggle the guard hit the intruder with a piece of board, killing him.

Knowing that thievery was rife in the area, volunteers had assisted in putting a chain link fence around the property. Even then, thieves could slip under the fence at places or cut it, so we had a full-time guard at night.

After work, we put most tools in the two containers in which we had brought materials and supplies from the US. We had kept them and placed them near our house. We locked them with padlocks at night. Occasionally someone would leave tools outside. This thief had found some of them.

This was a tremendous blow to me, since Carlos was away for a meeting. Another missionary had taken volunteers to Dar for their return to the US and would bring another group back

Trying to keep everything going was nearly more than I could manage, but to have such a tragic event was unnerving. All I could think about was how something like this could affect our relations in the community. We tried hard not to let such things hinder our Christian witness and our influence in the area.

The police stated that we would be responsible for burying this man. They had asked around the village and no one even knew who he was. One of the neighbors said they knew that he had come from Zambia some time back. The police took the body to the small hospital morgue and told me I must pick it up for burial later on that afternoon.

They released the guard since there was proof that this man had been stealing and the guard's response was to injure and not to kill.

Trying to be calm and work out the plans for burying a stranger, I immediately thought of our Convention's home missionary, Anosisye, who lived in town. When I arrived at his house, I learned that he had gone to Rungwe to care for some family matters. I was in a crisis, having to bury a man with no help.

Driving in the area where I knew some of our new Christians lived; I was pleased to see one sitting outside his house. After telling him of the problem, he agreed to find some men to help dig a grave in the local cemetery and assist with the burial.

He refused to hold a service. "I haven't been a Christian long enough to know what to say at a funeral," was his response. However, he agreed to go with me to pick up the body and cover the grave with soil.

Knowing the new group was coming later that afternoon, I scheduled the funeral for after they arrived. I did know that one of the pastors from Nashville would be in the group, as well as several of his members. When he arrived, I would ask if he could do the service.

"Bill, before you get settled and we eat supper tonight I want to ask you to have a funeral for us."

Rather taken back he responded, "What is happening here?"

After I had shared with him the problems, he agreed to do the best he could. "I never dreamed I would be having a funeral, I only expected to help in the construction."

Later I took the African men with me to pick up the body at the hospital, wrapped it in the blanket, which I bought, and transported it in the back of our Land Rover. Since I had carried a body before it did not bother me. We went by the Center to lead the way for the volunteers and Bro. Bill in the minivan to the burial site. In spite of being such a tragic situation, the funeral became an evangelistic opportunity to many who were passing by and gathered around as we buried the body. God provided what we needed and was faithful to his Word.

"And we know that in all things God works for the good of those who love him, who have been called according to his purpose," Ro 8:28

C: Water Tank

I sat on the scaffold, adjusting the huge jack on my side of the tank. My legs were hanging between the tank and me. Two volunteers were equidistant around the tank, adjusting their jacks. We raised the tank a fraction of an inch at a time.

A dozen men on the ground below held on to ropes fastened to the top of the tank keeping it balanced. Myrtice and two other volunteers were taking pictures. Everyone was tense knowing how dangerous our job was.

A construction project in the US no longer needed this twenty-two feet long storage tank weighing nearly two tons. They contributed it for use at the Conference Center. Because it was so heavy, our people in the US cut it in half and we welded it back together in Iringa.

We had raised the tank from ground level to where we were at the time—nearly twenty feet off the ground. We still had five feet to go and then we had to shift the tank onto a concrete block platform, which we had ready.

I was about to begin my turn at raising my jack when suddenly I noticed that the tank was shifting, slipping in my direction. I knew that there was neither a way nor time enough for me to pull my legs free and get away from the tank. Even if I were to get my legs free, I would fall backwards to the ground twenty feet below. I simply froze.

I could hear those on the ground, "No, no, no, no!"

Everything was happening so fast.

Still frozen in place, I watched the tank as it so slowly moved in my direction. When it was less than two inches from me it stopped. It was as if God had placed his hand on it and held it back.

Still much in shock, I held onto the scaffold and pulled my legs free. Those on the ground brought two long ladders and placed one on each side of me. One man climbed to me and took hold of my hand. We slowly descended the ladders to the ground.

After a time we built additional scaffolds. Another man took my place. He and the other two men raised the tank to the intended height and we were able to shift it onto the platform. We welded cables to the top edges of the tank and fastened them to metal stakes securely fixed in the ground. A giant task finished, we were relieved and took a well-deserved break. We thanked God that likely the most dangerous task in the Conference Center project was behind us.

> *"He set my feet on a rock and gave me*
> *a firm place to stand." Ps 40:2b*

M: Pumpkins and Corn

The new church was growing near the Center. Some Sundays the volunteers visited there, but most preferred to go out into the villages where we had three new preaching points. They enjoyed visiting in the villages, seeing the homes and life style. They would visit for a while before the services started. It was a blessing for them to meet the people and bring a message in English that one of us translated into Swahili. They felt like real missionaries and we were proud of their participation.

My duties included preparing meals every day of the week including Sundays. Hence I stayed in town most of the time and I started a women's Bible class before the worship service. Our group grew rapidly and the interest was strong.

"Mama, I must take my sick husband back to his village for the family to help care for him. He goes out of his head and I can't manage him," one of my class members told me one day. "The doctors have done all they can do here."

I knew she was a schoolteacher and that he was in the town school. "We certainly will be praying with you about him," I responded. "Is there anything else we can do for you?" I asked seeing her distress while she spoke to me. She would likely be away for several months.

"My money is nearly finished but we do have a large field of corn in front of our home. It is nearly ripe now. Could you help with it in any way? I am afraid it may all be stolen if I leave it too long."

Ideas whirled in my head. We could never buy fresh corn even in the market. The natives always leave their corn until it is hard before they harvest it for food. They enjoy roasting the hard corn. The rest is left to dry for making their corn meal. Perhaps I could buy the corn from her and harvest it myself when it was ready.

I put this idea to her. She was excited that I could use it and pay her money for her crop. We made an arrangement by judging how much corn was there.

The next day she stopped for her money. She could not thank me enough. Now she would not lose all her work in the field. I asked her to please tell her neighbors that I would be picking it when it was ripe.

Two weeks later, I took several burlap sacks and headed to the field, which was near by. I checked the corn for ripeness. It was just perfect, tender and ready to eat. I proceeded to pick it, going up and down rows and filling the sacks.

Shortly, an old ragged-dressed man came to greet me. I quickly assured him that I had bought the corn from my friend. We talked a short while and he disappeared. I continued picking the corn imagining how delicious it would taste.

Again, the old man came to me. He had his three wives and several children with him who all looked so very poor. He kindly introduced me to them for he wanted them to greet me. He seemed very proud of his family.

"They have brought you gifts. I hope you will receive them." He said, showing me several pumpkins the ladies had put on the ground.

"Oh, I am so grateful for your gifts, but I know your family needs these good pumpkins for food." I said, trying hard not to accept their generous gifts.

"You must accept them. We know you need them." They quickly put the pumpkins near me and disappeared into the rows of corn.

I was astonished! Why would these poor people be giving me their food? I knew they needed these items far more than I.

After plucking all the corn in the field, which took nearly two hours, I returned to our kitchen in the Center. Margaret, the local pastor's daughter, helped me unload it. She was a great helper in the kitchen, smart and quick to learn. We both pulled up chairs and started husking the corn. I was pleased to have a good quantity extra to freeze and to use for later meals.

As we sat working and talking, I told her about the poor old man who had given me his pumpkins. "I don't see how he could give away his food when he has such a large family to feed," I told her. "They seemed so very poor."

She nearly fell off the chair laughing. "Mama, you were gathering 'green' corn. Only people who are really starving will eat soft corn. We wait until it is hard. He thought you were starving, since you told him that you were getting the corn to eat! He just wanted to help you have enough food since you were hungry."

Such a generous and kind people you will not find anywhere else in the world.

"A generous man will himself be blessed, for he shares his food with the poor." Pr 22:9

C: Mattresses

I stood looking at the bunk frames. We had worked diligently, had them all finished and in their places in the rooms. They really looked nice. There were sixty frames— 120 beds.

Pillows had come from the US in a container along with building materials. Volunteers had brought material for sheets and pillowcases and had sewed them on the site. The only problem was that there were no mattresses and the opening and dedication was only three weeks away.

As I stood looking, I silently prayed.

God had provided two truckloads of cement from Zambia when none was available in Tanzania. Food was available for the volunteers when we wondered from where it would come. We had different materials just in time on several occasions. What would we do about the mattresses?

More than fifty visitors would be coming from the US. Missionaries from other stations would come. A full mission meeting of over a hundred missionaries would follow in the next week. They would all need places to sleep. Important

Government officials would also be present, but fortunately, for us we would not have to provide places for them to sleep.

I had already heard that there were no mattresses anywhere in Tanzania shops and that the factory in Dar es Salaam had closed for the lack of materials. As mattresses were bulk, bringing them from Zambia would be prohibitive cost-wise.

When I got back to the house I told Myrtice, "I'm going the Dar tomorrow."

"What is the use? From what we know, there are no mattresses in Dar and they have closed the factory."

"I have a feeling that there is a way. I've been praying and just have that feeling."

"OK. You go and I will stay here and pray."

The following morning I left early on the eight-hour trip to Dar. Paul had said that we should pray without ceasing and I did that. Jesus said that if we prayed believing, we would receive the things for which we pray. Somehow, I believed that we would have mattresses for the opening of the Conference Center.

Down the escarpment and through the Ruaha Valley I prayed. All the way through the game reserve, I prayed. Along the way, I saw an occasional animal grazing near the road. There were the giant anthills and the massive baobab trees. There were the acacia trees from the tops of which the giraffe grazed and herds of zebra grazing not too far from the road. Once I had to stop and wait while a herd of elephants crossed the road. I took notice of all these and prayed.

Many Africans walked along the roads with various loads on their heads. African villages were sparse. With each village I saw, I took note of their activities. As I moved along, I prayed.

Passing through Morogoro and getting closer to Dar I saw massive sisal fields and the kapok trees. Sugar cane patches appeared along the way usually quite near houses. Even closer to Dar I saw more and more banana trees, some with heavy stalks ready for harvest.

Occasionally a man, a boy or a woman walked alongside the road with a stalk of bananas or some other load on their head.

As I drove into Dar es Salaam, I made my way to the Industrial Park. I knew that the mattress factory would be there.

Driving into the park, I saw workers doing various jobs near the road.

Spotting one man not too far from the road, I stopped and asked in Swahili, "Where is the mattress factory?"

"Just ahead on your right," he called out in a rather loud voice.

As I drove on slowly, I saw a rather large sign indicating that I had arrived at the mattress factory. I pulled up next to the gate, a large metal frame covered with chain link fencing. They had closed and locked the gate with a piece of chain and a large padlock. A guard stood inside the gate near a small shed.

I got out of the car and greeted him in Swahili, "Hello! How are you?"

"I am fine. What do you want?"

"I want to speak with the manager."

"What is your name?'

"Tell him that I am Carlos Owens from Iringa."

The guard turned and went into the nearby building and soon returned, unlocked the gate and swung it back so that I could drive in.

Parking the car, I got out and the guard took me to the building. The manager was standing at the door. He told me that his name was Patel and invited me in. He asked, "What can I do for you?"

I told him of our need for mattresses, to which he replied, "We have no materials to make mattresses. All the workers are gone and the factory is closed."

"Mr. Patel," I said, "we are finishing the Huruma Conference Center in Iringa and are in big trouble if we can get no mattresses in time for the dedication."

He interrupted, "I've heard about the Center. I understand that it is to be quite a fine thing for Iringa. I have friends there." After some hesitation he added, "I wish I could help you but there is nothing I can do. We closed the factory when our materials ran out."

I proceeded to tell him that government officials as well as missionaries from all over Tanzania would be there for the dedication. I told him that some very important people from the US were to come—more than fifty.

He turned and motioned that I follow him. We walked through the back door of his office and into the factory area. I could see in a far corner of the large room a pile of tiny, off-colored plastic beads.

Mr. Patel said, "This is what we had left over when we closed the factory. We swept most of it from the floor. As you can see most of it is not very clean."

I asked, "Sir, could you make mattresses from this material?

"Yes, but they would not be first grade."

"How many could you make?"

"We might get fifty or maybe sixty. Not more than sixty five."

"How long would it take to make them?"

"Two or three days if I can get my workers back." He said that he was willing to try.

I was already saying in my heart how grateful I was that God was answering our prayers. If all went well we would have mattresses by the time of the dedication. God was using Mr. Patel, a Hindu worshiper, to provide needs for our Christian institution.

I told Mr. Patel that I knew haulers in Iringa who would come for the mattresses. He promised to call me when they were ready.

I left Dar es Salaam for Iringa without thinking to inquire about the size of the mattresses. As I drove back, I recalled that most local mattresses were five or six inches wider than the ones for which we had planned. I thought, "That is ok. We will make out with whatever we get."

The mattresses arrived in Iringa three days before visitors would come for the dedication. There were still so many things to do and, sure enough, the mattresses were five inches too wide. I had to make a plan quickly.

At first, I tried cutting away the extra five inches with a sharp knife. That worked but it was very slow. On thinking, I tried placing a piece of plywood on the mattress and using a circular saw to do the cutting. It worked beautifully. The blade cut only halfway through so we turned the mattress over and ran the saw again on the other side. In a relatively short time we had the mattresses trimmed and glued the leftover pieces together to make additional mattresses.

As covers were ready, each mattress at the right size got a cover and found its way to one of the waiting bed frames. All that were to stay had a mattress. God continued faithful to answer our prayers.

> *"Declare his glory among the nations, his marvelous deeds among all peoples." Ps 96:3*

C: Dedication

"Huruma (who-ROO-ma) Conference Centre" was visible from quite a distance back down the road. The large stone and painted sign was just inside the fence at the corner of the property before the entrance gate. The leaders of the Convention had chosen the name, Huruma, for its inherent meaning; compassion, concern, kindness. They chose the way the British and most locals spell 'Centre' instead of 'Center,'

Though exhausted from having worked hard to be ready for the opening, we were exhilarated to know that so many would be arriving to participate in the dedication. We hurried here and there, checking to see that everything was in place.

Myrtice and her helpers had seen that the rooms were ready for the multitude that would be sleeping over. She had stores of food, which she and her helpers would prepare, cook and serve to over two hundred who would be eating with us following the ceremonies. The dam and pool in the stream at the bottom of the hill was ready for Buddy's baptism. Therefore, when the people began arriving we were ready to welcome them.

Missionaries came from stations in both Tanzania and Kenya. Convention leaders came from their respective areas. Representatives from The Foreign Mission Board flew into Dar es Salaam and came on to Iringa in our mission's small plane. Government officials came in their big cars. Lesser officials, neighbors, church members from nearby, and distant churches walked in. Some arrived on the day before the opening and others came in time for the ceremonies. The program, which the Mission and Convention had approved, was printed and ready. We were about to celebrate the two and one-half years of planning and hard work so many people had helped in doing.

As the meeting began, we explained what the Conference Center was all about—how the Convention and Mission had conceived it and how it came to fruition. It was for the people of Tanzania, a place where the church people could meet, have fellowship and plan their work. It was a place where travelers of any church or no church at all could stop over and sleep.

One by one, board, mission and government officials spoke of their appreciation for the Center. Representatives of the churches from which volunteers had come spoke of having received joy and blessings from having worked on the project. The program lasted one and one half hours.

The last item printed on the program was Buddy's baptism. For this climatic event, everyone filed out of the hall and down the hill. Buddy and his pastor from South Carolina walked into the water where the pastor baptized him in a most impressive ceremony. As they came up out of the water, most eyes were tearful.

Walking back up the hill, many left but others stayed for food. Those who stayed had time for visiting and fellowship as Myrtice and her helpers served the food cafeteria style.

Everything moved along well and soon a big dining room was full with those enjoying their food.

When everyone had left or gone to their rooms and the dining room, kitchen and meeting hall were back in order; we went to our house and rested. It had been a marvelous celebration of our work, too. It was as if we were hearing those words....

"Well done, thy good and faithful servants." Mt. 25:21&23

Chapter Eleven

Namibia I

Tsumeb (SUE-meb), where we lived in the north of Namibia was hot most of the year but cool enough for a light jacket in the evenings in the winter, June through August. Although the area was semi-desert with hardly any rainfall, there were unusual cacti, desert flowers, giant flowering aloes and exotic flowering trees. Unusual birds of fantastic colors abounded.

Namibia's largest industry, mining, was centered in Tsumeb. Tsumeb Mining Corporation produced large amounts of copper, lead and some gold, and circulating underground water served to cool the mine. Excess water from the mine supplied the town's needs.

The vast Namib Desert stretching along and back from the coast has its unique rock formations, desert plants, prehistoric cliff paintings, desert animals and the highest sand dunes in the world—all a wonder of beauty. On the coast and to the south Namibia has one of the world's largest deposits of diamonds, in the sand along the shore and in the coral beds offshore.

Windhoek, ('Windy Corner' in German), Namibia's capital city, is a modern metropolis nestled between two ranges of mountains in the center of the country.

C: Studying Ndonga (Nn-DOAN-gah)

We knew that we must learn the language of the people if we were to communicate well. Of the related tribes in the North, the Kwanyama (Kwa-NYAH-ma) and the Ndonga composed over half the population of the country. Their languages were similar. There being more Ndonga than Kwanyama, we decided to learn their language.

No one in our mission had learned the language before us. With neither language school nor dictionary available, we set out to develop our own program for learning the language.

When we arrived in Tsumeb, our loads had not arrived. We got permission and moved into the Methodist Manse. Since they were without a pastor, the manse had no occupant, but there was furniture. Our not knowing Ndonga and there being no other English worship in the town, we attended services with the Methodists. Their church was in what had been a school building in the north part of downtown, later to become our meeting place.

When we first visited the Methodist church, we learned that Petrusi (Pay-TRUE-see) Nyambali (Nyam-BAH-lee) worked in the mine as an interpreter for expatriates. He was of the Ndonga tribe, knew and spoke the language well. As he had spent time in East Africa he also knew Swahili. His knowing both Swahili and English would be most helpful to us. His English was exceptionally good but he had never been a teacher. He agreed to come to our place three afternoons a week after work. This seemed to be an excellent arrangement for us.   We soon learned that Ndonga and Swahili had many similarities. Both were Bantu languages and some words had the same roots. For instance, the word for day in Swahili is 'siku.' In Ndonga, it is 'esiku.'

All words in Swahili end in a vowel. All words in Ndonga begin with a vowel. The accent in both languages is usually on the next to the last syllable. There were so many similarities that we would eventually find difficulty in determining whether a word were Swahili or Ndonga.

From the beginning, we made our own dictionaries. With two notebooks, we would enter every new word we encountered, in both the English and Ndonga notebooks. Since Petrusi had not been a teacher he did not know what direction to take. Each day we told him what things we wanted to learn.

We spent many hours learning Ndonga and by the end of the third month were able to begin services in the language in a nearby village. Myrtice taught Sunday school with the help of flannel graph stories and I preached. Did we make mistakes? Yes, we made many. Often someone from the congregation would supply a word for us if we hesitated or made a mistake, many laughing with us. Their being involved in helping us speak correctly brought them and us into a close fellowship. We thanked them continuously for their assistance. By using the language, we soon were able to express ourselves freely and the people responded favorably. They prayed with us about our learning the language and we knew that God was answering those prayers.

> *The prayer of a righteous man is powerful and effective." Ja 5:16b*

M: Queen and Chief

At Livuyu, a village far in the north of Namibia, there was a group of people who had had a church but lacked a leader. The missionary who had been there had unexpectedly left the country, leaving them with no guidance. Upon coming into their village and telling them who we were, they were delighted that we had come and asked for whatever help we could give them. We spent several hours with them and made plans to return.

Knowing the importance of getting permission to do work in a village, we inquired about their headman or chief. They told us that their paramount chief was Chief Shashipopo (Shah-she-PO-po) and told us where he lived. They assured us that he was very friendly to missionaries and would be happy to see us.

On our way home, we stopped by to see the Chief. We located him in his very large and sprawling compound about a mile off the main road in a very sandy area. He was a very old man, small and bent over, using a cane but carrying himself with dignity. He greeted us warmly and invited us into a rather large open building with a tin roof and dirt floor. Several guards or assistants stood inside surrounding the room. This was where he normally held court and greeted people. We were delighted at his receiving us so warmly. He had many questions about our mission and appeared eager that we assist his people in having a church at Livuyu.

While we were talking with Chief Shashipopo, a small kitten came into the room, purred and rubbed against his foot. He, in turn, called a servant and requested a bowl of milk. The servant brought the milk and handed it to the Chief who put it on the floor. The kitten began drinking immediately.

The Chief observed the cat with intensity for a moment and then said, "I am proud that you have come. It is like this milk with this kitten. You place a bowl of milk on the floor and the kitten will come to it." Then he continued, "If you come to our village with your work, our people will come to it. What you have will be good for our people." From that time, we had a superb relation with the Chief and all the people in his area.

In the same general vicinity as Chief Shashipopo, but closer to Rundu, there was a woman Paramount Chief known as Queen Maria. On the day we went to visit her for the first time, we waited over an hour before being invited in. Moses told us later that this was the protocol in her area. No one gets to see Queen Maria quickly.

Eventually, a servant came and ushered us through long winding grass-covered corridors (as protection from terrorists) into a very large room where the Queen was awaiting us. She was a small, old woman, with a much wrinkled face, wearing a knitted cap and cotton dress. After we curtsied to her, she smiled as she motioned us to take seats on beautifully carved stools, which a servant had placed for us near her.

She asked, "How can I help you?"

We explained that we were new in the area and wanted to express our greetings to her and to help her people.

She asked, "What is it that you want to do with my people?"

We shared with her about our mission and our desire to start churches among her people. We also told her that Myrtice was a nurse and could have clinics to help the sick.

Smiling, she welcomed us and offered her assistance in any way we needed.

While we were talking, I had noticed a hen on a nest in a cardboard box in the corner of the room. We were just about ready to leave when the hen, having laid an egg, started cackling, flew off her nest and out the door.

The Queen laughed aloud and said, "See, even the hen is happy that you are here!"

"You will go out in joy and be led forth in peace," Isa 55:12a

M: Greater Witness in Death

God's Word spreads in an unusual manner. In South Africa, a fellow missionary promoted Christianity with a Bible Way Correspondence School. Writing to the promoters, a person could have an opportunity to study a book of the Bible, have a test and even get a certificate of recognition for the study, all by mail.

An outstanding middle aged Namibian in Katima Mulilo, a town at the end of the Caprivi Strip, went to South Africa for business and found a copy of this study. After inquiring about it he found that we also had the same thing in Windhoek with a missionary couple there. Linus (LEE-nus) Matongo (Mah-TONE-goe) then began studying God's Word earnestly.

Linus was well educated and evidently very smart since he secured a position as Post Master in the local post office. Rarely did the South Africans use Namibians in such positions, since they still had political control of the government. We learned of Linus through fellow missionaries in Windhoek. Katima was a place they wanted to begin a new work and it was in our area.

Linus seemed enthused about having a church and promoting more study of God's Word. He had been a nominal Christian but studying the Word had stirred his heart and spirit.

We encouraged Linus to begin a small group in his neighborhood, which he did. We were excited about a beginning of a good work in this remote town about twelve hours from our home. He helped open doors to new contacts in other area villages.

One morning, Carlos answered the phone. I heard him say, "Excuse me, please repeat that." They told him that Linus had died in a car accident and that the family wanted him, his pastor, to conduct his funeral.

The news was a complete shock. We had just started the ministry there and felt that Linus was so important to the ongoing of the work. Although we questioned the timing of this unfortunate accident, we knew God was in control. Immediately we made plans to leave for the funeral. Burial had to be in twenty-four hours, since there was no embalming in this area.

In Katima the next morning, we went to the large, open community center for the funeral. The massive crowd overwhelmed us. Even an hour before the service over 1500 people had gathered and more were streaming in. They placed chairs for the dignitaries, family and a few extras. Most people brought their own or sat on the floor. Many stood. Government officials from all over the region were present and several had comments to make on Linus's life. A local impromptu singers' group formed and began singing Christian songs. There was much trilling and many tears flowed.

In his funeral message, Carlos witnessed to over 2500 in the crowd who had come to mourn the passing of this dear man. He had a great opportunity to share about Linus's life and the need of God in everyone's life. Linus truly had a greater influence in death than life. Afterwards, we went to the home to be with the family for the traditional feast.

Linus had a precious son about nine years old who was overcome with grief. We tried to console him with words and hugs. When we asked about Linus's wife, we found that she was sitting on the floor in the middle of the room completely covered up under a large blanket.

Seeing movement under the blanket, I whispered to Carlos, "Do you see that there are two forms under the cover?"

"Surely, there couldn't be!"

Shortly Carlos went outside to talk to some of the men of the family. He found that Linus had been hiding from us that he had two wives. He had introduced us only to the older, who was the son's mother. The other was younger and had his two small children with her.

This shook us up realizing that Linus had without doubt been hiding the truth but was searching for a way to handle his family situation in a Christian way. Most of the town people did not know about the second wife, who had lived out of town on a small farm. His secret would stay with his immediate family and us. We did not want anything to harm his tremendous witness to the town, for he surely had a great witness in death.

> *"Everyone who believes that Jesus is the Christ is born of God." IJn 5:1*

C: Baptizing with Leeches

After numerous visits to Livuyu for preaching and teaching, many had made professions of faith and were awaiting baptism. We faithfully examined each to determine his or her readiness. Of the more than seventy who wanted baptism, we approved thirty-eight.

The river was more than two miles away. We knew that if we were to go there on foot, baptize, return and organize the church, the day would be well spent before we finished. We asked if there were a place nearby with enough water to baptize. Mwema (Mm-WAY-mah) said that there was a water hole just over the first hill where the cows and other animals drink. He said however, that they always went to the river to bathe and to collect water for household use. We agreed to go to see if the waterhole were suitable.

We filed across the field and up the incline, the people singing with jubilation as we walked along, in celebration of this special time. On arriving at the water hole, I waded out into the middle in search for the deepest water, which was only knee deep. I had baptized in less water before and felt this would be adequate. The candidates entered the water in single file to where I was standing.

After some words and praying, I began baptizing, asking each to kneel so I could put them completely under the water. After baptizing only three or four, the women back at the end of the line began jumping up and down and screaming.

I stopped and asked, "What is happening?"

The women quickly let us know that there were leeches in the water. They were attaching themselves to their feet and legs.

Knowing the potential danger from blood-sucking leeches, I asked that we go to the river. They begged that I carry on with the baptism. They said that they would manage to keep the leeches off. I was pleased that I still had on socks and trousers, as protection. We completed the baptism with a sense of urgency.

On the way back to the church, I told Myrtice, "Guess that was the fastest baptism I have ever performed"!

We also discussed the fact that we had thirty-eight new baptized converts with none who could read. We went on, organized the church, and promised them that we would be back in two weeks to teach about being a church. One of the things we wanted to do was to teach them how to read.

During the next two weeks, we prepared materials to help us in doing that. We would be teaching a language we did not know. Theirs being a Bantu language, the sounds and the grammar were the same that of Swahili and Ndonga. We used the Luchazi Bible (their language) to find basic words, made up simple dictionaries with hand-drawn pictures to illustrate and put the Luchazi name under it, etc. and simple sentences on the back. We felt that we could help them learn at least the fundamentals.

On returning, we found all thirty-eight new church members present along with many more who wanted to read. We worked diligently, and at the end of four days more than half could read. They were obviously very keen and intelligent. They had never before had an opportunity to learn. In the group was old Matias (Mah-TEE-aas). I had baptized him and he wanted very much to read. We had doubts about his ability to learn at his age.

At the end of the four days, each had a Scripture verse to read. When Matias took his little red book of Bible verses, he held it in one hand and placed the index finger of his other hand on syllable by syllable and successfully sounded each one. Then he went back and slowly pronounced the word, and having done so, his face lit up. He had pronounced a word, which he already knew. Having finished each word correctly, he went back and slowly read the verse. He pronounced every syllable with a vowel and every word correctly.

He then looked out to us, flipped his booklet into the air, jumped up, clapped his hands and said, "This is the most wonderful day of my life. It is as if I were blind and now I can see."

He then stooped down, picked up his booklet, and slowly read his verse again in his language. We were thrilled as he slowly read John 3:16 and shouted Amen.

> *"For God so loved the world that he gave his only begotten son . ." Jn 3:16a*

M: Be Saved Now

As we visited new villages, we were impressed with the welcome and interest of the villagers. The second time to visit Folesti (Foe-LAY-stee) near the end of the Caprivi strip we decided to first walk around through the village to invite all we saw to come join us for the service.

As we walked, many children and young people followed closely with us. We stopped to talk with everyone we could find sitting outside the huts on grass mats. Men were playing bao. Most of the men really enjoyed the game of moving round stones from hole to hole in the board. Everyone was very cordial and friendly. When we were about half way around the village on our walk, we met three older ladies sitting on the ground. One of whom was blind, one was an invalid and the third had severe arthritis and was very bent over. They seemed so pleased to talk to us.

"It is very hard for us to come to your service. Could you have a service with us here? We would be happy if you would."

"I don't know why we couldn't. Let's invite your neighbors to join us here under your tree."

Many joined us, some sitting down on the sand and others on buckets or on any item they could find handy. After we began singing, more joined us along with the crowd who had been following us. We had special prayer for these three afflicted ladies and others that may be ill in the village. We noticed several older youths sitting together observing rather than participating.

Carlos began a short message on humanity's basic need of knowing God. He became more emphatic on the work of Jesus Christ and His sacrifice for us, and everyone's need of salvation. When he was about halfway through his message, one of these young men jumped up and spoke, interrupting Carlos.

"I want Jesus as my Savior now. Can I have Jesus in my heart now?"

"Yes, right now you can trust Him," Carlos responded, and included an invitation to all. Six people came forward to ask Christ in their hearts that day even before the sermon was over.

We should never be amazed at the spontaneity of hearts that are ripe and ready for the Gospel.

"The harvest is plentiful but the workers are few." Mt 9:37a

C: Translating Songs

Since Jesaja (Yea-SAH-yah) had accepted Jesus after hearing our songs, we realized how important it would be to translate more songs into the Ndonga language. Wherever we introduced these songs, the people readily and enthusiastically accepted them. They loved to sing them and asked why we did not translate more.

The task was not easy. We attempted to convey the writer's meaning but found it difficult. Finding words with the right number of syllables is complicated. We would spend days and sometimes weeks in translating a single line or verse trying to get it just right.

We found that while traveling was a good time for the tedious jobs. If I were driving, Myrtice would write down what we decided as a good way to express something. If she were driving, I would do the writing. We would rejoice when completing one line or one verse. We sang them repeatedly until we got just the right order of words and rhyme.

When a song was ready, we would try it out in the churches. The people would tell us if the song were good or if it needed more work. When the people and we agreed that a song was good, we would make copies and circulate it among the churches. When we had twenty-five songs, we made up a booklet for use in the churches. Each time we came up with something new, the people rejoiced with us. All loved to sing and sang beautifully.

When we had translated 126 songs, we requested the mission for funds and permission to publish them in a permanent book. An office worker in Johannesburg entered the songs into her computer and provided copies suitable for publication. We then handed them over to a printing company in Windhoek.

While we were waiting for the songbooks to be printed, we planned to record them on tape so that the churches could not only have the words but also the tune. The mission's Director of Communications agreed to bring his recording equipment to Tsumeb and do the recording. He would make

as many copies as we needed. Missionaries and
representatives from each church agreed to come and to
assist.

We met at the Nomsoub (NOME-soob) church. More
than thirty people came from all over the area. Some slept in
the church. Myrtice prepared the food for everyone. We
worked for the next five days, in day and evening sessions.

The group sang a song repeatedly until everyone felt that
it was right. Then the Communications Director recorded it.
We went through this process for all 126 songs. Each time
we recorded a song, the group expressed satisfaction for
having done a good job.

The Communications Director took the recordings with
him to Edenvale and made the copies. When we received the
tapes, we sent them with tape players and songbooks to each
church which used the Ndonga language. They became a
tremendous source of worship in the churches.

"Sing to the Lord for he is highly exalted." Ex 15:2lb

M: Down the Road

After some of the main roads in the northeastern part of
Namibia were cleared from terrorists and patrolled regularly,
we ventured out to find new areas where we could bring a
witness. We prayed fervently that the Lord would show us
where we should go.

We drove a very long distance through partial desert
country without seeing any villages. For miles and miles, all
we could see were thorn bushes, small thorn trees and dry
parched ground. Occasionally we saw some very small
settlements but we were not impressed to stop.

After several hours we began seeing more vegetation and
behold, a tremendous village loomed before us! Beautiful
mud houses with grass roofs filled the cleared area. Only
sand surrounded the houses, for the people cleaned around
their houses to minimize the number of animals, snakes,

scorpions and insects coming into their homes. We could see goats, dogs, and naked children running about. Yes, we felt strongly in our hearts that this looked like the right place.

Speaking in Owambo, we inquired where to find the chief of the village. A chief is in full authority of large areas, and his permission is necessary before beginning work in his area. Two young men directed us to a large kraal (compound) where he lived. The chief's compound had several huts surrounded by tightly-placed, crooked poles made from small tree trunks to form an enclosure. After we called out for admission to come in, a young man came out to find out who we were. These people are very disturbed to see white faces, for they identify the South Africans as whites with whom they were fighting for freedom for self-rule.

After some delay, a tall, erect man with shoulders pulled back proudly came out, a strong scowl on his face. He certainly did not look like he welcomed us.

Carlos graciously introduced himself.

The chief seemed concerned that we might be spies of the South Africans.

Knowing that women are expected to be subservient and normally curtsy or bow to men, I felt that I needed to show all respect to him, so bowed very low on my knees before him. Suddenly, he relaxed and broke out into a wide smile. He was immensely pleased to see a white woman bowing respectfully before him. The expression of submission of a woman can really make a difference!

The chief invited us to an open room with a dirt floor. He had his servants give us two low, round, hand-carved stools, inviting us to sit down.

Quickly, he asked, "What can I do for you?"

Carlos simply stated, "We would like to start a church in your village."

"Well, we don't have any churches in this area, so I guess that would be okay. What else can you do to help us?"

"Since you are a long way from any towns, we could help you with medical care. My wife is a qualified, registered nurse and has helped many villages in the past."

Sadly, he said, "Many of our children die from malaria, even diarrhea, measles; and all sorts of things. Please come and help us. I beg you to come help my people with their physical needs."

He paused then said, "What else can you do for us?"

Holding out his Bible, Carlos said, "I don't see any schools in your village. Perhaps we could help some of your people read, even read God's book."

"Good! Good!" Enthusiastically he asked again, "What else can you do for us?"

Carlos scratched his head and warmly answered, "We want your people to know our Heavenly Father. We want you to have everlasting life."

Thoughtfully pausing, the chief then began slowly rubbing his chin and asked, "Can I have everlasting life?"

This opened the door for witnessing to this important man, sharing with him the message of Jesus Christ and His love for him. After a time of teaching and explaining to him, as well as answering his questions, he responded genuinely. We all bowed on our knees on the dirt floor.

He prayed the prayer of repentance and accepted Jesus Christ as his Lord and Savior. Our hearts jumped for joy with the moving of the Spirit in this most important leader. The door was now open to proclaim the Good News in this area.

Shortly, this man took us outside and gestured with his hand, "I want my whole village to hear this message and especially my own family."

He motioned with his hand to call a group that was nearby to gather around and instructed that some men bring logs for seats under a large tree next to his compound. Many others joined as they saw the people sitting together.

We proclaimed the Christian message that day and many days following. Many made professions of faith and accepted baptism. God worked His miracles in the hearts of these people. We assisted the chief in establishing a church under this same tree.

Later, these same villagers asked us to go down the road to the next village to share about God. They said they had aunts, uncles, and friends who had not heard the message of salvation. Down the road, we found another large village open to the message. Later these people pointed us down the road to their families and friends who had not known about our loving Father. Again, we continued down the road, sharing the magnificent message of our Lord. This began as a fire burning quickly in dry bush. God continued to open doors through his people.

At Livuyu, on down the road, a church began meeting under a large baobab tree for several months. Then the rains started. On our next visit we were pleased to see that they had built a nice building out of the stalks of millet, a staple grain much like corn that grows in the short rainy season. They made such a cool building where winds could blow through the walls.

On one of our visits later, we were startled to see that the building was gone; only some small poles leaning to the ground.

"What happened to your church?"

One of the leaders quickly responded, "One day last week when we were not around our cows got hungry and ate it up."

It was not long before we assisted them in building a permanent church frame. They finished the sides. They were so proud to have a house of worship.

> *"Unless the Lord builds the house,*
> *Its builders labor in vain." Ps 127:1*

C: Biggest Witchdoctor

We had spent Saturday night at Kaisosi (Kai-ee-SO-see) in our pickup truck next to the church. Very early on Sunday

morning, people began arriving from every direction. Soon
the church was filled with more than eight hundred people
with many congregated outside, near windows, in order to
hear what would be going on inside. Since there were few
benches, many had brought chairs, stools, small benches,
boxes and buckets for seating.

When the service began, the people sang with
exuberance, some swaying to the rhythm of the drum beat.
They sang with happiness and joy. There were
announcements. Various choirs sang, (some visiting),
swaying in tune by walking down the aisles to the front. Also
there were several testimonies.

More than forty parents stood across the front of the
church with their babies. Moses, the local missionary, and I
placed our hands on the babies and their parents, prayed with
them and dedicated them to the Lord.

I preached as the congregation listened in silence. From
time to time a woman would stand with her baby, move from
side to side as to rock him. Some took their babies and went
outside. For the most part there was little movement in the
church.

When I had finished my sermon, Moses and the deacons
stood at the front of the church facing the congregation. We
began singing and many came forward to express their
acceptance of Christ as Savior and their desire to become
church members. More than thirty stood with Moses and the
deacons at the front of the church.

I looked up and saw an unusual-looking man coming
down the aisle. His clothes were crumpled. He was shabby
and his hair was matted and dirty. He was holding a bundle
in his hands. People from both sides of the aisle were staring
at him. When he reached the front of the church, I saw him
hand his bundle to Moses and he began to speak. I could not
understand him but later learned that he was telling Moses,
"I do not need these any more. I am accepting the
missionary's Jesus."

I turned to one behind me asking, "Who is that?"

"Livingi (Lee-VEEN-gee) Chimuma (Chee-MOO-mah)!

I, not having heard that name before, turned again and asked, "Who is Livingi Chimuma?"

A man whispered in my ear, "He is the witchdoctor."

After the service, they told me that Livingi was the biggest witchdoctor in the area. Most people lived in fear of him. Many paid him large sums of money to 'cure' them and some paid him money to place curses on their enemies. Some had told us that he had threatened to curse us, as we were a hindrance to his work.

Livingi's two teen-age daughters had been coming to church and had become members at Kaisosi. They had told their witchdoctor Daddy about Jesus and begged him to attend church. Members said that for some weeks he would appear at the church after the services had begun and would stand outside, near a window, to hear what was going on inside. As he would slip away as soon as the service was over, no one had been able to speak with him.

On this Sunday, he had, for the first time, come inside and sat on the floor just inside the back door. He later shared his decision with us.

"As the church bell (a large piece of metal hanging by a wire from a tree limb) sounded this morning, I began to hurt. It felt like a hot spear was piercing my heart. My daughters had begged me many times to come to church and hear about Jesus. All I could tell them was that I hated the people of the church and especially the missionaries who had started it.

"Today, God was speaking to me and I made my decision. I went around the house, gathered up my goods of witchcraft, and bundled them in this old cloth. Today was the day that I would follow Christ."

Assuring us he would not practice witchcraft again, he left the church that morning a changed man. He not only had given his heart to God but his profession as well.

On our next visit to Kaisosi, a clean and well-dressed man greeted me. He had combed his hair. He had on a clean and well-pressed shirt and tie. When I introduced myself to him he said, 'You have already met me. I accepted Jesus the last time you were here."

Myrtice and I spent the night again in our pickup as we had already planned to have church leadership training and a clinic the next day. Many had walked in, on Sunday evening, from several churches. I would teach while Myrtice would hold clinic.

Livingi, who had previously been using his concoctions of bones, parts of animals and skins and other articles for treating people, now came with his medical problem. He told Myrtice, "My chest hurts. May I have some of God's medicine?"

"As surely as I live, says the Lord, 'every knee will bow before me; every tongue will confess to God.'" Ro 14:11

Chapter Twelve

Namibia II

Our work expanded until we had followers from among seven different Namibian tribes and with others from Angola to the north and Zambia to the east. Many being ancestral and spirit worshipers readily responded to our Spirit God.

We saw the marula trees with fruits the size of golf balls. Elephants and baboons ate the fermented fruits and became drunk. Their staggering around fascinated and amused anyone who saw them.

Corn crickets, large and plump grasshopper-like creatures, appeared in large numbers at the end of the rains. They would mate; lay their eggs in the ground for the next season and hang around until they died or other corn crickets ate them. Vehicles crushed many on the roads and in turn, other corn crickets ate them. We could do little to get rid of them. We waited until they disappeared after six or seven weeks.

One of Africa's grandest game parks, the Etosha (Aa-TOW-shah) Game Park north of Tsumeb attracted visitors from around the world. A wide variety of animals lived there and visitors could easily see them at the water holes.

M: Ghost at the Water Tap

As many churches came into being, we were aware of their needs for buildings. Meeting under trees was adequate until a group was established, but a building added stability and prestige in the villages. We devised a plan of providing the basic frame with a metal roof, doors and window frames while the church was responsible for the sides, seating and flooring. The mission graciously provided the needed funds.

While building the basic structure we camped in the village to see that the materials were there, to supervise the work, and worked side by side with them. As the only woman of the crowd, I did my share with 'go-fer' work, finding tools and handing things to Carlos while he was high on a ladder. I also provided food for the volunteer workers -- sweetened hot tea with bread, butter and jam in the mid-morning. Later I cooked a one-pot, main meal, such as stew with meat and vegetables. We stayed in the village the three or four days that it took to complete the basic work. I also did some first aid and needed medical work for the villagers. Again, we slept in our pickup, with limited bathing facilities and outdoor toilet facilities; a hole in the ground enclosed with a tall grass fence.

After we had completed two church frames, we moved, with our supplies, to the Deli (DAY-lee) village to begin work on their church. We were both absolutely exhausted from the heat and work, but wanted to stay with it until the last building in this area was completed. I was feeling the grime, especially bothersome in my hair. Being in such heat with dust blowing everywhere, I knew I had to wash my hair to be able to live with myself.

After we arrived in early afternoon, several men came out to assist with unloading the building supplies. I knew this was my chance to find a tap in the village. Since villages of this size in this area had only one or two taps, I knew there would be a long line of women waiting with their buckets and clay pots for water. Seeing that Carlos did not need me right then, I was going to search out a tap so I could wash my hair.

This being the hottest time of day, I could see many taking their siesta on grass mats outside their huts.

"Oh, good," I thought. "Maybe there will be a short line."

I began following the heaviest traveled path searching for the tap. Over half mile back in the village, I suddenly saw the tap without a soul around. "How wonderful this is," I thought as I knelt down at the base of the tap, which was about two feet high.

Just to feel the cool, clean water flowing on my head was heaven itself for the moment. I poured a little shampoo to proceed to wash my hair thoroughly. As I was near to finishing with my head down I heard talking and buckets clanking. Some ladies were nearing the tap. As they neared, I raised up, throwing my head back and squeezing the water from my hair.

Screams and running followed. I could not imagine what was happening. Then two ladies slowly edged back staring at me. Then they burst out laughing.

"We thought you were a ghost! We have never seen a white woman in our village before."

Then, I began to tell them why we were here. They had three little children with them. Each one had infected eyes.

"This afternoon we are having a service at our church under the trees. Please come and join us. Also I could give you some medicine for your children's eyes."

They told me that they lived about three miles on the other side of the village but they would like to come. They said they had never been to a church.

Much to my pleasure, they did come to the service. Afterwards, I talked to them about our Lord, while I gave them medicine for the eyes of their children. This was not the end. They came later that week at the dedication of the building. One of them came forward, making a confession of faith. The other one told me later that she too wanted to come but wanted to try to get her husband to come with her in the next service.

It is amazing how God uses all such encounters for His glory?

> *"Now to him who is able to do immeasurably*
> *more than all we ask or imagine, According*
> *to his power that is at work within us." Eph 3:20*

C: Wiping away Salvation

We met Ndiana (Nn-dee-AH-nah) on our first visit to Buffalo, an Angolan refugee camp and army camp set up by the South African army on the cliff high above the Great

Kavango (Kah-VAHN-go) River. Moses had gained permission for our visit by knowing some of the Christians who lived there. They had requested his assistance in starting a church.

Ndiana was among the group of seven with whom we first met. She readily appeared to be the spokesperson and leader of this small group who wanted a church and had a desire to share their witness with others in the camp. We read and discussed Scripture and encouraged them the best we could. The visit lasted well over two hours. After praying, Ndiana called me aside before we left.

She quietly said, "I do not know whether or not I am a Christian."

"Why do you say that?"

I stood quietly as she told her story, "A missionary came and preached in our village in Angola. When he finished preaching, he asked those who wanted to be Christians to lift their hands. I lifted mine. He then said that to be Christians he would have to baptize us.

A woman brought a pan of water and placed it on the little table in front of him. He said that if we wanted him to baptize us we must come and stand in front of him. I was one of the first to go. He then took water from the bowl in his two hands and began pouring it over our heads each time saying, 'Now you are a Christian.'

She continued, "When it became my turn I was so happy. I was anxious to hear him say that I was a Christian but when he poured the water on my head, it ran down into my eyes. I took my hands and wiped it away. Afterwards he left and I did not see him again. The war came to our village and we all ran away and came here to Buffalo.

I waited patiently as she continued, "I keep thinking of what I did. I feared that by wiping the water from my face I had wiped away my salvation, so I really do not know whether I am a Christian or not."

She paused. I waited a moment and then said, "Ndiana, if you believed and accepted Jesus in your heart, nothing can wipe that away. The water did not make you a Christian."

In the next several minutes, she assured me that she had trusted Jesus as her Savior and said that she still trusted him. She convinced me that she had received Jesus in her heart and that she had been born again.

We left assuring them that we would return—that God would lead them and us in their having a church and witness at Buffalo.

"For I am convinced that neither death nor life . . anything . . will be able to separate us from the love of God that is in Christ Jesus our Lord." Ro 8:-38-39

M: Headman's Grandson

As we were working in the Lozi villages in the Caprivi Strip, we were aware that there were many small Bushmen tribal people in the area. Anytime we tried to encounter them, they ran away in fear. We began to have a burden to reach them with the message of Christ.

The Bushmen were unique in their appearance with their small statures, near Oriental facial appearance with light yellowish brown-colored skin. Their language was of clicking sounds. They lived mainly in the desert areas of the Kalahari and the Namib Desert. During the terrorist war, the South African army had brought them to the Caprivi Strip to assist in identifying the track and direction the terrorists were passing. Being keen trackers, they knew the signs of every animal and person passing an area. Their very survival in the desolate desert depended on their expertise. The SA army had brought them to the area where they had temporary villages with their wives and children.

During a service in the Wayawaya village, under some trees, we asked for prayer needs of the group. The leader immediately asked us to pray for a Bushman headman's grandson who was dying. They were just behind and over a way from this village. After the service, we asked if we could go over to pray with them ourselves.

A group from this little church escorted us to the area of the village where the headman lived. The headman arose and came up to this delegation. After our pastor introduced us, we asked about his grandchild. He nodded to a group of women sitting near the middle of the compound. With his approval, we gathered around this young mother, about fifteen years old, holding a dying child. We had our prayer and the men stepped back.

I drew close and could see the child was glassy eyed, his skin grayish in color, and his breathing labored. I knew he was at the point of dying. My medicine would not be adequate. I asked her if I might take her to the hospital at Katima Mulilo about forty miles away. She shook her head, "No!" I began begging her to let me take her, for I felt that there was still a possibility of saving the child. Again, she shook her head, "No!".

I noticed an older woman nearby. I asked if she were the baby's grandmother. "Yes," she said.

"Please, beg your daughter to let us help. Otherwise, the child cannot live. Our God is good and He will have mercy on you and give you help."

Without another word, the grandmother grabbed the child out of the mother's arms, went to a bucket of water and began briskly bathing the baby. She then wrapped him in a fresh cloth. "Let us go now."

Without hesitation, I led the way to our pickup truck. The mother and grandmother, with the baby, sat in the front with me while other women filled the back of the truck.

We sped down the road with the accelerator to the floor. Cows, goats, bicycles and many people filled the roadway. Trying to be as careful as possible, I felt the Lord was shooing them out of the way. I prayed fervently for this child.

Upon arrival at the hospital, I drove right into the emergency area. We had prayed for someone to help us and God provided a nurse, on her break, standing outside.

As soon as I told her what was happening and seeing the child, she took him and raced inside the ER.

After a short time, we saw that he was on oxygen, IV's, and antibiotics. We all went to the room where he was alone with his mother. As we gathered around, I asked again if I could lead in prayer. The mother nodded, 'yes' this time as tears ran down her cheeks. I prayed asking God to provide healing, if that were His will, and that this little life would glorify Him.

All the women filled the truck again and we went back to the village leaving only the mother and baby.

After three more days of ministry in the area, we both went to the hospital to check on the child. He was surviving and looking much better. The mother had a faint smile now, when she saw us.

"I had just given up for my child. I wanted him to live so very much, but I felt like there was no chance for him. Thank you for bringing us to the hospital. Now I feel like he may make it."

After a short visit and prayer, we assured the mother that we would continue to lift up her child to the Lord for his merciful healing. We knew we would be away for a short while but would return to see about the child. We returned home that day continuing to pray for the baby.

Before we could see the baby again, Carlos slipped a disc severely, while we were building another church frame in the area. He took a small plane back to Tsumeb from where he flew to South Africa for emergency surgery. I wanted to check on the child but had to return home immediately in order to go to Pretoria to be with Carlos.

Moses, with church members, finished the church frame. He and I drove the five hundred miles back to Rundu.

When we stopped in Rundu at Moses' house, his children ran out to greet him saying they had a new baby.

His wife, Rosa, had given birth to a little daughter while we were away. On seeing us, Rosa said, "I want to name the baby after you. We will call her Myrtice."

I was shocked but pleased that they thought enough of me to name their child after me. They were some of the dearest friends and co-workers anyone could have.

I drove the 250 miles on to Tsumeb.

After surgery and six months of recuperation, Carlos felt that he was able to visit the churches in the Caprivi Strip again. One of the first places we wanted to go was the village of the Bushmen chief.

This time, as we drove up into the sandy village, dozens of children came running out, jumping with joy, to greet us. Immediately I asked one about the chief's grandson.

"Look, here his mother comes."

She was holding this beautiful healthy-looking boy in her arms. I reached out to hold him, and to give the mother a hug.

"I am so thankful to the Lord for your child! He looks beautiful!" I told here. "What did you name him?"

"Oh, we call him Owensi, after you. He wouldn't be alive without you."

"I think it was completely the Lord's work of healing and mercy that your child is alive. I just want to praise God for his saving the life of your baby."

She responded with a big smile, understanding the truth of my words. That very day she stepped forward, in the service, to profess the Lord as her Savior and joined the church.

From this encounter with the Bushmen and reaching out to help them, we saw God do amazing things to save many of their lives with their trust and belief in Jesus Christ as their Lord and Savior. Several churches came into being and many lives turned to Christ in this unique tribal group. We must remember that a dying baby opened the way to these Bushmen.

"Let them know that you, whose name is the Lord—that you alone are the Most High over all the earth." Ps 83:18

C: Timo's Dream

We stopped at the gate to Owamboland to our north west and asked the soldier guard if there were a headman in the village.

Pointing to the right the soldier said, "Yes. His name is Timo (TEE-mow). He lives right over there."

We thanked him, pulled through the gate and over to the house to which he had pointed. A small, elderly light-colored woman greeted us fondly. We asked about Headman Timo.

"He has gone to see about the cows. Please come in. He will be back soon. I am his wife, Betty."

We went in, sat down and she served us sweet African tea. She asked about why we had come. When we told her that we were missionaries and wanted to see about a church in the village she became excited and said that she would send her grandson to call Timo. The boy ran quickly away into the bush.

Only a short time passed when Timo and his grandson came in. He was an elderly, tall, large and an important looking African. His grandson had told him about us on their way back to the house.

Betty handed Timo a glass of water and, sipping on it he said, "So you are missionaries?"

"Yes. We have come to visit you and to see if there is a need for at church at Oshivelo (O-she-VAY-low)."

Headman Timo shook his head slowly as if in disbelief and said, "While I was in Cape Town, I dreamed of coming back to Namibia and having a church near my home. God has sent you to bring an answer to my dream."

Timo explained that he had some years before gone to Cape Town to find work. While there he had married but longed to come back to Namibia. When Namibia was about to gain independence he came home. He wanted to assist in any way he could in a new, independent government.

When he got back to Oshivelo, the village people recognized him as being a good leader and chose him as their headman. He said that he had been back more than two years and often recalled his dream about a church. He said that he was not a Christian but wanted to be one.

"If you will help me to have a church, I will give you land for the church and for a cemetery."

We came back the following Sunday and found a large group waiting for us under some trees not too far from Timo's house. After preaching and explaining as best we could how people become Christians, most of those present expressed a desire to be Christians.

We came often after that and taught the people. After about two months, we planned to have a baptizing. We would baptize Timo, his wife and more than twenty other villagers.

As there were many other places for us to go, Timo took the leadership of the church at Oshivelo. The church grew. In less than a year, we assisted them in putting up a simple church building.

In less than two years after our going to Oshivelo Timo became sick and died. I was to have his funeral in his home village several miles from Oshivelo. We wondered how the village people there would take to us, as we were complete strangers to most of them. We knew that Timo's having been a headman, there would be many important people at the funeral, including government people from Windhoek, the capitol of Namibia.

On the day of the funeral, we were amazed to see masses of people gathered under trees in a large open place where all stood around at the edge of a schoolyard. The homemade wooden casket was on cement blocks in the middle.

Family and friends brought wild flowers from the fields and placed them, unarranged, at the base of the casket. Some brought bougainvillea from their yards. We brought an arrangement of silk flowers, which we placed on top of the casket. Many were in tears and women's trills were heard throughout the crowd.

Several local and government people spoke before I did. To my surprise and pleasure, each spoke of Timo as being a leader of his church and of me as his leader. Each one seemed to be proud that Timo "had his church."

I told the people of Timo's dream and that we were proud to have been a part of its fulfillment. I said that he would continue to influence his village even after his death.

When Timo was gone, those in the small church remained faithful and others took the leadership role. The dream came to fruition to the glory of God.

> "...*an angel of the Lord appeared to him in a dream...*" Mt 1:20b

M: Waiting for water

After the church at Omutsegonime (lion's head) was organized, we always had to pass by the house of their pastor, Raimund, to get to the church. We would stop to see if any were still at home to give them a lift to the church about another mile or so away. The sand is very deep in this area and even walking is very tiring.

On one Sunday we were passing the hand-dug well when we saw the pastor's wife, Marta, come running to wave us down.

"I have been here since first daylight but the water is so little and so many people are waiting. I cannot go to church without washing the faces of my children. I want to go to church but my family must be clean." Marta sounded so pitiful. She had six small children.

We waited patiently for her, knowing she would otherwise miss the service. The buckets were dropped into the wells and water pulled up slowly. Because so little water seeped through the ground, they had to wait for each bucket to have even a little water.

The whole hillside was bone dry, no vegetation survived. It had been a severe drought this season. The cows were so thin that all their ribs showed.

Finally, Marta had enough water. We helped her load her two small buckets into the truck and drove to her house. She quickly cleaned up her children and we were off to the church down the sandy road. The people packed the church singing with great enthusiasm. We were glad that Marta cared enough to keep her family clean for church.

On another day, we were going to the church heading up to pick up Marta and her children again. This time we stopped suddenly in the sandy tracks when we saw a donkey lying in the road, loaded with two large ten-gallon tins tied on his back. Over to the side was the five-year-old son of Raimund and Marta, with tears running down his face. He was so small and distressed that he could not get the donkey to stand up so he could get the water home in time for church. He could not even speak.

We both got out, untied the water cans from the donkey's back and placed them in the truck. Then we picked up the boy and put him with us in the front seat. The donkey just lay there, for he was weak from the drought with little food and water.

When we arrived at their house, the little boy ran to his mother shouting with joy that he had gotten the water home, even when the donkey would not go.

Marta, too, was happy to see us. She had been worried that her son had not come home. She was a remarkable woman living in such a difficult situation.

On another day when we dropped by her home to carry her to church, she came running out with a new baby.

"Marta, you have had your baby. We are so happy for you."

"Yes, but I did have a difficult time. Raimund was away when I went into labor and the older children were in school."

"What did you do?"

"Well, this time I had to have the baby all by myself. However, I am thankful that it all went well. I did not even have time to call a neighbor. God was with me and I am so thankful!"

Yes, Marta is an amazing woman!

"But a woman who fears the Lord is to be praised.
Give her the reward she has earned, and let her
works bring her praise at the city gate." Pr 31:30b-31

M: Bible Business

Looking through the bookstore in our little town, I asked, "Do you have any Bibles in the local languages?"

"Sorry, none of the stores have Bibles. The only place you can get them is in Windhoek."

"Do you really mean that in all the northern area of Namibia there are no Bibles for the local people?"

"That's right. We cannot get them up here. You'll have to go to Windhoek to the Bible Society office."

We knew that the only source of the written Gospel needed to be in the hands of the people. We were amazed that no distributors existed in the northern area where the largest population of the country lived.

Immediately, we made plans to visit the Bible Society and place orders for Bibles in seven languages of the people with whom we worked. Some were only partial translations of one book of the Bible, or just a few books. We wanted extra Bibles to distribute among the church people and others who wanted them. We would sell them at a minimum price, for we had money to subsidize them. The most important thing was to have Bibles available to all people.

Word spread through the town of Tsumeb where we lived, and soon we had many calls, even for English Bibles, from local people. The bookstore referred people to us who had come in asking for Bibles. Hence, we always carried boxes of Bibles, in all the languages, with us, in the truck, ready when someone wanted to buy one.

As we approached the Folesti (Foe-LAY-stee) village, many people were waiting for our arrival and a worship service that day. After a great time of sharing, we announced for the first time that we had Bibles in several languages to sell. As soon as the service was over, a huge group gathered at the back of the baki (BAH-kee), our pickup. I would sell them since Carlos had much planning and discussions with the church leaders.

As one older man waited, he asked if we had a Bible in the Lozi language. I assured him that we did. I looked around and pulled out the Bible he wanted and handed it to him.

"We have never seen one in our language. Are you sure it is Lozi?'

"Oh, yes. Here in the front, it says: Bible in Lozi Language."

"Whoopee" (translated into English) he began hollering loudly as he looked into the Bible. "Yes, yes this is Lozi. Wonderful, now I can really read God's Word. I'm so excited. I'm so happy!"

Everywhere we went people were hungry to own their personal Bible. All were excited to be able to read the Word in their own language. We were so thankful that we could help.

In fact, we used the Bible as witness to the South African army who stopped us frequently for major roadblocks. As they pointed their guns into our faces, demanding to see what we had with us, we gladly opened the boxes of Bibles, asking if they would like one in their language. Most times, they accepted them gladly and waved us on our way.

Surely, God's word opens up hearts and lives for the Savior.

> "So is my word that goes out from my mouth: it will not
> return to me empty, but will accomplish what I desire
> and achieve the purpose for which I sent it." Is 55:11

C: Pastor's Uncle is Witchdoctor

Sitali (See-TAH-lee) and his family accepted Jesus and I baptized them in the Zambezi River before we knew that crocodiles infested the waters. When the converts in his village became a church, they chose him as their pastor and he led them well. He knew little about Christianity but learned quickly.

Coming to Tsumeb for pastor training was, for Sitali, an enlightening experience. Fellowship with other church leaders and learning from the Bible meant much to him. He would never forget traveling to and from Tsumeb. On the way, he saw donkeys for the first time and talked about that so much that I sometimes found it difficult to keep on track in the classes.

Since it was more than 500 miles from Tsumeb to Katima Mulilo where Sitali lived, we did not go there as much as we would have liked. When we did go, we tried to spend enough time to visit all the churches in the area and have time with church leaders. Sometimes we would stay in a small, simple guest house in the town, instead of sleeping in the pickup.

On one occasion, we checked in at the guest house to spend the night to find that of their six rooms, none was available. The manager allowed us to sleep on cots in the eating area, where people fixed their own meals. In the middle of the night, red biting ants disturbed our sleep. Jumping up and trying to remove the ants was quite a hassle. We ended up sleeping in the pickup again.

The next morning, we drove out to Sitali's village. We found him quite ill with a high fever and lying on a mat next to his hut. There was a cow tied to a tree near by. Not having seen his having animals before, I asked him about this one. He tried to avoid talking about the cow. I could tell that things were not just right.

"Sitali, tell me about this cow."

"I am afraid to tell you."

"Don't be afraid. Tell me about the cow."

He began what was to be quite a lengthy explanation,"My uncle is a witchdoctor. I had not seen him in a long time. When he heard about my being sick, he came to see me. He was unhappy and angry when he found out that I was a Christian and especially when hearing that I was the leader of our church.

"He told me that I must buy a cow and give it to him in order for him to make me well. Otherwise, he said that I would die.

"I know that witchcraft is wrong. It is of the devil. I told him that I could not do what he wanted. He said that I would die, and, then he walked away.

"After he left, my wife and children begged me to do what my uncle wanted. They believed that I would die. Finally, I sent one of my sons to look for a cow. He bought this one. We sent word to my uncle that I have the cow. We are waiting for him to come."

At this point, I asked that we pray. After prayer, I opened my Bible, read and talked about how Jesus and our God are greater than the witchdoctor. I told him that I was confident that he would not die if he trusted Jesus and took the medicine which Myrtice would give him.

We also talked with his wife and children. He agreed to trust Jesus and take Myrtice's medicine.

Myrtice had already perceived that Sitali had a bad case of malaria. She had the needed medicine and gave him what she felt he required. We prayed again and left to visit some other churches.

The next morning when we came to Sitali's village we found that his fever had subsided. He was still quite sick but better.

We saw him daily for the remaining days we were in the area and each day he was better. He and his family were pleased with the decision he had made with our help.

When we came again after several weeks, he and his family were praising God for his healing and preaching about it everywhere he went. He sold the cow to friends who operated a meat market.

"The acts of the sinful nature . . witchcraft . . and the like will not inherit the Kingdom of God." Gal. 5:20

M: Christmas at Kaisosi

For new Christians in Africa, Christmas is the day of big celebrations at the church. They rejoice in the birth of the Savior and enjoy the fellowship of the body of believers. There are no trees or tinsels or even gift giving, but true rejoicing in the remembrance of the birth of the Savior.

One Christmas, we wanted to be at the Kaisosi Church in Rundu for the weekend with special revival services leading up to Christmas day. All the nearby churches came to participate, so the crowds were huge, well over one thousand attending. Those who had come long distances on foot slept on the church floor bringing their own blankets and some food.

We felt that a great pageant of the Christmas story would be very appropriate. I made plans for costumes and props and wrote the simple story, using someone to read the Scripture dialogue, with choirs singing at designated times. While Carlos was busy with affairs of the church and visitation, I gathered a few together to rehearse the scenes beforehand. I knew it would be a very meaningful and beautiful way to convey the story.

We were astonished that the church planned to start very early -- at four a.m. We questioned if they really meant this time but we were firmly reassured.

We were up and out of our sleeping place in the pick-up truck on time. As we entered the church, we could not believe it. The house was packed. Yes, they really meant to begin so early. Shortly after prayers and a song or two, we went out to the side of the church for a continuation of the service.

Since there is no electricity or lights, it seemed very dark, but we could vaguely see enough to understand what was happening.

By flashlight, someone read the Scripture about Mary and Joseph going to Bethlehem. A young woman, sitting on a donkey, led by a man in flowing clothing, passed by to a small area, then to another and finally to a tent area with straw. They had found the stable, where they got down and sat in the straw.

A few minutes after singing and more Scripture, a light came rolling down from one tree to a place right over the stable. They had tied one end of a long rope to a place high in a tree with a flashlight that would slide down to the right place. Their ingenuity amazed us, as they portrayed beautifully the scene of the birth. The "star" came to rest over the baby, a real, tiny newborn in the arms of its mother.

Then we went inside for the pageant that I had prepared, the scene in the stable with the child while choirs sang of Christ's birth, "Away in the Manger." Wise men also came to present gifts.

In spite of gaudy dress and crowns, they performed proudly. We had lanterns all around to lighten the stage with breathtaking beauty. All began to sing "Joy to the World" with strong emotion and meaning.

About daybreak, we dismissed and enjoyed hot African tea with bread. Each person brought his or her own cup for the tea. Several ladies had tended the roasting of two oxen above open fires.

After a short break, we all went inside for the regular worship service. With many choirs and several sermons, the service lasted into the afternoon. Then we all went out for the big feast of meat and corn meal mush for our Christmas dinner.

This was one of the most significant Christmases we ever experienced; a day when we really celebrated the birth of our Savior and honored His name.

'For unto us a child is born, to us a son is given . .' Isa 9:6

M: Big Boots

After the South African army commander had told us to be always alert to terrorists in the region, we observed closely those who attended the clinics. The army was fearful that the terrorists would kidnap me to care for their wounded, as they had done with several health workers in the rural areas.

One of the most remote areas we visited was Omakolombongo (Oh-ma-ko-low-mm-BOW-nn-go), miles deep in the Owambo region from where many of the terrorists had come. It took us nearly an hour to weave our way back into the remote area of shrub bush, tall anthills towering 10-12 feet high, and winding sand roads.

An existing church, having been begun only a few years before by a group and abandoned, invited us. We found an old lady, Rebeka, who was leading the church and kept it going.

She lived in a typical Owambo kraal surrounded by poles from tree trunks. The entrance was like an inverted cow's yoke, through which one must step up to pass over. She said it was to deter lions from coming into the kraal.

Rebeka lived alone most of the time but had some of her families' children stay with her to help in planting her fields with millet. She had a large pile of millet heads drying in the sun. Holding the heads one by one, she would beat the seeds out, and then pound them into flour.

The church was a strong looking, mud building with a heavy grass roof. We were pleased to see the small congregation singing and reading the scripture. At that time, they only had a schoolgirl who would read the Scripture and speak briefly from it. However, they were very fervent in their prayers. They welcomed us royally and were attentive to the sermon on our first visit.

After many visits, we began clinics and assisted them in building a more permanent building, since the termites had eaten the poles of their building and the mud walls were falling away. The church membership was growing and they definitely needed a larger room for church services.

On the day after the church frame was up, we were able to have a full day, preaching in the early morning and clinics for the rest of the day. Of course, the building still had only poles to hold up the roof. The sides were open, waiting for walls of some sort, which the people would provide. The winds blew strongly through the open place but they helped cool the 105-degree weather.

Profuse drops of sweat dropped off our faces but no one thought anything about it. There were so many patients coming from every direction through the bush that I got too involved to think about the heat or even terrorists.

Later in the afternoon, I was caring for an old man who had a cut on his foot. As I was bending down to treat it, I looked to the next feet and saw a pair of very heavy army boots. I was startled, knowing that these were the feet of a terrorist, for no one else wore this kind of boots. Everyone else was barefooted except us. When he came for his examination he was dressed as most of the men of the area, only the shoes were different. I wanted to send word to Carlos who was out visiting with one of the leaders. All I could do was pray hard that this man had come alone.

After examining him and giving him the medicine he needed, I asked if he would like a book to read about our Savior who wanted to bring peace to our world and to our hearts. He said "yes" in very correct Ndonga. Looking into his eyes all I could see was a kind and courteous man with a tender heart. I shared with him a tract on salvation and the book of John. He smiled and thanked me profusely.

"I am so glad to have something to read." he commented and quickly moved out of sight into the heavy scrub brush surrounding us.

However, I kept a keen eye open for any more wearing big boots. I was so thankful that on this day I was able to witness to a man who needed the Lord and who did not use his gun on me. I am sure he had one hidden in the bush.

"But I trust in you, O Lord; I say, "You are my God."
My times are in your hands; deliver me from my
enemies And from those who pursue me." Ps 31:14-15

C: Youth Start Churches

When Kaisosi had grown to have a membership over five hundred, youth choirs began to develop. Eventually the four youth choirs all expected to sing at every service. Each choir made up songs with messages for every occasion. They would prepare a new song to honor their missionaries each time we came.

With four to six songs ready for every service, it became necessary to limit the number of songs a choir could sing. Eventually the church world tell each choir that they would be given time for only two songs.

The youth outsmarted the church by marching in with a song and after singing their two songs before the church, marching out with another song. The marching in and out eventually became very slow, in order for them to get in a few more verses. Since they sang well, there was little complaint. The services just became longer and longer. Other churches in the area heard about the youth choirs and invited them to sing in their churches.

After a time Moses decided to use these choirs to go to villages without churches. Sometimes they would walk a full day to reach a certain village, sing in the evening, sleep over and sing the next day and evening, being gone from their homes over two nights.

Moses and other church leaders would accompany the choirs. The youth infiltrated the village, sharing about the Lord and teaching them to sing. Moses would preach and many accepted Christ, opening doors for beginning new churches. The young people would have the new village's youth to sing with them for the services. In turn, each of the new churches organized their own youth choirs and some of them became missionary singers, going into more villages without churches.

"I want men everywhere to lift up holy hands in prayer."
ITi 2:8

M: Livuyu Baby

With many young churches beginning, we knew we had to spend extra time in teaching them and their leaders to strengthen their faith. We began by making rounds to all the churches in the northern strip, spending at least a day or so at each village. These were all far from any town and actually in the 'bush' areas and long distances apart. Often we traveled over 1500 miles for the two weeks of ministry each month. We had to carry food and water for the whole time, medical supplies for the clinics, and boxes of Bibles in seven different languages.

This type of ministry required some 'rough' living but we did not mind doing what it took to strengthen the young churches. Just immersing ourselves in the work was our trademark. We found that it was best to sleep in the back of our pickup under the canopy. We removed our supplies from the pickup at night and put them in the front or under the truck. Africans were always very gracious to invite us to sleep in their homes but we had found that it was more comfortable with less mites, fleas and mosquitoes in the pickup. We bathed from a pan of water behind the truck after dark when we could be free from 'visitors.'

Our food was mostly canned goods cooked in a pot for dinner over our little gas burner. It was a struggle to keep the flame going in the hard winds which are customary in this semi-desert area. The people were so poor and had so little, we asked that we prepare our own food. Otherwise, they would kill their only chicken to serve us while the family went without food. All day, even to late evening, people surrounded us. We needed some time for unwinding as well as planning for the next day.

After being out for twelve days we were very exhausted and supplies were nearly finished. We pulled up into the Livuyu village late one afternoon for preaching that evening. For the next day, we had planned for pastor training, including those from surrounding churches. The enthusiastic welcome of singing and clapping in rhythm by a great crowd lifted our spirits, eased our tiredness and recharged our souls.

Shortly the church began to fill up with people coming from every direction. The joy of the congregation and anticipation of a great service flowed over into our hearts. After singing, prayer and all the preliminaries they wanted to do, Carlos stood behind a rough wooden pulpit and preached a powerful sermon that touched hearts. Several came forward making a commitment to Christ. All this lifted our spirits so high that we could hardly sleep that night.

As the early morning light streaked the sky, someone calling us to get up awakened us unexpectedly.

"We're hungry for the Word, and we want to hear more preaching."

We had planned only pastor training for that day, but with that invitation we could not refuse. After a quick breakfast, we gathered with the congregation for an early morning service. What a delightful way to start a day, in worship!

After the service, Carlos, pointing to the large group of children sitting near the front on grass mats, said to me, "I think you had better take care of these sick children instead of teaching with me today. I can manage by myself."

Many had infected eyes with flies swarming around them. Others had deep coughs, and some had open sores or white skin fungus. My tender heart did not delay. I quickly pulled out the boxes of medical supplies and set up a clinic inside, while Carlos took the group of men to meet together under a large tree. Many villagers joined each group. Over one hundred and fifty waited for treatment for medical problems. I worked as quickly and thoroughly as I could by examining whole families together. Often, the same problem went through the family.

Before I knew it, evening had come and Carlos was calling me to close up so we could move to the next village.

It was late afternoon and I still had several patients waiting to be seen. I knew I had already treated the most severe cases and the rest had only minor complaints. I felt pulled to finish up, but he quickly reminded me that even Jesus left the multitudes when it was late. I asked the others to forgive me for we must move to the next church.

As I nearly completed packing all my medical supplies, a small, Bushman woman came running through the open back door screaming out, "Please help me. My baby is dying!"

I quickly looked over at Carlos and he nodded for me to help her.

I reached out for the little one all wrapped up in an old cloth. He felt as if he weighed less than five pounds, but the mother said he was six months old.

As I took the cloths off his body, all I could see were bones with skin wrapped around them; the crevices of his skull, all the little ribs showing, and tiny bones for his limbs, all so prominent. I could feel his fever through the cloth, and his breathing was labored.

As I looked at the mother, I realized that the child was starving to death and now most likely had pneumonia. Her breasts were flat and had little milk supply. I continued to examine him and found that she had already taken him to the witchdoctor. Fetishes, called "hirizi," consisting of bones, skin, shells and parts of animals in little bags were tied about his neck, arms, waist and legs. The witchdoctor had also cut multiple inch-long gashes across his swollen stomach to "let out the evil causing his illness."

"Why did you take him to the witchdoctor? You are killing him,"

"I had no place else to go. The hospital is very far away. Even today, when I heard that the nurse was in Livuyu, I rushed to find a canoe to cross the river. Then I ran most of the way, for fear you would be gone. Please help my baby!"

"Your baby needs more help than I can give. Do you mind if we ask our Heavenly Father to help us?"

"I don't know the Father but you just do whatever you need to do."

I prayed a short prayer that God would put His hand on this child and bring glory to His name in the healing. I asked the large group seated in the church that were watching me at work to pray silently for this baby.

Having seen several hundred patients in these last twelve days, my supply of medicines nearly depleted, I feared I could not find enough to help him. When I began to dig into the boxes searching for antibiotics, etc., suddenly my hand found a vial for injection, also a bottle of oral antibiotics that she could take home, as well as a large can of whole, powdered milk, a baby bottle, and all the other needed medicines.

I silently praised the Lord for providing our needs and for the churches who had helped buy them. After giving the appropriate medicines, carefully explaining their schedules to the mother, I asked her to come back on our planned visit in one month.

"I will keep praying that God will bring healing to your son"

"I hope so, I hope so."

As we returned on the scheduled date, the whole congregation and many villagers were outside the church waiting for us. As soon as they saw our white pickup truck, they started showing enthusiasm. When we got near the church, they began circling the truck while singing and dancing. We stopped abruptly to keep from hitting anyone.

They were singing a song, made up especially for us: "We love our missionaries who have come to bring the Word of God. We thank our missionaries for helping us and showing the way to heaven. We love our missionaries who teach us God's way and salvation for eternal life. Thank you, missionaries, for coming to us."

It always made us feel so blessed with their gratitude and their beautiful way of expressing it.

After nearly five minutes, we tried to get out but the singing and dancing people continued circling our vehicle. Finally, I edged the door nearly open. There, right beside me, was the little Bushman woman who literally threw the baby into my lap. The tiny one was beautiful and well.

I burst out, "I just praise the Lord for your child's healing."

"I want to thank you for coming. I do not think your God would do anything if you had not come. Your God has power, and I want to know your God."

It was not long before I was able to speak to her and explain how she could know our Lord. She committed her life to Christ that day. She found the Lord of power and love.

How beautiful are the feet of those who bring good news!"
Ro 10:15b

Chapter Thirteen

The Hard to Reach

In 1990, Namibia became Africa's last nation to receive independence. Freedom, peace and self-rule finally came to the region. Mission work spread dramatically. Many new churches throughout Namibia had already come into being and had united to become an association of churches. They, in turn, led in beginning and developing more churches. The need for church leadership increased and, while still visiting and working with the churches in the north, we spent much time in developing and producing material for training leaders.

Eventually, the distance between the last churches in the west to the last in the east, across northern Namibia, was a thousand miles. This meant that more time lapsed between return visits to churches. As the work expanded, so did problems. However, churches continued to grow and became more involved in planting new churches.

C: With Crocodiles

On the day I baptized Ndiana (Nn-dee-AH-nah) and others at Buffalo there was much celebration. She and the others agreed that they wanted me to baptize them in the Kavango River next to their camp.

Everything seemed to be going very well. I had finished baptizing and we had come out of the water onto the shore when Myrtice slipped over to me, touched my arm and said, "Look," as she pointed to a large crocodile not more than thirty feet offshore, gliding slowly near the surface. You could easily see that it was nearly twenty feet long. Not just a little shaken, we finished the service and headed for home, thinking of how to avoid going into the river again for baptisms.

Back in Tsumeb, I purchased a plastic children's swimming pool and cut the metal frame down to the right size, keeping in mind that water is scarce in some places. I made it so that a person could kneel and I could baptize with a minimum of water. I then made a folding stepladder with steps on both sides on which one could get into and out of the pool. We would use it instead of going into the rivers.

We used the portable pool many times. Where there was running water, it was easy to fill. In other places, we would put it up at the church and the women and girls would bring water in clay pots, pans or pails to fill it. At times that would take many hours.

On one occasion in Katima (Kah-TEE-ma) Mulilo (Moo-LEE-low), we set up the pool on Saturday afternoon near a water tap at the church. Very little water was coming from the tap but we trusted that there would be enough overnight for the baptism. In the morning, however, we found that only a little water had come through the pipes, not enough for baptizing.

Katima was more than five hundred miles from Tsumeb and we came there only occasionally. We did not want to wait for another trip to baptize the new converts. As crocodiles infested the Zambezi River, I did not want to go there.

Myrtice said, "We will just have to have faith and go to the river."

"Honey, you can have faith but I am the one who will have to go into the river." After a while, we did decide to go to the Zambezi for the baptizing.

We had a number of Bushmen in the church who were trackers for the South African Army and had keen eyes. I chose two of the ones who appeared to be the sharpest and assigned them to stand on the bank near where I would baptize.

"You stand here and watch the water. Do not look away even for a moment. If you see the slightest ripple, call out and we will come out of the water."

Although nervous, I went into the water with the candidates and I admit that though very happy I was relieved when the baptizing was over.

"According to your faith will it be done unto you." Mt 9:29

M: Churches' Concerns

All of the new churches were young in the Lord and striving to grow. We met with them as often as possible, diligently teaching the truths of the Word to the individual church leaders and members. From time to time we invited pastors, whom they had chosen from among their own congregation, to meet in a central place for training. The congregations were growing, but the devil kept busy trying to disrupt the churches.

In the Mbeyo (M-BAY-yoe) church, along the main road south of Rundu, we were pleased to see their building always filled to capacity. Their joy and enthusiasm were contagious. Many of the men carved beautiful African objects to sell to the army and other visitors passing on the road.

One day when we arrived, we noticed the pastor was not there. "Where is your pastor today?"

"Many problems have taken him away!"

"What problems? He said nothing about problems the last time we were here."

Two of the men took us aside. They began sharing how he was doing a very good job of preaching, but the devil got into him.

"He left his wife with three children and decided to get a new wife. Our church was very upset about it. You had taught us that the Bible said the pastor was to be the husband of one wife. We did not think what he was doing was pleasing to the Lord. So, we called the congregation together to decide what we should do. We all agreed that he did a very wrong thing and that he must not be the pastor anymore. We told him and he left. Now we are praying and asking God to show us who should be the pastor of our church."

"We are very pleased with you for applying the Word of God. The Lord will surely bless you for standing faithful to his Word."

We were proud of their standing firm in God's teachings.

The Kenyemo (Kay-NYA-mow) church, north of town and not far from the largest church at Kaisosi, was a faithful group under Samueli's leadership. He stood firm in the faith and wanted to strengthen his congregation in God's teachings. We had been with them many times in deaths of key church leaders, as well as in major conferences in church training.

The church first built in the middle of the village where there was deep, loose sand. Their first mud-walled and grass-roofed building was soon too small for the group. We were able to help them have a nice, larger frame building with a tin roof. They were more industrious than some churches and had enclosed the building with slats from a nearby sawmill.

The sand in the whole area was treacherous to us. We did not have a four-wheel drive vehicle and never failed to be stuck. Often we reduced the air in the tires. However, most often we would get started going a short ways and then mire down in the sand, having to walk back to the village for help.

When we merely wanted to see pastor Samweli for making plans for something, we really had problems since most of the men of the village were out working or in town. Usually we would call out the men of the congregation to give us a push, but when no men were around, women and children as well as I, pushed while Carlos drove in low gear.

When we came to celebrate the church's completion, we had a two-day meeting with preaching, teaching and singing. At least we would be in one spot and not have to worry about the sand.

The church prepared African food, tea and bread, in the morning, while later in the day, the meeting stopped and we ate corn meal mush and some kind of sauce with vegetables. They were all very poor but a few did have jobs in town. Some carved wooden animals, chains or drums for sale.

The choir of young people was unusually talented in their singing and swaying as they came into the church for the service. The whole congregation and many visitors attended this great celebration. At the end, the pastor baptized many new believers in the improvised plastic pool. They rang their big tire-rim church bell. All the church joined in a circle, dancing and singing praises to God. It was a special time to remember how God changes hearts and brings joy to His people. As the meeting was completed, all the men started pushing off our pickup truck even before we got stuck, singing and running after us waving their farewells.

The Babati (Bah-BAH-tee) church began in a village south of Rundu where they had to cut through the shrubby bush area to begin their first building. As there was much witchcraft in the area, the church had to stand strong in face of the challenges.

When we arrived one morning for services, we found the building empty. Our hearts sank. We could not imagine what could have happened. We started walking to the houses and one of the members came running to us.

"Our pastor's son has just passed away."

"He looked strong and healthy as he led the singing the last time we were here. What has happened to him?"

"He was fine until he complained of a severe headache and fever yesterday. This morning he was gone."

We found the whole congregation at the pastor's home, all in mourning with them for the loss of his seventeen-year-old son. Our hearts were burdened that this new pastor had experienced such a terrible tragedy. We expressed our deepest sympathy to him and his wife and sat with them. Most likely this young man had died of cerebral malaria which often quickly hits the brain.

The pastor then started sharing with us. "Some in the village say that our son died because we have a new church here. Some in witchcraft are afraid we will spoil their business. We will not let the devil succeed. We will stand firm in the faith. Our church will keep on preaching the Word."

The church did continue to grow and witness to God's love and power in the area.

*"For I have not hesitated to proclaim to you the
whole will of God. Keep watch over yourselves
and all the flock of which the Holy Spirit has made
you overseers. Be shepherds of the church of God which
he bought with his own blood." Ac 20:27-28*

C: Damara Couples

Many Damara (Dah-MA-rah) lived and worked on farms
owned by Europeans. They were, like the Bushmen, small in
stature and lighter in color than other African tribes. They
spoke with a clicking language similar to the Bushmen,
although different. Few of them had any opportunity to go to
school, attend church or to learn anything about Jesus. We
found, when going onto the farms that these Damara workers
and their families longed for spiritual guidance.

With permission from the farm owners, we began
services, usually under trees near the labor camps. Soon we
had many accepting Jesus and wanting baptism. The groups
were usually small but became meaningful churches. They
chose their own church leadership from among themselves.

After I had preached on marriage and the family one
Sunday, a man came and told me that he and his wife wanted
to marry "like Christians marry." He had had a pagan
marriage and had three children. As we talked, others joined
us and some of the other men said that they also wanted
Christian marriages. We set a time and prepared.

On the set day, many attended. Members came from two
other farms where we also had churches, and some had
walked more than twenty miles. There was much jubilation
and the singing was exceptionally good. Choirs from the
three churches sang together. Their unique clicking language
gave beautiful sounds in songs.

When the preaching was finished, those wanting to be
married stood with me at the front. There were four couples,
each with their children standing before me. I had decided to
make this a group marriage with grooms and brides
responding together to my questions. Having practiced and

knowing exactly what was to happen, all went smoothly. It was wonderful hearing all the men together and the all the women together saying, "I do" or "I will." There was no kissing, as the Africans never kiss in public. They, with the entire church, clapped their hands and shouted with joy.

"Our prayer is for your perfection." 2Co 13:8b

M: Dopie (DOE-pee) Woman

"Where are the ladies in your camp?" I asked the men and children standing around after we had driven in and greeted those present in this Bushmen camp.

Carlos was talking with the men but I could not see a single woman. I always like to make contact with them, hoping I can minister to them in some way.

As a young boy was pointing back, over through the bush, to show me where the women were, red biting ants starting covering my feet and lower legs. I danced a jig trying to get them off and out of their way, but to no avail. Ants were crawling everywhere. My open sandals certainly gave me no protection. The ants hurt and stung terribly, still covering my legs.

The same little boy grabbed my arm and pulled me onto an old rubber tire lying over to the side. After I got onto it with the boy and balanced myself by holding to his arm, I was able to brush off the rest of the ants. I thanked him profusely. Then he led me across the sandy opening, both of us dodging ants, through some small trees and shrubs. He pointed to the women all standing around in a tight group.

I could not imagine what was going on. I called out my greeting in the clicking sound of their language. All of them immediately turned to my direction. I was a complete stranger to this village of Bushmen called Dopie.

They responded in greeting and invited me over to join them. There, in their midst, was a very old woman crying in pain. Her wrinkled face showed she was very dehydrated.

She was lying on a grass mat with her right leg exposed. To my horror, I saw the deep, smelly burn that she had from her waist to her knee on the right side.

Immediately, I knelt down beside her to comfort her and examine her burn. Asking her how she got her burn, she told me that she had stumbled and fallen into the fire where she was preparing her food for cooking.

I asked if I could help her. With pleading eyes filled with tears that flowed down both cheeks, she begged with a nod. I asked if they had put any of their medicine on it. She shook her head "no." One of the women indicated, with holding up five fingers, that she had fallen about five days before.

I rushed back to the pickup truck to find my boxes of medicines. We had been visiting several church groups and new places on this trip and had used my medicines several times. I was so thankful that I had them with me. Since this was a new place for us to visit, we had not planned any ministry, merely to introduce ourselves and get acquainted with them.

Keri (KAY-ree), one of the strong Bushmen church leaders, was with us and had showed us where this group was camping. In the Caprivi (Kah-PRE-vee) Strip, we had already established several churches among the Bushmen and were attempting to find some new villages among them.

Gathering my medical supplies needed, I quickly hurried back to the dear suffering woman, being careful to avoid the biting ants.

Giving her painkillers first, I cleaned the burned area and applied an excellent ointment that hastens the healing of burns. I had plenty of bandages and some ointment-soaked gauze, so I could cover all the exposed areas in order that blowing sand and insects, especially flies, could not get on the wound.

Burns are one of the biggest problems that these people have, since they cook over an open fire and use it as light in the evenings. Many children and older people stumble and fall into fires.

Finishing my care, I carefully explained to the one holding her head in her lap, most likely one of her daughters, how she must give her one antibiotic capsule three times a day by pointing to the sky in the positioning of the sun. In addition, I went over her care several times, of when she needed to change the bandage and put on fresh ointment. The old woman tried to get up to thank me.

"No, no, you must rest. I am pleased that I was able to help you with your problem."

Repeatedly, all the women expressed their gratitude. They begged us repeatedly to come back to their village. They agreed that they would love to hear about God and his love for people. They appeared surprised that He loved them.

Two days later, we returned to Dopies. After checking my burned patient and giving her more bandages and medicines, I returned to join the group setting up for our church service. They brought out anything they could find for seating -- logs, low hand-made stools and a few rickety chairs that someone must have salvaged.

Around sixty Bushmen villagers sat mesmerized with the sermon. They knew some god had made all the things that kept them alive and now they heard about the true God in Heaven who wanted to be their heavenly Father. That day many of them made decisions to trust the Creator God, the Loving God, and Forgiving God. These uninhibited people, so expressive, will now have the real joy of the Lord.

> *"And foreigners who bind themselves to the Lord*
> *to serve him, to love the name of the Lord, and*
> *to worship him. These I will bring to my holy mountain*
> *an give them joy In my house of prayer." Is 56:6a, 7b*

C: Food is finished

We stood with this pleasant, small Bushman woman, next to a fence of brush and sticks, which she had put up to keep the goats out of the field. On the other side of the fence, the withered millet stalks were only half the size they would have been if there had been enough rain. We could readily see that there would be no harvest.

"Our food is finished. We do not know what we will do."

We left Mavis at Menzasuvila (Main-zah-soo-VEE-lah) and drove to Bushman Camp No. 7. Keri, the Bushman leader in the area, walked with us through the camp. Soon we came upon blind Margaret, sitting on a grass mat in front of her hut. Someone had placed a pile of weeds next to her. With nimble hands, she was feeling of each weed, taking off the little leaves, and placing them in a basket in front of her. It was an emotional experience for us.

"You do not eat those, do you?"

"We have no other food. We eat anything we can find. We eat grass, these weeds and sometimes roots and bark from trees."

When we got home to Tsumeb, I called Edenvale in South Africa, and told James, our area leader, of the plight of our people. I asked if it were possible for us to get some of the hunger relief funds our churches collect each October.

"Carlos, we must get permission from Richmond. I will see if I can do that. Go ahead and see if what you need is available, but do not buy anything until you hear from me. I will call you when I find out."

I went straight into town and made inquiry about the possibility of getting corn meal, beans, cooking oil and salt—basic food for our people—from South Africa, as these items were not available in Namibia in the quantities we would need. I was pleased to find that we could get them.

When I got back to the house, James had already called. He had called Nairobi. From there a call had gone to Richmond. A committee came together and made their decision. They called Nairobi back and Nairobi called Edenvale. James, in Edenvale, called us in Tsumeb—all in less than two hours, to tell us to go ahead and order what we needed. This was somewhat of a miracle, since phone calls were very difficult in this part of the world. Sometimes, it takes days to get through.

During the following four months we distributed, once a month, food to more than 15,000 people, preventing what would have been a disaster otherwise.

We went from village to village with truckloads of food and gave to each family enough to last one month. At each place, we had a service, telling them about the love of God and His care for them. Because of what we were doing, many turned to God.

We came back a month later and did the same. At the end of four months, the rains having begun, people had planted, cultivated, and near to harvesting crops. We were grateful that we were there to help -- grateful that our people back at home loved and cared enough to provide what we needed to prevent that disaster.

"For I was hungry and you gave me something to eat."
Mt 25:35a

M: Women's Stand

The women in all our churches are a very deep concern in my heart. Most of them have never had a chance to go to school. They labor in the fields to plant, weed and harvest their crops. They are responsible for cooking and feeding the family. Most spend hours searching for firewood and carrying water from long distances for household use. Hard work is their daily routine.

I wanted to have some special times with them to teach them how they can serve the Lord and be a part of the Kingdom's work. I was able to teach the women in our churches in Tsumeb, near our home, in sewing, knitting, nutrition, home-emergency care and Bible study regularly. The churches scattered through the more distant areas were too far to give them regular assistance. We had to spend our time teaching the whole congregation and caring for their medical needs. I had apologized to many of the women for not being able to assist them. I had discussed ways they could serve in their churches and communities while we were visiting but failed to have any regular planned activities.

Rosa, the wife of Moses Tololi, was interested in helping the ladies, though she had very little schooling. I encouraged her to do whatever she could but I failed to assess her abilities. I expected her to try to help the ladies at Kaisosi (Kah-ee-SO-see), the first major church there.

When we came to minister to the church one day, Rosa was all smiles. I asked her what was happening. She told me that she was so excited about her women's meeting the past weekend.

"Please tell me all about it"

"We had over two hundred ladies who came from many of our churches to spend three days for inspiration and discussions on ways we, as women, can serve the Lord."

"That is terrific! I'm so proud of you, Rosa, for leading such a needed conference."

"The women brought their own food and blankets for sleeping in the church. We had a great time of learning about how we can minister in the church and to each other." Rosa continued to tell many funny and serious moments of the conference.

My faith surely was too small in assessing the abilities and determination of this pastor's wife. God had used her in an amazing way to reach out in teaching the ladies to be involved in serving the Lord. God has such a special place for the women who have been so faithful in His service. Since women were so effective in traveling with Jesus and his disciples, supporting and serving them as we read in Luke 8:1-3, women have a vital part in God's service.

"Mary Magdalene, . Joanna the wife of Cuza, . Susanna and many others . . were helping to support them out of their own means." Lk 8:2b-3

C: "Blessed are the Poor"

It was our last day at Omutsegonime (Omm-say-go-NEE-may) before leaving for the US. We would not be coming back for we would retire at the end of furlough. It was a very emotional time. We had spent nearly eleven years in Namibia and most of those present had accepted Jesus during that time. There were many tears and some cried aloud. The congregation listened intently as I preached. They were very somber. When I finished preaching, many expressed appreciation for what we had done with and for them.

I will never forget what Seunike (Say-oo-NEE-kay) had to say. It went something like, "You are going away to America. When you get there please tell all the Christian brothers and sisters that we thank them for sending you to us. Tell them that many of us would have already died in our sins if you had not come. You taught us about how Jesus cleans us from our sins. We trusted in him and you baptized us.

"The rains did not come. The Christians in America sent money for you to buy food for us. Without it, many of us would have died of hunger. Thank them for doing that.

"We sat on logs under trees to hear you preach. You used money from America and bought materials so we could have a church building and the benches on which we sit. We would never have had a church like this if you had not come. Thank the people in America for that."

She went on and on but before she finished she opened her Bible to Matthew 5:3. She did not know how to read so we knew that someone had found the verse for her.

With her finger firmly on that verse she said, "The Bible says 'blessed are the poor.'"

After a pause she continued, "We are the poor of whom the Bible speaks. We do not have anything. We live in poor houses and have little food. We have poor clothes. Most of us have no shoes. We have no cars or bicycles, so we walk wherever we need to go or if we have money enough we can get a bus to go to the town. Yes, we are the poor of whom Jesus speaks but we are blessed. God blessed us because you came. Please tell the people in America that we thank them for sending you."

Seunike sat down, placed her face in her hands and wept.

It was hard for me to respond but I finally said, "We are the blessed ones. You people here at Omutsegonime and all over Namibia have blessed us by allowing us to come and share Jesus with you. We will tell the people in America all about you. I will tell them about today and about what each of you has said."

As long as we shall live we will thank God for allowing us to spend those years in Africa. We will look forward to seeing Seunike and all the rest in Heaven one day.

"Blessed are the poor in spirit, for theirs is the Kingdom of Heaven." Mt 5:3

C: Omutsegonime Girl

On that very last day at this village, many other situations arose.

"Please give us some water. We have so very little and we are always thirsty," cried out the people from the village.

It was the dry season and had not rained for more than five months. Water was difficult to find anywhere in the area and especially difficult at Omutsegonime. Most families made do with very little. Even their skin seemed to show more wrinkles and they lost weight.

We collected all the containers we could and wherever we went to a church, took as much water as we could. Following a church service, we would give each family a container of water—the only clean water they had had since we had been there before.

It was interesting to see a man take his container of water, remove the cap, sip just a little from it, and hand it to each member of his family for a sip before putting the cap back on and walking away, proudly holding his water next to his side and with his family following close behind him..

"Oh, this is so good" they all seemed to say in unison.

On this Sunday morning when we arrived at Omutsegonime to give our farewell, a young boy met us outside and told us about a girl who had died the day before.

"She has been coming to Sunday school and church. She accepted Jesus two weeks ago. She was waiting for you to come and baptize her. I want to help the family but don't know what I need to do."

"I am so sorry. Let us see if we might go and visit her family after church."

This pleased him very much.

After the service different members told us that the girl had left home early in the morning with a bucket, looking for water. She was gone most of the day and arrived home only late in the evening with the small amount of water she had found. She gave the water to her mother, telling her that her head hurt very badly. She went into the hut, lay down on her mat and did not get up.

We suspected that she had cerebral malaria, which comes and kills quickly. The entire church agreed to visit the family, though none had attended the church except the girl.

We walked quite a long distance under the terribly hot, tropical sun. There was no shade. All the trees had lost their leaves due to the heat and lack of water. The sand was deep adding to the difficulty of walking.

After a time we could see, in the distance, some people sitting under a tree. As we drew nearer, we could see that it was the girl's family. Getting closer still, we could see a mound covered with thorny branches near where they sat.

They had buried the girl in a shallow grave, as it is their custom, placing thorn branches over the mounded grave to prevent wild animals from disturbing it. There was only the father, mother and four children. No one else was there to comfort then and to mourn with them.

We approached the family and I went and sat on the ground next to the father. Myrtice sat next to the mother. The church members sat around in the nearly unbearable hot sun.

We sat silently for a while and then I said to the man, "I would like to pray. Would that be all right?"

At first, he appeared puzzled. Then with a faint smile on his face, he said, "That is what you do at church isn't it?" Pointing to the grave he continued, "She said that you pray at church. She said that it is talking with God."

Then, looking to me, "Can you talk with God?"

"Yes, we talk with God when we pray. We talk with God at church and we can talk with him here, too. Would you like for me to talk with God now?"

"Yes, please talk with God."

I prayed for a time and, with my Bible in my hand, asked if it would be all right for me to read from it.

Staring at the Bible he asked, "Is this the book from which you read at church? My girl said that God talks to you out of this book. Can God talk to you out of this book?"

"Yes, He can. Would you like to hear him speak to you out of this book?"

"Yes. Please read it to me."

I read. We sang some hymns and talked with the family for awhile, seeking to comfort them. We bade them farewell and left with most of the church members going their separate ways to their homes. When we reached the church we got into our pickup and drove away, getting home well after dark.

As we were finishing up our time in Namibia, we spent most of the following week putting things together and packing crates which we would ship home. Each day we prayed for the family whose girl had died. Our hearts went out to them

The following Sunday we attended church at another place and came home to continue our packing. On Monday of the following week, some church members came from Omutsegonime. After greetings, we immediately inquired about this family. They responded that they all came to church on the next Sunday after we visited them.

"They all came again yesterday," one said.

Another continued, "When the pastor gave the invitation they all came forward, saying that they wanted to trust the Jesus that their little girl loved so much."

At that we paused and prayed, offering thanks for our God who could and would bring about good things from the bad.

> *"They were harassed and helpless, like sheep without a shepherd." Mt 9:36b*

M: Jumping like Crickets

When we visited Bushman Camp No. 7, we realized that only a few people were around.

"Where are all the people?" I asked the first ones who came running out to greet us.

"They cannot find enough food, like roots and berries in this area, or find enough ground to plant any crops here. Many of them have moved out to the Menzasuvila (Mane-zah-sue-VEE-lah) area to begin a new village."

After we had a wonderful service with those remaining in the camp we asked where we could find this new one.

"It is about twenty-five miles down the road towards Rundu. You can find it by looking for the soft-drink can on a bush near the road."

Finding a soft-drink can in so much scrubby bush was nearly impossible. We drove very slowly, straining our eyes. We must have passed it and went several miles beyond when we realized we had gone too far. Then we decided to return and try to search it out again. As we slowly went down the road, we suddenly spotted a can. What a relief!

We turned into an opening in the thorny bush area and soon spotted the children running toward us. They started jumping up and down like a bunch of crickets with the joy of seeing us. Yes, we were in the right camp. These were our sweet little children from Bushman Camp No. 7. They always jumped like no one else. As soon as we pulled close, others started running up. They expressed their joy at seeing us, without any inhibition. We loved this trait of the Bushmen people.

As we greeted them in their clicking language and hugged them, they nearly rolled over in laughter. They always laughed at our clicking sounds, which were far from perfect. Repeatedly, they would laugh and tell us again the sounds we should make. Specific clicks must come from either the right side or the left side of the mouth. Some are guttural-sounding clicks produced by the tongue at the roof of the mouth. Their joy was so contagious that we loved just being with them.

They had cleared only part of the camp. None of the huts was finished, only part of one or two walls in most cases. A few had army canvas over some leaning poles in a small area for a place to sleep. Most had been very busy trying to carve this new village out of the rough bush. The shrub brush was thick and difficult to remove, but they were persevering.

Shortly, Mavis shared with us that they already had a church.

"Since we came here we have been meeting every afternoon late. The newcomers who were not in the other village are now joining us. We are teaching them our songs and I read Bible stories to them. We are so happy that you have come and found us."

Mavis called all the others to come together under the trees, which she had already prepared for their meeting place. Since her husband was away, she alone was leading the group.

"We want our own church here, too!" She expressed and seemed proud of her faith.

As over eighty gathered, they began singing the songs she had taught them. Carlos was able to lead the service with Mavis interpreting from Owambo into the Bushman clicking language. At the end of the service, Carlos gave the customary call to come forward to confess their sins and to accept Lord Jesus as their Savior.

To our amazement, nearly all made a profession of faith. The others who remained on the seats had already made that decision. Yes, our faithful little Mavis had been very faithful in sharing her faith and helping the others to know and to follow the Lord.

"Help these women who have contended at my side in the cause of the gospel" Php 4:3

C: Sleeping on the Ground

The civil war in Angola had been severe for a number of weeks and daily news reports were grim. We knew that the most intense fighting had been in southern Angola where our churches had been flourishing. We prayed daily for them. Angola was just across the river from Rundu, and many of our church members had come over several years before because of the fighting.

Moses called at dusk one evening from Rundu to tell us that four men from there had showed up at his house. They had neither shoes nor shirts. Their shorts were scanty and ragged. They had walked for more than seventy miles and found someone who agreed to bring them across the river in a canoe. Moses said that his church people had found clothes for them but they and their families back in Angola were in dire need for help.

At daybreak the following morning, I left for Rundu and on to Kaisosi. I arrived at Moses' house at one o'clock to find that three of the men had been with us previously for pastor training on two different occasions. Their stories of fear, carnage and brutality were heart rendering.

They told us of when the soldiers arrived in their village, burning their huts and stealing their cattle, chickens, goats and whatever else they could take. Upon the approach of the soldiers, the families had run away into the forest with nothing—far away enough to escape the brutal war. Family groups were together, but having no food they foraged in the forest for berries, edible roots and anything else they could find.

One said, "Our women sleep on the bare ground at night holding our babies next to them but with nothing for cover."

Another said, "It gets very cold at night."

Many of our Christians in Kaisosi gathered around to hear of the plight of their brothers and sisters in Angola. Many were shaking their heads in unbelief and many women were weeping.

I asked, "What can we do? How can we help?"

"We do not need money as there is nothing to buy. There are no shops in the area where we are staying. Though there is little food, we do find enough to survive. We need blankets—blankets to cover our women and babies at night."

As they spoke, I thought of ways to get blankets, clothes and food for them and their families.

"If we get blankets for you, how will we get them to your families in Angola?"

"We have talked with the rebel soldiers. They told us that if we were to get help of any kind and could get it across the river, they would take it in their trucks to our people in the bush."

"Won't the soldiers take it all for their own use?"

"No, some of them are our people. They know that we support their cause. They will help us. We know that they will. They have large trucks and will take anything we get."

"You stay here with Moses while I go back to Tsumeb and see what we can do to help."

I asked Moses to assess with the men how much they felt the rebels would be able to take, if we were to get it together. I asked him to find men with canoes who would be willing to take what we get across the river and to check with the wholesalers to see if they had corn meal in stock. It was late afternoon when I left for Tsumeb. It was nearly midnight when I arrived home.

As soon as the shops opened the next morning, I was in town looking for blankets. Myrtice was on the phone calling our European friends and neighbors, asking for used clothing. By noon, I had 220 blankets -- all that four different shops had in stock.

Hearing my story, two of the storeowners gave them to me at their cost. The other two gave them to me for less than what they had paid for them. In the meantime, Myrtice had collected many used clothes. By daybreak the next morning, I was on my way back to Kaisosi with the pickup packed full of blankets and bundles of used clothes.

Moses and the four men joined me in going to the wholesale house, where we filled Moses' pickup with corn meal, beans, cooking oil and salt. We both drove to the river where men were waiting with their canoes to ferry across what we had. We could see the waiting trucks on the other side.

We loaded what we had into the canoes and watched as they crossed the river. We watched as the rebel soldiers took the loads from the canoes and put them into their truck. As they drove out of sight, we prayed -- that what we sent would arrive safely. I drove back to Tsumeb.

During the ensuing weeks, we went about doing our work and wondering daily about those four men, their families and our doing what we could to help. We were elated to hear that the men and their loads arrived safely and that the people were doing better. They were establishing new homes and churches in the areas into which they had fled.

"I needed clothes and you clothed me." Mt 25:36a

C: No Food for Five Days

We arrived at Livuyu in mid-afternoon, as we wanted to worship with the people and talk with them prior to our distributing food the following morning. The drought had been so long that the people had used up their spare food for extra planting and eating. Now they were without adequate food. Knowing that we were coming, many had already gathered when we arrived. We joined them inside the church for singing and worship and told them how our Christian brothers and sisters in America had given money so that we could buy food for them. We then began registering those present.

We wrote down every family name with the number of adults and children to determine how much basic ration each would need for a month. The plan was to return after one month with a ration for another month. When we had finished registering those present, it was about dark. We sent them away, telling them to return in the morning.

We slept in our pickup truck and got up early to fix some breakfast. Before we had finished eating, the people were gathering in great numbers. We expected the truck to arrive between 8:30 and 9:00 o'clock but it did not come. Ten o'clock and then eleven passed and the truck still had not arrived.

At about 10:00, seeing that there were many sick in the group, Myrtice took from the pickup what medicines she had brought and started treating them. Many of the children were severely malnourished and very thin. Adults showed signs of weakening and loss of weight. When one o'clock came, the truck still had not arrived.

Myrtice, having used up most of her medicines, sat with the women in the shade of the big baobab tree. The rains had come, and the millet they had planted was coming up. It would be at least four or five months before they would begin to harvest. Most of them said that they were weeding their millet. Some spoke of expecting a good crop if the rains continued. They spoke with joy of our bringing food for them. They said that they would die before getting a harvest without our help. Seti (SAY-tee) sat without speaking.

Myrtice asked her, "Seti, are you weeding your millet?"

She shook her head and said faintly, "No!"

"Why are you not weeding your millet?"

"I have not felt like it."

"I'm sorry! I could have given you some medicine to make you feel better."

"That is not the problem. My food gave out five days ago. I have had nothing to eat for five days."

While Myrtice was telling me about Seti, we heard the truck in the distance. We also could see the cloud of dust as the truck drew nearer. Soon the truck was leaving the main road and coming toward the church. The people began cheering.

Church members assisted in taking the corn meal, beans, salt and cooking oil from the truck and giving it to families as Myrtice called their names and told us how much they would receive. Church members and other families in need received their ration for a month.

Many had come, received food and gone away when I saw Seti standing before me. Two men placed a fifty-two lb bag of corn meal on her head and handed her the oil, beans and salt, which she held close to her body with both hands.

She looked up at me and said, "Thank you! Thank you! Thank you!"

As she turned and walked away, I watched in disbelief that she was able to carry the heavy load. I looked up to heaven and said, "Thank you so much, Heavenly Father, for those who make this possible."

"Jesus went through all the towns and villages, teaching in their synagogues, preaching the good news of the kingdom, and healing every disease and sickness." Mt 9:35

M: Hands Reaching Out

"Thump, thump, thump," roared the rear tire of our pickup truck.

"Not again! This just cannot be possible -- three blowouts in one day! What in the world can we do now?" I loudly questioned Carlos over the roar of the pickup truck driving on the loose gravel as I braked to a stop.

He responded, "We'll just have to trust the Lord to work it out."

Pulling to the side of the hot, dusty road, we got out to see how much damage there was. Indeed, the rim had cut through the rubber of the tire.

Carlos, shaking his head, said, "No more spares. We brought two. They are both used now."

The tires and the spares were in good shape when we left home. The intense heat of the road had brought about this scenario. The temperature was up to 105 degrees or more. The gravel was so hot that we could feel it through the soles of our shoes. The only thing to do was to wait for someone to come along who would be willing to help us.

We were right in the middle of the Caprivi Strip of northern Namibia. This area was on the northern border with Angola and Zambia, where the terrorists normally crossed to attack the South African army. We were glad that the doors of our truck had a bold sign of our mission, with a cross over a Bible emblazoned on it.

After a long wait in the unbearable heat, we were getting discouraged. We kept a vigilant eye for any sign of terrorists as well as wild animals, knowing that both were numerous in this area. Traffic was minimal and no vehicles were in sight for hours. We prayed and waited. Because we had planned to meet with a new village that afternoon, we were also bothered that we would fail them.

On our last trip out, while making rounds to say our farewells to the churches before going on leave, we had met three young men who had come to sell dried fish in this village. Someone had told them about us and had invited them to the service.

After the service one said, "We came to sell some of our dried fish but we heard about Jesus. We have never had a missionary come to our village to tell us. Could you please come to our village to teach us about the Lord?"

Carlos responded, "I don't think that is possible. We are closing up our ministry now because we are going home and there is no one to take our place. We are sorry but there is no time for a visit to your village."

In disappointment, one responded, "I guess there will never be a missionary to teach us about this Jesus."

As I looked at Carlos, and he at me, we both had a feeling of guilt in not being able to assist these pleading men.

Thinking of how we could work it out, we agreed to visit their village, knowing we did need to come to this general area one more time for farewells to other churches. We would come to their village first and then visit the other churches. We asked them to meet us at a certain place on the main road late in the afternoon for a service around 5 p.m. We did not want to miss this opportunity, but now because of this third blowout it looked impossible.

Finally, we saw a large cloud of dust in the distance down the road. A truck was coming our way. Carlos went to the side of the road to wave the truck down. We were hopeful, as throughout the country people were always helpful in stopping to assist when a car was broken down.

The driver pulled up and heard about our problem. He agreed to take Carlos back to the last place that had tires -- about sixty miles back. The riders, four Damara women and five children, climbed from the back of the truck to wait with me.

My time with the Damara ladies and children was rather comical. They are very much like the Bushmen; small, light colored and a little oriental looking, but I did not know any words of their clicking language except the greetings. We said the greetings many times and laughed.

I started using my hands to express some conversation and they tried the same. We sat down together on the side of the road under a nearby tree while just smiling at each other.

The children gradually moved closer and closer to me until they were actually touching my body with theirs. They took turns feeling my skin and hair. I would pull grasses nearby and chew their tender part. The children would do the same. I shared water and some cookies that we had in the truck. They were very expressive while they enjoyed them. It was a touching time to feel close to strangers when we needed each other.

After about two hours, they returned with a new tire on the rim. The men quickly put it on in place of the torn up shreds of a tire. We profusely expressed gratitude to our good Samaritans and gave them a monetary gift of appreciation. We were so very grateful to these dear people. We left, knowing it would be late into the night before we could possibly get to our destination.

When we neared the village at nearly eleven o'clock, we suspected that the people waiting for us might have given up hope and gone back to their homes. It was very dark.

Suddenly, in the lights of our pickup, we saw three men standing on the roadside vigorously waving. They had faithfully waited for us. We apologized for being so late. We told them that we would meet with their people the next morning.

"Oh, please, come greet our people tonight. Let them know you have come. They are waiting for you now. They have been so happy that you are coming. They started gathering at noon today."

Locking the pickup and leaving it on the side of the road, we began following the men, into the darkness, to the interior of the village, amazed that these people would wait nearly twelve hours for our arrival.

The night was as dark as could be, neither moon nor lights in the village. All we could see were a few coals left over from cooking the evening meals in front of huts.

We followed our leaders closely, fearing we would step into a hole or fall in the rough areas. After walking about a quarter of a mile, we could hear the sound of those waiting for us. It was so dark we could not see anyone.

Then we had to cross over a small ravine. Our leader took Carlos' hand and I, his. Climbing out of the ravine, we sensed that people were right there but we could not see them. You cannot see black faces on a dark night.

All of a sudden, as if God were touching the embers of a nearly extinguished fire next to our path, a blaze flared up, its light revealing the many hands reaching out to greet us. Hands over hands were extending to us for their greetings, with the palms catching the light of the fire. We looked again. In amazement, all we could see were these hands reaching out of the darkness. We could not see faces, only dozens of hands to welcome us to share the Gospel with them. This powerful image has remained vividly in our memory.

Those hands represented the hunger and desire of many of the villages that wanted Jesus Christ in their lives. Those hands and those lives are the reason we went to Africa; to share the love and salvation of Christ. Those very hands are the ones who readily accepted the Way. They are the reason for our serving our Lord Jesus Christ when He said, "Go into the uttermost parts, preach the Gospel."

"I will make you a light for the Gentiles that you may bring my salvation to the ends of the earth." Isa 49:6b,

Made in United States
Orlando, FL
17 October 2023

37979396R00196